Learning and Practice:
Agency and Identities

This Reader is one of a series of three which form part of *Curriculum, learning and society: investigating practice* (E846), a course belonging to the Open University Masters in Education programme. The series consists of the following books:

Learning and Practice: Agency and Identities (edited by Patricia Murphy and Kathy Hall)

Pedagogy and Practice: Culture and Identities (edited by Kathy Hall, Patricia Murphy and Janet Soler)

Knowledge and Practice: Representations and Identities (edited by Patricia Murphy and Robert McCormick)

The Open University Masters in Education

The Open University Masters in Education is now firmly established as the most popular postgraduate degree for education professionals in Europe, with around 3000 students registered each year. It is designed particularly for those with experience of teaching, the advisory service, educational administration or allied fields. Specialist lines in leadership and management, applied linguistics and special needs/inclusive education are available within the award. Successful study on the Masters entitles students to apply for entry into the Open University Doctorate in Education programme.

Details of this and other Open University courses can be obtained from the Student Registration and Enquiry Service, The Open University, PO Box 197, Milton Keynes MK7 6BJ, United Kingdom; telephone: +44 (0) 845 300 6090; e-mail: general-enquiries@open. ac.uk.

Alternatively, you may wish to visit the Open University website at http://www. open.ac.uk, where you can learn more about the wide range of courses and packs offered at all levels by The Open University.

Learning and Practice: Agency and Identities

Edited by
Patricia Murphy and Kathy Hall

Los Angeles • London • New Delhi • Singapore

The Open University

First Published in 2008

SAGE Publications Ltd
1 Oliver's Yard
55 City Road
London EC1Y 1SP

SAGE Publications Inc.
2455 Teller Road
Thousand Oaks, California 91320

SAGE Publications India Pvt Ltd
B 1/I 1 Mohan Cooperative Industrial Area
Mathura Road
New Delhi 110 044

SAGE Publications Asia-Pacific Pte Ltd
33 Pekin Street #02-01
Far East Square
Singapore 048763

Library of Congress Control Number: 2088920073

British Library Cataloguing in Publication data

A catalogue record for this book is available from the British Library

ISBN 978-1-8478-7365-1
ISBN 978-1-8478-7366-8 (pbk)

Typeset by C&M Digitals (P) Ltd., Chennai, India
Printed by The Cromwell Press Ltd, Trowbridge, Wiltshire
Printed on paper from sustainable resources

Contents

Acknowledgements vii

Introduction ix

Section 1: Mind and Learning **1**

1 Curriculum: The Case for a Focus on Learning 3
 Robert McCormick and Patricia Murphy

2 Neuroscience and Education 19
 Usha Goswami

3 Meaning 31
 Etienne Wenger

Section 2: Culture, Tools and Learning **47**

4 Thinking with the Tools and Institutions of Culture 49
 Barbara Rogoff

5 A Sociocultural Analysis of Organisational Learning 71
 Nick Boreham and Colin Morgan

6 Gender Issues in Testing and Assessment 87
 Jannette Elwood

7 Portfolios and Assessment in Teacher Education in Norway:
 A Theory-based Discussion of Different Models in Two Sites 102
 Olga Dysthe and Knut Steinar Engelsen

8 Participationist Discourse on Mathematics Learning 120
 Anna Sfard

Section 3:   Identities, Agency and Learning   **133**

  9 Literacies and Masculinities in the Life of a
     Young Working-Class Boy   135
     Deborah Hicks

 10 Positional Identities   149
     *Dorothy Holland, William Lachicotte Jr, Debra Skinner
     and Carole Cain*

 11 Gender and Subject Cultures in Practice   161
     Patricia Murphy

 12 Science Education as/for Participation in the Community   173
     Wolff-Michael Roth and Stuart Lee

 13 Growing Up Digital: How the Web Changes Work, Education
     and the Ways People Learn   193
     John Seely Brown

Index   202

Acknowledgements

We would like to thank the authors who contributed their chapters, as well as colleagues within and outside The Open University who helped with the preparation of the manuscripts. Special thanks are due to the following people for their assistance in the production of this book:

Sally Jones (course secretary)
Fulden Underwood (course manager)
Professor Valentina Klenowski (external assessor)
Gordon Bloomer (critical reader)
Gill Gowans (copublishing–media developer)

Chapter 1

From: Moon, B., Ben-Peretz, M. and Brown, S. (eds.) *Routledge International Companion to Education* (© 2000, published by Routledge). Reproduced by permission of Taylor & Francis Books UK.

Chapter 2

From: *British Journal of Educational Psychology*, 74 (2004), pp.1–14. Reproduced with permission from the *British Journal of Educational Psychology*, © The British Psychological Society.

Chapter 3

From: Chapter 1 in Wenger, E., *Communities of Practice Learning, Meaning and Identity* (Cambridge: Cambridge University Press, 1998). © Cambridge University Press 1998, reproduced with permission.

Chapter 4

From: Chapter 7 in Rogoff, B., *The Cultural Nature of Human Development* (Oxford: Oxford University Press, 2003). By permission of Oxford University Press, Inc.

Chapter 5

From: *Oxford Review of Education*, 30 (3), 2004, pp.307–25. Reprinted by permission of the publisher (Taylor & Francis Ltd, http://www.informaworld.com).

Chapter 7

From: *Assessment and Evaluation in Higher Education*, 29 (2), 2004, pp.239–58. Reprinted by permission of the publisher (Taylor & Francis Ltd, http://www.informaworld.com).

Chapter 8

Chapter 9

Chapter 10

Chapter 12

Chapter 13

Introduction

Patricia Murphy and Kathy Hall

This book is the first of three Readers examining relational views of learning, knowledge and pedagogy from a sociocultural perspective. Sociocultural approaches to learning transcend typical boundaries, such as school/workplace or, home/school and emphasise the socially negotiated and embedded nature of meaning-making and how learners learn to use the cognitive tools of their cultural community through participation in social activity.

In the last decade, debate about mind has seen an emerging consensus about its agentive nature. Neuoroscientific research into the physical basis of mind has supported this, revealing the unique nature of human experience: memories and mind are inextricably linked (Greenfield, 2000). Further, if mind is agentive and experience unique then learning and being in the world involve a process of negotiation of meaning. This has challenged theories of mind that see language mirroring reality and mind and body as separate (Bredo, 1994). In a sociocultural perspective, language only has meaning in the context of its use and meaning-making is an essential aspect of being in the world. What remains particularly contentious is how the relationship between the individual and society – the collective – is understood in this process of meaning-making.

Drawing on Vygotskian theorising that individual functioning has sociocultural origins and as such 'patterned collective forms of distinctly human forms of doing are understood to be developmentally prior to the activities of the individual' (Sfard, 2006: 157), socio-culturalism challenges assumptions that individual minds are the primary source of development. This treats the individual and the collective as a duality, a unity (Wenger, 1998). The significance of this shift is in where mind is understood to be located. In the socio-cultural perspective adopted in the book, mind is situated between individuals in social action in cultural settings and within cultural, historical relationships (Cobb, 1999). As such, the perspective 'reformulates relations between the level of analysis of social practice in the everyday world and that of the constitutive order in relations with which experience in the lived world is dialectically formed' (Lave, 1988: 171).

In viewing mind as non-local, learning and knowing are understood as relations among people in activity and learning, rather than a process of acquiring knowledge which involves a movement into and through social existence (Lave, 1988). Wenger (1998) argues that identity is the pivot between the individual and the collective. Taking this view focuses attention on the affordances made available to learners to negotiate ways of being a person in a context within the possibilities made available by the systems of relations. In the book, 'becoming' and 'belonging' encapsulates the key perspectives within a socio-cultural account of learning as a movement deeper into practice, and as a transformation of identity, where identity is understood as evolving forms of competence. This duality has significant implications for how pedagogy and assessment are understood and practised.

A sociocultural view of learning and knowing also recognises the cultural variations in the nature of learning and what constitutes valued knowledge and the way that individuals draw on cultural legacies and the connections made by prior generations, often mediated by the cultural tools they inherit (Rogoff, 2003). To enable learners to develop novel affordances, those who support learning have to recognise the funds of knowledge drawn on by learners, and create hybrid pedagogical spaces, where points of intersection between these and institutional practices and values are enabled (Hicks, 2001).

In a social practice view of learning, which is concerned with achieving particular relations with others, experiencing mutuality and sustaining mutual engagement is critical. It is this aspect of participation, which further highlights the need to consider, from a sociocultural perspective, the histories of participation and identifications that participants bring into settings in communities in which they choose to, or are required to, engage.

In the first section of the book in Chapter 1, Robert McCormick and Patricia Murphy highlight significant differences in views of mind, which remain dominant in educational discourses, and some of their epistemological and pedagogical implications. Thinking about curriculum, they argue for a focus on learning in line with a sociocultural, analytical perspective. This leads them to foreground subjective experience suggesting that this has profound implications for how the specified curriculum, particularly subject domains, and the enacted curriculum are considered. In Chapter 2, Usha Goswami examines some of the advances made in neuroscience and how these might support the exploration of educational questions. Of particular interest are the alignments she demonstrates between educational theorising and neuroscientific evidence, and the potential of the methods and instruments of neuroscience to illuminate educational practices. She also opens up new ways of thinking about learning in relation to local neural plasticity, which substantiate the notion of the life-long learner. Chapter 3 is from Etienne Wenger's influential book *Communities of Practice*. The chapter focuses on meaning and how it is understood, in particular its distributed nature, which places emphasis on the social mind and how knowing comes into being through negotiation with others. Wenger conceptualises two processes, participation and reification, arguing that it is in the convergence of these two processes that negotiation of meaning takes place. In arguing for the processes to be understood as a duality, Wenger opens up a way of analysing learning situations, arguing that different mixes of the processes become differentially productive of meaning.

In the second section of the book, Chapter 4 is an edited excerpt of Barbara Rogoff's chapter, 'Thinking with the Tools and Institutions of Culture', from her book *The Cultural Nature of Human Development*. In referring to culture, Rogoff considers how it plays out at the level of the constitutive order and how it emerges in practice. She does not, in this excerpt, focus on lived experiences as manifestations of particular historically accumulated funds of knowledge (González, 2005). Rogoff explores how cultural values influence perceptions and constructions of intelligent behaviour and come into play in any observation of thinking. She argues from a sociocultural view of cognition that the focus of learning should be the development of adaptive expertise where learners, through associating certain practices with being particular types of people, learn how to act in different circumstances. In looking at cultural tools for thinking, she examines cultural variations and changes over time within cultures. She argues, in a similar way to Wenger, how artefacts or reifications form and are formed by the practices of their use, and how they serve to amplify as well as constrain human activity. In Chapter 5, Nick Boreham and Colin Morgan report on their study of organisational learning in a petrochemicals manufacturing complex. Applying a sociocultural approach, they identify dialogue as the fundamental process by which organisations learn and the relational practices of opening space for the creation of shared meaning, reconstituting power relationships, and providing cultural tools to mediate learning as the social structures which embed the dialogue.

In Chapter 6, Jannette Elwood examines views of mind to explore their implications for how gender is understood and assessment practised. She identifies literature that she locates along a continuum depending on the interpretation of the relationship between the individual and the collective. She argues that in a sociocultural, non-local view of mind, gender is a fluid social representation and assessment and testing as cultural activities can only describe students' learning in relationship to their teachers and their 'forms of life'– their histories of participation. Olga Dysthe and Knut Engelsen, in Chapter 7, continue the discussion of a sociocultural view of assessment in their examination of portfolios and assessment in two teacher education institutions in Norway. They confront the dilemma of how to assess the transformation of identity alongside evolving forms of competence when the formative assessment aspects of portfolios are dominated by their summative purposes. They found that the use of digital portfolios brought new dimensions to the learning environment and describe how students built new knowledge utilising the distributed knowledge of their fellow students. Finishing the section, Anna Sfard, in Chapter 8, compares two discourses about learning, acquisitionism and participationism, and applies them to understand mathematical learning and thinking drawing on data from observations of young children. In particular, she takes forward understanding about the nature of thinking as she argues from a participationist, sociocultural view that, as communication between people is the source of individual thinking, then individual thinking is an individualised form of communication. Therefore, how we understand collective communication will influence how we interpret individual thinking.

In the final section of the book, consideration is given to identities and agency in learning. In Chapter 9, Deborah Hicks, arguing for hybrid discourses on instruction, draws on the narrative history of one young, male, working-class reader struggling to find cultural spaces at school in which the values and practices he lived at home came together with classroom values and practices. The gap between his identity as a failing reader at school contrasted markedly with his evolving identity and competence as an apprentice in family projects and his father's business and he increasingly identified with the latter in imagining his future. Chapter 10 is an edited excerpt by Dorothy Holland and her colleagues from the chapter on 'Positional Identity,' from their seminal book *Identity and Agency in Cultural Worlds* (1998). In the excerpt, two aspects of identity are considered. Narrative identities draw on social representations of how people figure in the world and the signs which invoke these. Positional identities are to do with the day-to-day relations of power. How individuals take up narrative identities influence how they position themselves, and are, in turn, positioned. Aspects of positional identities become objectified and available for reflection as people learn to play the game. However, individuals vary in their success in this.

Chapters 11, 12 and 13 highlight the implications of a sociocultural perspective for enabling participation. Patricia Murphy draws on her research with her colleague Gabrielle Ivinson and uses extracts of ethnographic case studies of single-sex groups studying science and technology in a co-educational setting. She draws attention to how teachers, when confronted with a problem of gender without support or insights into its operation, draw on cultural legacies about gender in relation to their subjects, so that rather than extending the means by which students mediate the boundaries of self, they unwittingly constrain them. Wolff-Michael Roth and Stuart Lee in this edited version of their extended article report on an ambitious community project, which redefines how scientific literacy is understood by involving students in contributing to the solutions of contentious, everyday-life issues. In this way there was no gap created between community and school to be bridged. Roth and Lee argue that this approach prepares students for life-long learning and by giving students autonomy over the nature and form of their engagement and ways of representing what is salient, it also engages students hitherto excluded from scientific practices. However, the project raised challenges for assessment and positioned science as just one of a number of forms of useful knowledge. John Seely Brown concludes the book with his discussion of how the web is changing work, education and the ways people learn. He reflects on the shift away from using technology as a support for individuals towards using technology to support relationships between individuals. Along with other authors, he sees this as a way in which new tools and social protocols will develop to support life-long learning.

References

Bredo, E. (1994) 'Reconstructing Educational Psychology', *Educational Psychologist*, 29 (1): 23–45.

Cobb, P. (1999) 'Where Is the Mind?', in P. Murphy (ed.) *Learners, Learning and Assessment*, London: Sage.

González, N. (2005) 'Beyond Culture: The Hybridity of Funds of Knowledge', in: N. González, L.C. Moll and C. Amanti (eds) *Funds of Knowledge: Theorizing Practices in Households, Communities and Classrooms*, Mahwah, NJ: Lawrence Erlbaum Associates.

Greenfield, S. (2000) *The Private Life of the Brain*, London: Penguin Books Ltd.

Holland, D., Lachicotte Jr, W., Skinner, D. and Cain, C. (1998) *Identity and Agency in Cultural Worlds*, Cambridge, MA: Harvard University Press.

Hicks, D. (2001) 'Literacies and Masculinities in the Life of a Young Working-class Boy', *Language Arts*, 78 (3): 217–26.

Lave, J. (2008) 'Everyday Life and Learning', in P. Murphy and R. McCormick (eds) *Knowledge and Practice: Representations and Identities*, London: Sage.

Lave, J. and Wenger, E. (1991) *Situated Learning: Legitimate Peripheral Participation*, Cambridge: Cambridge University Press.

Rogoff, B. (2003) *The Cultural Nature of Human Development*, Oxford: Oxford University Press.

Sfard, A. (2006) 'Participationist Discourse On Mathematics Learning', in J. Maasz and W. Schloeglmann (eds) *New Mathematics Research and Practice*, Rotterdam, Netherlands: Sense Publishers.

Wenger, E. (1998) *Communities of Practice: Learning, Meaning and Identity*, Cambridge: Cambridge University Press.

Section 1

Mind and Learning

1

Curriculum: The Case for a Focus on Learning

Robert McCormick and Patricia Murphy

Introduction

'Curriculum' is understood in many ways and has been the subject of study from a number of perspectives. Three levels of analysis have become evident over the years, namely that of the *specified*, the *enacted*, and the *experienced* curricula. Early perspectives focused on the aims and content of what was to be taught; the *specified curriculum*. This focus on the specified curriculum led to analyses that sought to establish the relationships between educational knowledge and the social and economic interests of a society. These analyses have since been expanded to consider the socio-historical influences on the production and validation of the knowledge specified in curricula. More recently, this has focused attention on how knowledge is selected, organised, transmitted and evaluated (Bernstein, 1971); and the extent to which worldwide processes are at play in this, in terms of the emergence of standardised models of society and of education (Benavot et al., 1992). These developments had a twofold effect; they extended the context of the curriculum debate in relation to the mediating influences that were identified. They also, and importantly, extended the levels of study of curriculum to include the arena of the 'classroom', i.e. the *enacted curriculum*. In this sense, curriculum and instruction were seen as inseparable, reflecting Goodson's concept of curriculum as 'constructed, negotiated, and re-negotiated at a number of levels and in a number of arenas' (Goodson, 1994, p. 111).

Implicated in this shift of perspective were changing views of pedagogy, and of teachers' roles within it, based on developments in understanding about the nature of human action and learning, which led to a focus on a further level of curriculum definition: that of the learners and the curriculum they experience. The *experienced* curriculum has largely been ignored in curriculum debates and it is our contention that this reflects the limited understanding about learning of those involved. If learners are the passive receivers of the enacted curriculum, then the received and the enacted curriculum correspond. What distinguishes these levels is the ability of the learners to learn or receive. If, however, learning is a social process and if learners' agency, like teachers' agency, is recognised, then what is experienced is determined by the participants and the nature of their participation in the arenas in which curricula are enacted; for example, the learning activities and associated assessment. Furthermore, as Murphy (1990) argued, theories of how students learn

[This is an edited excerpt of an extensive chapter]

From: Moon, B., Ben-Peretz, M. and Brown, S. (eds.) *Routledge International Companion to Education* (© 2000, published by Routledge). Reproduced by permission of Taylor & Francis Books UK.

and develop help determine: *what* is selected for inclusion in the curriculum; *how* it is taught, including which classroom resources, organisation and pedagogical strategies are judged to be appropriate; and the *nature* of the teacher's role and relationship with learners (Murphy, 1990, p. 35), i.e. all three levels of curriculum definition.

To understand curriculum then, it is necessary to consider the mediating influences and their effects at all three levels of curriculum negotiation: the specified, enacted and experienced. Furthermore, central to these influences are views of learning and associated views of knowledge.

There has been an international trend towards legislating for curricula in schools (Skilbeck, 1990), though this is not universal, with some countries such as France going in the opposite direction (i.e. allowing more local control of the curriculum). The focus in the early 1990s, in those countries where legislation existed, was therefore on the specified curriculum. However, these curricula were invariably accompanied by assessment systems that *enacted* national proposals. This appeared to leave curriculum considerations at the level of policy-makers, with the job of teachers only to follow prescriptions. Work on curriculum change has, however, made it clear, even at policy level, that there is no mere transmission from proposals to classroom activities. Teachers' agency is reflected in their views about the curriculum, about learning, knowledge and pedagogy, and these all affect the way curricular proposals and assessment systems are implemented and valued. The enacted curriculum is consequently unlikely to correspond to the specified curriculum. [...]

New understandings about learning have made possible a more profound analysis of the curriculum than hitherto. We shall argue that this understanding affects all levels and elements of curriculum considerations and, paradoxically, emphasises the enacted and experienced curriculum to an extent that the specified curriculum is less important; teaching and learning take centre-stage. This serves as the justification for the involvement of teachers in curriculum discussions at a time when it appears they have least say. It also implies that policy-makers need to have a more explicit and justified view of learning than is usually evident in their pronouncements on curriculum issues. Furthermore, assessment systems need to reflect these views of learning and learners, and the systems' limitations [are] as a consequence made explicit. [...]

We shall argue that [...] our understanding of learning has transformed how we should consider the curriculum. This transformation links learning, culture, knowledge, assessment and pedagogy in a way that requires us to rethink our views of the curriculum [...]

There have been significant developments in our understanding of learning, not just since the days of Dewey or early twentieth-century behaviourism, but since the 1960s and 1970s, when issues of learning were being explored for their implications for the curriculum. Our current understandings have, in our view, great significance for contemporary views of the curriculum. [...]

When we examine the curriculum considerations and issues, we shall try to show how the interrelationship of the specified, the enacted and the experienced curriculum is achieved through a focus on learning.

Contemporary views of learning: two approaches to mind

Bruner's [...] book sets the scene of his consideration of learning by sketching out two views of mind; computational and the cultural (Bruner, 1996). Others have characterised these as *symbol-processing* and *situated* views of the mind (Bredo, 1994). The symbol-processing view, as the name suggests, sees the mind as a manipulator of symbols. These symbols are learned and stored in memory; when confronted with a problem, a person searches the memory for symbols to represent the problem and then manipulates them to solve the problem. There are, of course, different views of how these symbols are learned, i.e. of what constitutes the learning process. At one end of the spectrum is the information-processing view, where the learner is a passive processor of information. But the most widely held view sees learning as a knowledge construction process, i.e. learners make meaning from experiences. This places learners in an active role and problem-solving as a central process in knowledge construction. Bredo (1994) characterises symbol-processing in terms of three dualisms: language and reality; mind and body; and individual and society. Under the first (language and reality), symbol-processing sees the symbols as mirrors of reality and, as such, these representations are transmitted to, or at least acquired by, learners. The mind–body dualism from a symbol-processing approach sees thinking as separate from the actions the body takes, while the individual–society dualism sees thinking as an individual process. There are, however, variations between the different theorists in how the knowledge construction process is understood and what are its ends.

Through the latter part of the twentieth century, there were those theorists who focused increasingly on the social aspects of knowledge construction and the social nature of knowledge, and hence minimised the individual–society dualism. These led to a group of theories labelled as social constructivist, a label which itself has many variations. What is common to this view of learning is the role of others in creating and sharing meaning. All constructivist approaches have some social element in the construction process. Thus Piaget, although focused upon individual internalisation of knowledge, saw a role for peer interaction to produce cognitive conflict that would result in a change in the thinking of the individual, leading to the internalisation of a concept or idea. By challenging the role of others in the construction of knowledge, social constructivists to varying degrees challenged views of the nature of knowledge and of culture. (Bruner (1986, p. 65) describes culture as the 'implicit semi-connected knowledge of the world, from which through negotiation people arrive at satisfactory ways of acting in given contexts'.)

A more radical challenge to constructivism has emerged in the last two decades from theorists who view learning as a process of participation in cultural activity. This approach to learning has been labelled as 'situated', and is contrasted with a symbol-processing view by Bredo (1994), although he includes all social constructivists under this label. However, those who take a situated approach see a different role for the interactions with others where 'participation' is a central process. This approach stems in part from Vygotsky and action theory (Bredo, 1997; Lave, 1996). Meaning is created through participating in social activity. In this sense there is no individual notion of an idea or concept, but a distributed one. Rather than seeing learning as a process of transfer of knowledge from the knowledgeable to the less knowledgeable, we have engagement in culturally authentic activity. Such activity is part of a 'community of practice'. To learn to be a doctor is not just to learn the requisite physiology, anatomy, etc., but to enter into the community of practice of doctors. A novice starts on the outside of the community and, as understanding increases, moves towards a more central participation in that community of practice, eventually taking part in its transformation; what Lave and Wenger (1991) rather inelegantly termed a movement from 'legitimate peripheral participation' to central participation. Mutual understanding, or 'intersubjectivity' comes through this participation (Rogoff,

1990), and with it a transformation of identity. A situated approach to learning also brings with it a particular view of how to analyse learning. Just as we have argued that curriculum needs to be understood at different levels of negotiation and definition, so too does learning from a situated approach.

Participation can therefore be understood in different ways, depending upon the level of analysis. Rogoff (1995) identifies three interrelated perspectives on learning associated with three planes of analysis. The three planes are 'community', 'interpersonal' and 'personal'; the view of the learning process associated with each of these is *apprenticeship, guided participation* and *participatory appropriation*. Lave and Wenger (1991) focus on the community level and hence the idea of the community of practice, with apprentices 'learning the trade'. At the interpersonal level, the process of guided participation focuses attention on the interpersonal activities that are 'managed collaboratively by individuals and their social partners' (Rogoff, 1995, p. 146). For both levels, the role of the 'expert' is important in the collaboration that takes place, with the learner and the expert involved in joint problem-solving. Nevertheless, at the interpersonal level, all participants in communal activity are significant. Participatory appropriation is the process 'by which individuals transform their understanding of, and responsibility for, activities through their own participation' (Rogoff, 1995, p. 150). Rogoff uses this term, rather than the symbol-processing idea of 'internalisation' (i.e. the individual construction of knowledge), to emphasise the interrelationship of the person and the social context. What is central to a situated view of learning is that all three planes of analysis have to be considered in developing understanding of any one plane.

To view learning as a transformation of identity and enculturation into communities of practice also requires a quite different conception of knowledge to that held by cognitivist or symbol-processing views of mind. In symbol-processing, 'concepts' are objects to be internalised (stored in memory); in situated learning, 'the activity in which knowledge is developed and deployed is not separable from or ancillary to learning and cognition' (Brown et al., 1989, p. 32). [...]

From this view of situated learning comes a central focus on collaboration (between peers and others) and problem-solving. Unlike the symbol-processing view, problem-solving in a situated view is a shared activity, even when it is undertaken with an expert; expert and novices jointly solve problems. Problems emerge from activity. Thus, they are not given (the assumption in most teaching situations) but experienced. Likewise the solutions to problems emerge from actions in resolving experienced dilemmas. The idea of a dilemma is important: 'a problem is a dilemma with which the problem solver is emotionally engaged' (Lave, 1988, p. 175). A dilemma has no unique or stable resolution and there may be no entirely satisfactory solution (Lave, 1988, p. 139). It is these dilemmas that become the *emergent problems* as the activity progresses. Collaboration is at the heart of this situated view, and the development of intersubjectivity. Intersubjectivity between participants arises from the 'shared understanding based on a common focus of attention and some shared pre-suppositions that form the ground for communication' (Rogoff, 1990, p. 71). (We shall return to some of these ideas when we consider 'group work'.)

In summary, to reflect on the situated view, we see that in taking such an approach, all three of Bredo's dualisms (Bredo, 1994) lose their distinctions: there is no mind–body dualism, nor is there a simple separation of individual and society, nor of language and reality, [rather they form a unity].

This leaves one important idea of learning, namely, *metacognition*. This is seen as including knowledge about cognitive resources (which would include concepts) and self-regulatory mechanisms (Duell, 1986). Knowledge about cognitive resources is seen as a form of reflection on learning. How metacognitive knowledge is understood is determined also by the view of learning that obtains. In a symbol-processing approach, planning precedes action. Metacognition is an element of this planning through self-regulation. (Self-regulation involves planning what to do next, checking outcomes of strategies, and evaluating and revising strategies.) In a situated approach to learning, planning is a dynamic process that both precedes and is a consequence of action. Central to this view of planning is a view of reflection that von Glasersfeld (1989) refers to as 'operative knowledge'. 'Operative knowledge is not associative retrieval of a particular answer [as in symbol-processing views of mind], but rather knowledge of what to do in order to produce an answer [a solution]' (von Glasersfeld, 1989, p. 12). If an individual is to be able to reflect on her cognition, then this requires further knowledge than she apparently has; you can't know what you don't know. In the situated approach to learning, collaboration and the need for intersubjectivity provide the means by which operative or metacognitive knowledge can be both deployed and developed. We are, however, straying into a discussion of the nature of knowledge.

Views of knowledge and views of learning

[...]

The nature of knowledge

The two dominant views of learning we have been considering take different views of knowledge. Table 1.1 takes the two views of mind and compares them on the three dualisms identified by Bredo (1994).
[...]
   Participation, in the situated approach, is more than just a social affair: activity takes place in a social *and* physical world. In contrast to the symbol-processing view, knowledge guides action, and action guides knowledge. Knowledge is integrated with activity, along with the tools, sign systems and skills associated with the activity. A classic study illustrating the interrelationship of knowledge and activity was of dairy workers (Scribner, 1985). One part of the study looked at how what they did in their various jobs (clerical, delivery or warehouse) affected how they thought about the dairy products, compared for example with consumers. Most consumers thought of the products in terms of 'kinds' (e.g. milk and cheese), whereas drivers thought about 'kind' and 'size' (e.g. quart), and warehouse workers in terms of 'kind', 'size' and 'location'. Each of the groups of dairy workers had their thinking organised by the kinds of activity in which they engaged. But their knowledge also guided action. When warehouse workers made up an order from an order form, they would group the items on the list to be brought for central loading in ways that reduced journey distance. They used the accumulated social knowledge that went into the layout of the warehouse, and individual knowledge that reflected the current stacking arrangement. Observations showed that they would take very efficient travel distances, and would group items on the order form in ways that aided this efficiency. Looking at this from the point of view of learning (i.e. to be a dairy worker), Scribner concludes that 'What you learn is bound up with what you have to do' (1985, p. 203).

Table 1.1 Ideas about knowledge as depicted by symbol-processing and situated cognition

Dualism	Symbol-processing	Situated cognition
Language and reality	Objective reality	Knowledge is not a mirror of reality
Mind and body	Knowledge in the head	Knowledge related to action
Individual and society	Knowledge as individual property	Knowledge as social

An increasing sense of identity is what it means to become a part of a community of practice, but not as an 'explicit objective of change' (Lave and Wenger, 1991, p. 112). Lave and Wenger claim that 'the development of identity is central to the careers of newcomers in communities of practice' (ibid., p. 115). They equate the outcome of learning (knowledge) with the process of learning (participation), because they state that 'learning and a sense of identity are inseparable', i.e. they equate learning and identity. The formation of a sense of identity is learning, and the identity itself is knowledge.

Identity and self-esteem are seen by Bruner as one of the nine tenets of what he calls a psycho-cultural approach to education (Bruner, 1996). These tenets reflect a situated view of the nature of mind and of the nature of culture. For him cultural learning lies at the intersection of these two. He considers identity and self-esteem as two elements, with agency leading to 'the construction of a conceptual system that organises ... a "record" of agentive encounters in the world' (ibid., p. 36). In the formation of identity, the agency of an individual builds up skills and know-how based upon successes and failures. For a young person, school will be an important institution that defines criteria for these successes and failures, through, for example, assessment. The second element, self-esteem, stems from such evaluations, and if schools do not nurture this self-esteem, other parts of life will, as various forms of disaffection with schooling show (for example, groups of truants, street gangs and drug users). These kinds of issues are not just applicable to the education of young people, although it is evident that the early years are formative in the creation of identities. Nurses (or doctors) will be forming an identity as 'carers', 'efficient professionals', 'upholders of life' or whatever may be the ethos that is part of the profession. (At the same time they may have and be forming other identities as student, wife, father or 'responsible adult'.) When individuals move into a new situation where they join a company or group, they may (or may not) want to become part of that and share the identity of those who belong. Developing an identity is thus the subject matter of all learning, and is therefore on the face of it 'knowledge'.

The identities that individual learners bring to learning activities will position them, and they will be positioned by them, in ways that will influence their participation and hence the experienced curriculum. A situated view of learning makes identity central to the study of curriculum, including the assessment of its outcomes. [...]

Implications for views of the curriculum

The discussion of learning and knowledge in the previous sections gives rise to some implications for how we should approach central curriculum considerations. We shall therefore examine these considerations through knowledge, assessment and pedagogy. For each of the considerations, we shall show how learning addresses and interrelates the specified, enacted and experienced curricula.

Knowledge

We have already argued that a focus on learning gives a different approach to the analyses that are necessary to view knowledge in the curriculum, either as an 'input' to the (specified) curriculum or as a consideration in the enacted and experienced curricula. The 'disciplines of knowledge' are superseded by the idea of communities of practice in the situated approach. Philosophical analyses have always tried to reflect knowledge that is culturally valued, but took a narrow view of what represented culture in terms of educational goals. The idea of *cultural authenticity* remains important; a critical idea in engaging in a community of practice is that activity is authentic. This means it is coherent, meaningful and purposeful within a social framework – the ordinary practices of the culture. Thus, learning activities must allow students to engage in this authentic activity. However, there is a second sense in which authenticity needs to be considered, that of *personal* authenticity; i.e. that is personally meaningful. Without this second element, no construction of knowledge or participation, which will lead to learning, can take place. These two aspects of authenticity are interrelated but they can be thought of distinctly. They are distinct in that personal authenticity relates to the view of the learners and not to the view of knowledge, which is what cultural authenticity refers to. This means that the experienced curriculum is bound to decisions about the specified curriculum through the enacted curriculum. In making a task that is set as a 'problem' personally meaningful, students must be involved in the context of the problem. They must also be given significant decisions to make, which allow them to create solutions. Thus, in making bridges between school learning and everyday experience, it is not essential that the situations in which school activities are set are 'real'. The central requirement is that they afford the students authentic dilemmas that, in Lave's words, 'furnish opportunities [to the students] to improvise new practice [i.e. to learn]' (Lave, 1992, p. 85).

We therefore have the two kinds of authenticity coming together to provide a focus for the specified curriculum (communities of practice representing cultural authenticity) as a selection from culture, linked to the experienced curriculum (learners engaged with dilemmas that have both personal and cultural authenticity). The enacted curriculum must in some sense mediate the other two levels. This can be done for particular elements of the enacted curriculum, such as a set of learning activities or more holistically through a complete pedagogic strategy, for example, by adopting a 'community of learners' approach (we shall return to this in the consideration of pedagogy).

A movement away from disciplines as the source of knowledge for education (i.e. as an input to the specified curriculum) requires a more universal term than the 'subject' that is so often the focus of knowledge issues in the curriculum. Using a philosophical analysis of disciplines, a domain will be seen in terms of concepts, procedures, skills, etc., that relate together in a way that can be characterised as having some identity. Yet a community of practice is also a domain. Terms that might be used to characterise a domain, such as 'bodies of knowledge', 'practices' and 'ways of organising our experience', encapsulate views of the nature of learning and knowledge. Whatever way we think about the idea of a domain, we must be clear that it has many guises. Glaser, taking a symbol-processing

[…] approach, has a vision of a domain that is not just a subject. He talked of 'chess configurations, functional interpretations of circuit diagrams or representations of anatomical abnormalities in x-rays' (Glaser, 1992, pp. 64–65), and said that the structure and organisation are 'tied to the goal structure' of the problems that experts meet (ibid., p. 67). In this sense, we are seeing the domain knowledge as situated, and hence it must be related to action and hence to practices. […] When we think of a domain as a subject, we also tend to think of it only in cognitive terms, i.e. devoid of affect. Greeno et al. (1997) indicate that it is not as straightforward as this. In the cognitive (or symbol-processing) approach there are 'beliefs', and in the situated approach there seems to be no separation of cognitive and affective aspects of knowledge (e.g. identity is made up of both).

The specified curriculum is therefore affected, not just by a philosophical or cultural analysis, but by a consideration of learning and associated views of mind. Again, we are simultaneously engaging with the specified and the experienced curriculum, with the former not just being an 'input' to the latter. Philosophical analyses of the nature of knowledge, or even anthropological ones of how knowledge is produced by say scientists (e.g. Latour and Woolgar, 1979), provide but one element of analysis at the global level (parallel to Rogoff's community level noted earlier). We also need to see the interrelationships of the discussion at the interactional and the individual level, to see how this knowledge is constructed through participatory appropriation or internalisation (depending upon the view of learning). […]

Thus, we have a level of analysis relating to the experienced curriculum […] that has profound implications for how we consider the specified curriculum (particularly 'domains') and the enacted curriculum (how these domains are treated in the classroom).

Assessment

In spite of attention to the role of assessment in the development of curriculum, only rarely have assessment systems been analysed from a perspective on learning. Increasingly, the specified curriculum is enacted to a degree in national assessment systems, yet seldom are the educational purposes and values of such systems considered in conjunction. It is common, for example, for constructivist rhetoric to underpin the specified curriculum, but to be noticeably absent from assessment of the curriculum (Murphy, 1996). The tensions that this creates are then manifest at the levels of the enacted and experienced curricula.

In recent debates, the view of knowledge and of learning underpinning most assessment practice has been challenged (Black and Wiliam, 1998; Gardner, 1992; Gipps, 1994; Murphy, 1995). Typically, assessment systems reflect the psychometric tradition that had its roots in views of mind that saw ability as an innate trait that could be measured. At its most extreme, this led to unidimensional views of ability encapsulated in notions of general intelligence. The 'measurement' approach tried to distinguish students according to ability, usually to match a 'normal' statistical distribution of such ability that was supposed to exist in the population. Thus, the task was to separate students, so they could be selected for curricula that would suit them, or for jobs that they would be able to perform. Challenges to assessment, derived from a Vygotskian perspective, have emerged through the 1980s and 1990s, but have tended to focus on the assessment of learning *in situ*, rather than on national systems; for example, Brown and Ferrara (1985), Newman et al. (1989) and Lunt (1993). Analyses of national, large-scale assessment based on situated views of knowledge have been rare and have tended to focus on equity in relation to gender

(Murphy, 1995) and on social class (Cooper, 1992). It is only recently that more general critiques have emerged, but these have typically been associated with subject perspectives, rather than assessment perspectives *per se*; for example, mathematics (Boaler, 1997) and science (Roth, 1997). [...]

[A] situated view of learning requires a radical rethink of assessment that would encompass, for example, shared understanding. At the very least it would make group assessment a central issue, rather than an issue of continual conflict with national assessment systems that overwhelmingly reward individual, rather than group, achievement (despite the apparent calls from those outside education for the opposite approach). [...]

Nature of tasks

If we take a symbol-processing view of learning, then an assessment task will have a stability that allows responses to be evaluated against an accepted 'answer'. The response will show an understanding of a concept or procedure that can be matched against an accepted view. A constructivist version of this sees learners on their way to understanding, and various responses could exemplify misconceptions that they have and indicate how future learning could be adjusted to confront these misconceptions and arrive at an accepted one. From a situated view, then, the stability of the task is an issue. Newman et al. (1989) refer to a task as a 'strategic fiction'. When a teacher sets a 'problem', then what is actually problematic is at issue. Also, what the student sees as salient in the information given can vary, not just depending upon their 'level of understanding' (what the task is trying to assess), but depending upon the qualitative differences in the communities in which they participate. For example, gender and race locate learners in different communities, and their interpretations of tasks reflect the qualitative differences between these communities (e.g. for gender, see Murphy, 1991; Gipps and Murphy, 1994). [...] Numerous examples of these differences in views of salience, and the consequences for what tasks students perceive and the solutions they judge to be appropriate, have been demonstrated in assessment situations (Boaler, 1994; Cooper, 1992; Murphy, 1991). That these same effects obtain in learning situations has also been demonstrated (Murphy and McCormick, 1997).

The dynamic nature of tasks means that interpretations of responses are made problematic, i.e. the central issue of validity in assessment. Furthermore, such a view leads one to anticipate variation in response from an individual to demands in assessment tasks, irrespective of the theoretical construct assumed. Consequently, the traditional notion of reliability is under threat in a situated approach to assessment. The implications of this for assessment methods are demanding, and beyond the scope of this chapter, but it will be evident that we must be more modest in what we think assessment is able to achieve, and at the same time more creative in the practices we implement. The need to expand the kinds of evidence that are used in assessment is obvious, to accompany the move to authentic assessments (such as work-based assessment). Thus, interpreting student responses to tasks can be seen in the context of the community of practice; it may imply more interrogation of the student to establish the context of response, along with the kind of evidence gained from such things as process-folios ('instruments of learning ... [that] contain full process-tracing records of a student's involvement in one or more ... works' (Gardner, 1992, p. 103)). The broader the range of assessment used to illuminate a complex achievement or performance, the better will be the understanding of the student. However, assessment information provides only an understanding of achievement, or an indicator of it, not actual achievement. Thus, how we use assessment to monitor progress in the experienced curriculum, or to determine the outcomes of the specified and enacted curriculum, depends crucially on how we understand learning and learners.

Self-assessment

As with many curriculum initiatives, the advocates of self-assessment may be driven by an ideology such as child- or student-centred approaches. Thus, self-assessment is seen in terms of empowering and valuing the students' view and the criteria they may bring to their learning. Our discussion of views of learning gives another and more powerful rationale. Metacognition, with its operative and self-regulatory elements, requires students to develop an awareness of learning, and to achieve this they need an involvement in reflecting upon their learning. Without some element of self-assessment, this awareness cannot be developed. Self-assessment, present in, for example, peer assessment (where students assess each other), is central to the development of a strategic approach to their learning. This is the constructive aspect of operative knowledge that is best demonstrated, according to von Glasersfeld (1989, p. 12) 'where something new is generated, something that was not already available to the operator'. Thus, learning to solve problems requires knowing when to solve them, or recognising particular kinds of problems, and when it is appropriate to use particular solutions. Children may be taught how to carry out a 'fair test' as a form of scientific investigation but, if they are unaware of when a fair test should be carried out, they will be unable to use this test without a teacher to tell them (Murphy et al., 1996).

Self-assessment is also a prerequisite for students learning the norms of a community of practice. Schoenfeld (1996) advocates conducting undergraduate mathematics classes in a way that is true to what he and other mathematicians do (Lave et al., 1988; Schoenfeld, 1996). Students, for example, have to convince each other about what constitutes a solution to a mathematical problem (as mathematicians do), not just produce 'right answers' (that is 'right' according to the teacher's judgement). In a similar vein, in critical literacy approaches, students are encouraged to examine texts to understand how identities are constructed in various discourses (Moss, 1996). Whether this constitutes a good model for other areas of the curriculum is of course a point for debate.

Validity

Finally we turn to the notions of validity of assessment that might flow from different views of learning. These different notions give different views of knowledge and hence of domains, as we have already argued. But such views of knowledge also imply that validity cannot come directly from how we see subjects or domains. Face and content validity are derived from teachers' or experts' views of a subject; for example, an assessment is judged valid if it reflects the content of a subject. If we are to take seriously the ideas on interpretations of tasks by students, and hence some caution in interpreting their responses, then we cannot judge validity only in terms of content. Messick (1989) argued strongly for the overarching importance of construct validity. This requires both a view of the theoretical construct (what is the model of achievement in the domain) and the empirical data of performance on the assessment instrument, upon which to judge the construct validity.

Messick did not argue this in terms of views of learning, as we would, but nevertheless his stance is an accepted one among assessment theorists. What is less evident, however, is the operationalisation of the theoretical constructs that are sensitive to different views of learning. Greeno and his colleagues (1997) laid out such theoretical constructs to reflect both the symbol-processing (what they called the 'cognitive') approach and the situated approach. Further, they outlined these for both literacy and mathematics. This we see as ground-breaking work, particularly with respect to the situated approach, and we hope that other domains could be elaborated, and assessment procedures implemented, that tried to assess achievement against these constructs.

Each of these three issues (nature of tasks, self-assessment and validity) reflects the different levels of analysis of the curriculum:

- validity draws on the specified curriculum through its articulation of the theoretical construct, and the experienced curriculum through the empirical data of students' responses to the assessment based upon the construct.
- the nature of tasks is central to the determination of the enacted curriculum, yet requires a view of learning drawing together the specified level of communities of practice and experienced curriculum in the interpretation of tasks.
- the discussion of self-assessment started with the experienced curriculum in terms of its role in student learning, yet with the example of encouraging students to participate in a community of practice (of mathematicians), we have this level feeding through to the other two levels.

Pedagogy

We have argued that changing views about the nature of learning and of knowledge have focused attention on the experienced curriculum. We have shown how, in many ways, the agency of learners and of teachers can lead to a diversity of meanings being constructed within any one curriculum level. We have also argued that, as a consequence, a situated view of learning creates new roles for assessment to enable the progression and diversity of these meanings to be monitored in order to support students' learning. What we consider here is how the teaching and learning process is understood in a situated view and the implications of this for understanding the curriculum. [...]

So why have we chosen to use [the term pedagogy]? The term 'teaching methods' carries with it a view that a teacher does things to learners (teaches them), and hence may have a connotation that these methods exist outside a view of learning and of learners. It is not just that particular teaching methods may only suit particular learners, but that they encapsulate particular views of learning. If we think that giving lectures is a way of teaching, then we must have some kind of view of learning as information-processing if the learner is not allowed an active role. On the other hand, the lecture might achieve such an active role in learners through controversial statements and tasks to be followed up with other kinds of activities. This starts to broaden to a consideration of a number of issues, including the role of the learner and the teacher, the kinds of learning activities that are provided, and the nature of the assessment of the learning. If we then put together these features with that of views of learning and knowledge, we have a pedagogic *approach*, or a pedagogic *strategy*. For governments to focus on teaching methods in isolation, as in the UK government's concern to increase 'whole-class teaching' (Reynolds and Farrell, 1996), is to ignore the other pedagogic dimensions that mediate the implementation of this method. A teacher who sees the learner as agentive (Bruner, 1996) would use such whole-class methods to engage students in interactions with one another and herself, to reflect the view of learning associated with the method. A teacher adopting a symbol-processing approach to learning may find the implementation more difficult, as the notion of the sharing of understanding is less important than the individual internalisation. Indeed, such a teacher may ironically (given the association of whole-class teaching with 'traditional' views of learning) have more difficulty with this approach!

The crucial notion of a pedagogic approach, then, is the coherence and consistency that exist among the dimensions of the pedagogy [...]:

1   goals of learning
2   knowledge that is the focus of learning
3   learning and assessment activities
4   the teacher–student roles and relationships
5   'classroom' discourse. [...]

Implications for curriculum issues

Transfer

The assumption of transfer of knowledge underlies much of schooling and indeed all education associated with educational institutions, at whatever level. The specified curriculum typically assumes that general-purpose knowledge is learned for use at another time and in another context. This assumption permeates many aspects of how we view curriculum. For example, we assume that students who learn mathematics in the mathematics lesson can use this in the geography lesson; that is, we make the assumption that knowledge learned in one part of the curriculum is available for use in any other part. This implies a particular organisation and enactment of the specified curriculum. Yet teachers and researchers will testify to the continual failing of this assumption, and our own investigations of classrooms have provided empirical evidence of this for some areas of the curriculum (Davidson et al., 1998; Evens and McCormick, 1997; McCormick et al., 1998). To take the view of 'transfer of learning' is to adopt a symbol-processing view of mind; symbols stored in memory are abstracted knowledge that can then be used when confronted with a problem in any context. We have already indicated that those who hold a situated view of mind reject this view, and in particular reject the idea of abstract knowledge devoid of context (Lave and Wenger, 1991); they hold a quite distinctly different view of generalised knowledge. Indeed, transfer lies at the heart of the dispute between the symbol-processing and the situated views. For those who support the idea of transfer, there is a certainty about the process, while others harbour doubts about the empirical evidence. For example, Lave (1988) reviews many of the studies of transfer and concludes that the evidence fails to show that the concept of transfer is a helpful one. Those who believe that we store in our minds symbol representations that we recall for use in particular situations dismiss this kind of argument and claim that there are many examples of transfer established in the literature (Anderson et al., 1996). The arguments between the two sides are extensive and continuing. [...]

Ultimately, the argument comes down to which view of learning is supported. However, there are two important points that come out of this argument. The first is that the conditions under which transfer will take place depend on a match between the situation where the learning took place and the situation where the knowledge is used. This doesn't look much like transfer ('transportation' might be a better word). The second point Anderson et al. (1996) make is that we need to pay more attention to the cues that signal the relevance of skill (or knowledge), i.e. the crucial issues are where and what the cues are. [...] Under these circumstances, learning the salience or the 'cues', as Anderson et al. (1996) describe it (or 'affordances' as Clancey (1993) puts it), is what should be the focus and not, in our view, transfer.

This argument is not merely academic, but it reveals some common elements about how transfer can be supported (Murphy et al., 1999, pp. 94–95):

- providing a bridge between novel and new contexts;
- enabling tacit and explicit communication using experts and peers who serve as resources in collaborative settings;
- using analogies to identify similarities between situations;
- explicit treatment of the features in a situation to point up alternative views of salience;
- teachers act as partners, coaches, modelling practices;
- self-monitoring of learning processes (i.e. develop metacognitive awareness).

But underlying the common strategies is the argument of whether the mechanism sees the transfer of the same knowledge between situations or an engagement in new learning.

The curriculum implications of this argument we have discussed are (a) that the teaching of abstract knowledge for later use may be flawed and (b) that the use of knowledge across the curriculum and hence the curriculum organisation may similarly be based upon an incorrect premise about the nature of that knowledge. [...]

Group work

This final issue is often seen as a question of which teaching method to adopt, perhaps for reasons only associated with classroom management (e.g. the amount of teaching resources available). We have chosen to use the term 'group work' because this is often how it is dealt with in the curriculum. However, we see underlying this the central issue of *collaboration*, which depends on intersubjectivity. This terms stems from views of learning, both as a *means* and as an *end* of learning. As a means, i.e. collaborating to learn, it stems from the views we discussed earlier, where the development of intersubjectivity was central, at least in the situated view. Even Piagetian approaches see symmetrical collaboration among peers as a prerequisite for knowledge construction through cognitive conflict and hence change. Collaboration is thus a central part of learning mechanisms. What a situated view brings to this is, however, the need for collaboration to be seen not only among peers, but also between experts (e.g. teachers) and learners. The collaboration from this approach is not just about purely cognitive issues (in the terms Piaget might have seen it), but also about relations among people, as the participation metaphor emphasises.

That, of course, relates to our second curriculum view of collaboration, namely as an end in itself. Here it is important for students to learn how to collaborate so that they will be able to identify and share common reference points and models of the situation. For collaboration to take place, students must engage in each other's thinking. But it also means that the tasks should enable this. The idea in the use of the term 'group work' is that it is a way of carrying out a classroom task, without there necessarily being any implication for the nature of this task. We would dispute this; tasks must give students the opportunity to share. Students inevitably reformulate tasks, and alternative perceptions of purposes and salience emerge. Collaboration is often gendered territory, and there is evidence that girls and boys not only bring different views of salience to activities, but collaborate differently (Murphy, 1999). Some argue that central to all collaborative activity is exploratory talk (Mercer, 1995). Thus, tasks must give opportunities for talk, including the sharing of information, joint planning, presenting of ideas to the group, joint reasoning, evaluation and decision-taking. If collaboration is also learning to participate, this talk cannot be separated from what is being talked about; the community of practice will have a language that reflects the domain of the practice. This kind of view of collaboration, with the need to learn skills (including collaborative talk), places great demands on teachers and learners, and is more complex than the mere arrangement of students into groups. Murphy (1999) provides a summary of the factors necessary for effective collaboration:

- a 'true' group task;
- a requirement to plan, record, act and communicate as a group;
- teacher support for both skills for collaboration as well as collaboration for learning;
- teacher provision of tools for making thinking explicit, including forms of the representation of tools, equipment, etc.;
- student autonomy;
- monitoring by the teacher of the dialectic between the students, and students and tasks;
- encouragement of reflective discourse between students;
- students' explicit awareness of the agenda in relation to the subject and to collaboration.

However, any changes to the way collaboration is supported through the nature of tasks and other features of pedagogy listed above, need to be accompanied by changes to all elements of a pedagogic approach, particularly assessment. Many of the developments in national curricula that have included assessment systems, have focused almost exclusively upon individual assessment. This means that the focus of tasks that include an element of assessment will detract from any collaborative effort. Further, there still seems to be a lack of routine assessment techniques that allow assessment of participation (and hence collaboration), despite the development of models of achievement for the situated approach indicated earlier (Greeno et al., 1997). A renewed focus on learning in relation to both assessment and collaboration may spur this development. [...]

References

Anderson, J. R., Reder, L. M. and Simon, H. A. (1996) 'Situated learning and education'. *Educational Researcher*, 25 (4), 5–11.

Benavot, A., Cha, Y.-K., Kamens, D. H., Meyer, J. and Wong, S.-Y. (1992) 'Knowledge for the masses: world models and national curricula, 1920–1986'. In J. Meyer, D. Kamens, A. Benavot, Y.-K. Cha and S. Wong (eds) *School Knowledge for the Masses. World Models and National Primary Curricular Categories in the Twentieth Century*. London: Falmer.

Bernstein, B. (1971) 'On classification and framing of educational knowledge'. In M. F. D. Young (ed.) *Knowledge and Control*. London: Collier-Macmillan, 47–69.

Black, P. and Wiliam, D. (1998) 'Assessment and classroom learning'. *Assessment in Education*, 5 (1), 1–75.

Boaler, J. (1994) 'When do girls prefer football to fashion? An analysis of female underachievement in relation to realistic mathematics contexts'. *British Educational Research Journal*, 20 (5), 551–564.

Boaler, J. (1997) 'Alternative approaches to teaching, learning and assessing mathematics'. Paper presented at the 7th Conference of the European Association for Research in Learning and Instruction held in Athens, Greece in August.

Bredo, E. (1994) 'Reconstructing educational psychology: Situated cognition and Deweyian pragmatism'. *Educational Psychologist*, 29 (1), 23–35.

Bredo, E. (1997) 'The social construction of learning'. In G. D. Phye (ed.) *Handbook of Academic Learning: Construction of Knowledge*. San Diego: Academic Press.

Brown, A. L., and Ferrara, R. A. (1985) 'Diagnosing zones of proximal development'. In J. Wertsch (ed.) *Culture, Communication, and Cognition: Vygotskian Perspectives*. New York: Cambridge University Press.

Brown, J. S., Collins, A. and Duguid, P. (1989) 'Situated cognition and the culture of learning'. *Educational Researcher*, 18 (1), 32 –41.

Bruner, J. (1986) *Actual Minds, Possible Worlds*. Cambridge, MA: Harvard University Press.

Bruner, J. (1996) *The Culture of Education*. Cambridge, MA: Harvard University Press.

Clancey, W. J. (1993) 'Situated action: A neuropsychological interpretation response to Vera and Simon'. *Cognitive Science*, 17, 87–116.

Cooper, B. (1992) 'Testing National Curriculum mathematics: Some critical comments on the treatment of "real" contexts for mathematics'. *Curriculum Journal*, 3, 231–243.

Davidson, M., Evens, H. and McCormick, R. (1998) 'Bridging the gap. The use of concepts from science and mathematics in design and technology at KS3'. In J. S. Smith and E. W. L. Norman (eds) *IDATER 98 – International Conference on Design and Technology Educational Research and Curriculum Development*. Loughborough: University of Loughborough, 48–53.

Duell, O. K. (1986) 'Metacognitive skills'. In G. D. Phye and T. Andre (eds) *Cognitive Classroom Learning: Understanding, Thinking, and Problem-Solving*. Orlando: Academic Press, 205–242.

Evens, H. and McCormick, R. (1997) *Mathematics by Design: An Investigation at Key Stage 3* (Final Report for the Design Council). Milton Keynes: School of Education, The Open University.

Gardner, H. (1992) 'Assessment in context: The alternative to standardized testing'. In B. R. Gifford and M. C. O'Connor (eds) *Changing Assessment: Alternative Views of Aptitude, Achievement and Instruction*. London: Kluwer.

Gipps, C. V. (1994) *Beyond Testing: Towards a Theory of Educational Assessment*. London: Falmer.

Gipps, C. and Murphy, P. (1994) *A Fair Test? Assessment, Achievement and Equity*. Buckingham: Open University Press.

Glaser, R. (1992) 'Expert knowledge and processes of thinking'. In D. F. Halpern (ed.) *Enhancing Thinking Skills in the Sciences and Mathematics*. Hillsdale, NJ: Erlhaum, 63–75.

Goodson, I. F. (1994) *Studying the Curriculum*. Buckingham: Open University Press.

Greeno, J. G., Pearson, P. D. and Schoenfeld, A. H. (1997) 'Implications for national assessment of educational progress of research and cognition'. In R. Glaser and R. Linn (eds) *Assessment in Transition: Monitoring the Nation's Educational Progress. Background Studies*. Stanford, CA: National Academy of Education, Stanford University.

Latour, B. and Woolgar, S. (1979) *Laboratory Life: The Construction of Scientific Facts*. Princeton, NJ: Princeton University Press.

Lave, J. (1988) *Cognition in Practice: Mind, Mathematics and Culture in Everyday Life*. New York: Cambridge University Press.

Lave, J. (1992) 'Word problems: A microcosm of theories of learning'. In P. Light and G. Butterworth (eds) *Context and Cognition: Ways of Learning and Knowing*. London: Harvester Wheatsheaf, 74–92.

Lave, J. (1996) 'The practice of learning'. In S. Chaiklin and J. Lave (eds) *Understanding Practice: Perspectives on Activity and Context*. Cambridge: Cambridge University Press, 3–32.

Lave, J. and Wenger, E. (1991) *Situated Learning: Legitimate Peripheral Participation*. Cambridge: Cambridge University Press.

Lave, J., Greeno, J. G. Schoenfeld, A., Smith, S. and Butler, M. (eds) (1988) *Learning Mathematical Problem Solving.* (Report No. IRL88–0006) Palo Alto, CA: Institute for Research on Learning.

Lunt, I. (1993) 'The practice of assessment'. In H. Daniels (ed.) *Charting the Agenda: Educational Activity after Vygotsky.* London: Routledge, 145–170.

McCormick, R., Murphy, P., Davidson, M., Evens, H. and Spence, M. (1998) *The Use of Mathematics in Science and Technology Education.* Symposium at the British Educational Research Association annual conference, September, Queen's University, Belfast.

Mercer, N. (1995) *The Guided Construction of Knowledge: Talk amongst Teachers and Learners.* Clevedon, UK: Multilingual Matters.

Messick, S. (1989) 'Meaning and values in test validation: The science and ethics of assessment'. *Educational Researcher*, 18 (2), 5–11.

Moss, G. (1996) 'Negotiated literacies: How children enact what counts as reading in a different social setting'. Unpublished PhD thesis. Milton Keynes: Open University.

Murphy, P. (1990) 'Learning and the curriculum'. In M. Lawn, B. Moon and P. Murphy (eds) *Curriculum, Learning and Assessment (E819). Study Guide.* Milton Keynes: Open University Press, 35–36.

Murphy, P. (1991) 'Gender and practical work'. In B. Woolnough (ed.) *Practical Work in Science.* Milton Keynes: Open University Press.

Murphy, P. (1995) 'Sources of inequity: Understanding students' responses to assessment'. *Assessment in Education: Principles, Policy and Practice*, 2 (3), 249–270.

Murphy, P. (1996) 'Integrating learning and assessment – the role of learning theories'. In P. Woods (ed.) *Contemporary Issues in Teaching and Learning.* London: Routledge, 173–193.

Murphy, P. (1999) 'Supporting collaborative learning: A gender dimension'. In P. Murphy (ed.) *Learners, Learning and Assessment.* London: Paul Chapman, 258–276.

Murphy, P. and McCormick, R. (1997) 'Problem solving in science and technology education'. *Research in Science and Education*, 27 (3), 461–481.

Murphy, P., Scanlon, E. and Issroff, K. with Hodgson, B. and Whitelegg, E. (1996) 'Group work in Primary Science – emerging issues for learning and teaching'. In K. Schnack (ed.) *Studies in Educational Theory and Curriculum*, vol. 14. Copenhagen: Danish School of Educational Studies.

Murphy, P., Moon, B., McCormick, R. and Leach, J. (1999) *Learning, Curriculum and Assessment* (E836 Study Guide). Milton Keynes: Open University Press.

Newman, D., Griffin, P. and Cole, M. (1989) *The Construction Zone: Working for Cognitive Change in Schools.* Cambridge: Cambridge University Press.

Reynolds, D. and Farrell, S. (1996) *Worlds Apart? A Review of International Surveys of Educational Achievement Involving England.* (Ofsted reviews of research.) London: HMSO.

Rogoff, B. (1990) *Apprenticeship in Thinking: Cognitive Development in a Social Context.* New York: Oxford University Press.

Rogoff, B. (1995) 'Observing sociocultural activity on three planes: Participatory appropriation, guided participation and apprenticeship'. In J. V. Wertsch, P. del Rio, and A. Alverez (eds) *Sociocultural Studies of Mind.* Cambridge: Cambridge University Press, 139–164.

Roth, W. M. (1997) 'Situated cognition and assessment of competence in science'. Paper presented at the 7th Conference of the European Association for Research in Learning and Instruction. Athens, Greece.

Schoenfeld, A. (1996) 'In fostering communities of inquiry, must it matter that the teacher knows the answer?' *For the Learning of Mathematics*, 14 (1), 44–55.

Scribner, S. (1985) 'Knowledge at work'. *Anthropology and Education Quarterly*, 16 (3), 199–206.

Skilbeck, M. (1990) *Curriculum Reform: An Overview of Trends.* Paris: OECD.

Von Glasersfeld, E. (1989) 'Learning as constuctive activity'. In P. Murphy and B. Moon (eds) *Developments in Learning and Assessment.* London: Hodder & Stoughton, 5–18.

2

Neuroscience and Education

Usha Goswami

[...]

The study of learning unites education and neuroscience. Neuroscience as broadly defined investigates the processes by which the brain learns and remembers, from the molecular and cellular levels right through to brain systems (e.g., the system of neural areas and pathways underpinning our ability to speak and comprehend language). This focus on learning and memory can be at a variety of levels. Understanding cell signalling and synaptic mechanisms (one brain cell connects to another via a synapse) is important for understanding learning, but so is examination of the functions of specific brain structures such as the hippocampus by natural lesion studies or by invasive methods. Brain cells (or neurons) transmit information via electrical signals, which pass from cell to cell via the synapses, triggering the release of neurotransmitters (chemical messengers). There are around 100 billion neurons in the brain, each with massive connections to other neurons. Understanding the ways in which neurotransmitters work is a major goal of neuroscience. Patterns of neural activity are thought to correspond to particular mental states or mental representations. Learning broadly comprises changes in connectivity, either via changes in potentiation at the synapse or via the strengthening or pruning of connections. Successful teaching thus directly affects brain function, by changing connectivity.

Clearly, educators do not study learning at the level of the cell. Successful learning is also dependent on the curriculum and the teacher, the context provided by the classroom and the family, and the context of the school and the wider community. All of these factors of course interact with the characteristics of individual brains. [...]

Teaching

It is notable, however, that neuroscience does not as yet study teaching. Successful teaching is the natural counterpart of successful learning, and is described as a 'natural cognition' by Strauss (2003). Forms of teaching are found throughout the animal kingdom, usually related to ways of getting food. However, the performance of *intentional acts* to increase the knowledge of others (teaching with a 'theory of mind') does seem to be unique to humans, and is perhaps essential to what it means to be a human being (Strauss *et al.*, 2002). The identification and analysis of successful pedagogy is central to research

From: *British Journal of Educational Psychology*, 74 (2004), pp.1–14. Reproduced with permission from the *British Journal of Educational Psychology*, © The British Psychological Society.

in education, but is currently a foreign field to cognitive neuroscience. There are occasional studies of the neural changes accompanying certain types of highly focused educational programmes (such as remedial programmes for teaching literacy to dyslexic children, see below), but wider questions involving the invisible mental processes and inferences made by successful teachers have not begun to be asked. Strauss suggests that questions such as whether there are specialized neural circuits for different aspects of teaching may soon be tractable to neuroimaging methods, and this is a thought-provoking idea. Teaching is a very specialized kind of social interaction, and some of its aspects (reading the minds of others, inferring their motivational and emotional states) are after all already investigated in cognitive neuroscience.

[…]

A quick primer on brain development

Many critical aspects of brain development are complete prior to birth. […] The development of the neural tube begins during the first weeks of gestation, and 'proliferative zones' within the tube give birth to the cells that compose the brain. These cells migrate to the different regions where they will be employed in the mature brain prior to birth. By 7 months gestation almost all of the neurons that will comprise the mature brain have been formed. Brain development following birth consists almost exclusively of the growth of axons, synapses and dendrites (fibre connections): this process is called synaptogenesis. For visual and auditory cortex, there is dramatic early synaptogenesis, with maximum density of around 150% of adult levels between 4 and 12 months followed by pruning. Synaptic density in the visual cortex returns to adult levels between 2 and 4 years. For other areas such as prefrontal cortex (thought to underpin planning and reasoning), density increases more slowly and peaks after the first year. Reduction to adult levels of density is not seen until some time between 10 and 20 years. Brain metabolism (glucose uptake, an approximate index of synaptic functioning) is also above adult levels in the early years, with a peak of about 150% somewhere around 4–5 years.

By the age of around 10 years, brain metabolism reduces to adult levels for most cortical regions. The general pattern of brain development is clear. There are bursts of synaptogenesis, peaks of density, and then synapse rearrangement and stabilisation with myelinisation, occurring at different times and rates for different brain regions (i.e., different sensitive periods for the development of different types of knowledge). Brain volume quadruples between birth and adulthood, because of the proliferation of connections, not because of the production of new neurons. Nevertheless, the brain is highly plastic, and significant new connections frequently form in adulthood in response to new learning or to environmental insults (such as a stroke). Similarly, sensitive periods are not all-or-none. If visual input is lacking during early development, for example, the critical period is extended (Fagiolini & Hensch, 2000). Nevertheless, visual functions that develop late (e.g., depth perception) suffer more from early deprivation than functions that are relatively mature at birth (such as colour perception, Maurer *et al.*, 1989). Thus more complex abilities may have a lower likelihood of recovery than elementary skills. One reason may be that axons have already stabilised on target

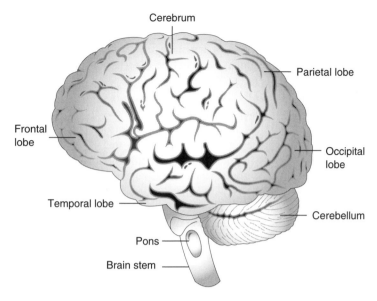

Cerebrum

Parietal lobe

Frontal
lobe

Occipital
lobe

Temporal lobe

Cerebellum

Pons

Brain stem

Figure 2.1   The major subdivisions of the cerebral cortex. The different lobes are specialised for different tasks. The frontal lobe is used for planning and reasoning, and controls our ability to use speech and how we react to situations emotionally. The temporal lobe is mainly concerned with memory, audition, language and object recognition. The parietal lobe controls our sense of touch and is used for spatial processing and perception. The occipital lobe is specialised for vision. Structures such as the hippocampus and the amygdala are internal to the brain, situated beneath the cerebral cortex in the midbrain

cells for which they are not normally able to compete, thereby causing irreversible reorganisation.

It is important to realise that there are large individual differences between brains. Even in genetically identical twins, there is striking variation in the size of different brain structures, and in the number of neurons that different brains use to carry out identical functions. This individual variation is coupled with significant localisation of function. A basic map of major brain subdivisions is shown in Figure 2.1. Although adult brains all show this basic structure, it is thought that early in development a number of possible developmental paths and end states are possible. The fact that development converges on the same basic brain structure across cultures and gene pools is probably to do with the constraints on development present in the environment. Most children are exposed to very similar constraints despite slightly different rearing environments. Large differences in environment, such as being reared in darkness or without contact with other humans, are thankfully absent or rare. When large environmental differences occur, they have notable effects on cognitive function. For example, neuroimaging studies show that blind adults are faster at processing auditory information than sighted controls, and that congenitally deaf adults are faster at processing visual information in the peripheral field than hearing controls (e.g., Neville & Bavelier, 2000; Neville et al., 1983; Röder et al., 1999).

Nevertheless, neurons themselves are interchangeable in the immature system, and so dramatic differences in environment can lead to different developmental outcomes. For example, the area underpinning spoken language in hearing people (used for auditory analysis) is recruited for sign language in deaf people (visual/spatial analysis) (Neville et al., 1998). Visual brain areas are recruited for Braille reading (tactile analysis) in blind people (see Röder & Neville, 2003). It has even been reported that a blind adult who suffered a stroke specific to the visual areas of her brain consequently lost her proficient Braille reading ability, despite the fact that her somatosensory perception abilities were unaffected (Jackson, 2000). It has also been suggested that all modalities are initially mutually linked, as during early infancy auditory stimulation also evokes large responses in visual areas of the brain, and somatosensory responses are enhanced by white noise (e.g., Neville, 1995). If this is the case, a kind of 'synaesthesia' could enable infants to extract schemas that are independent of particular modalities, schemas such as number, intensity and time (see Röder & Neville, 2003). If this mutual linkage extends into early childhood, it may explain why younger children respond so well to teaching via multi-sensory methods.

Neuroimaging tools for developmental cognitive neuroscience

Neuroimaging studies are based on the assumption that any cognitive task makes specific demands on the brain which will be met by changes in neural activity. These changes in activity affect local blood flow which can be measured either directly (PET) or indirectly (fMRI). Dynamic interactions among mental processes can be measured by ERPs.

PET (positron emission tomography) relies on the injection of radioactive tracers, and is not suitable for use with children. Brain areas with higher levels of blood flow have larger amounts of the tracer, allowing pictures of the distribution of radiation to be created and thereby enabling the localisation of different neural functions. fMRI (functional magnetic resonance imaging) also enables the localisation of brain activity. This technique requires inserting the participant into a large magnet (like a big tube), and works by measuring the magnetic resonance signal generated by the protons of water molecules in neural cells. When blood flow to particular brain areas increases, the distribution of water in the brain tissue also changes. This enables measurement of a BOLD (blood oxygenation level dependent) response which measures changes in the oxygenation state of haemoglobin associated with neural activity. The change in BOLD response is the outcome measure in most fMRI studies. It is very noisy inside the magnet and participants are given headphones to shield their ears and a panic button (the magnet is claustrophobic). Because of these factors, it has been challenging to adapt fMRI for use with children (who also move a lot, impeding scanning accuracy). However, with the advent of specially adapted coils and less claustrophobic head scanners, such studies are growing in number.

A different and widely used neuroimaging technique that can be applied to children is that of the event related potential (ERP). ERPs enable the timing rather than localisation of neural events to be studied. Sensitive electrodes are placed on the skin of the scalp and then recordings of brain activity are taken. Recording of the spontaneous natural rhythms of the brain is called EEG (electroencephalography). ERP refers to systematic deflections in electrical activity that may occur to precede, accompany or follow experimenter-determined events. ERP rhythms are thus time-locked to specific events designed to study cognitive function. The usual technique is for the child to watch a video while wearing a headcap (like a swimming cap) that holds the electrodes. For visual ERP studies, the video is delivering the stimuli; for auditory ERP studies, the linguistic stimuli form a background noise and the child sits engrossed in a silent cartoon. The most usual outcome measures are (i) the latency of the potentials, (ii) the amplitude (magnitude) of the various positive and negative changes in neural response, and (iii) the distribution of the activity. The different potentials (characterised in countless ERP studies) are called N100, P200, N400 and so on, denoting Negative peak at 100 ms, Positive peak at 200 ms and so on. The amplitude and duration of single ERP components such as the P200 increase until age 3 to 4 years (in parallel with synaptic density), and then decrease until puberty. ERP latencies decrease within the first years of life (in parallel with myelinisation) and reach adult levels in late childhood. ERP studies have provided extensive evidence on the time course of neural processing and their amplitude and duration are used to understand the underlying cognitive processes.

Selected studies from cognitive neuroscience with interesting implications for education

[...]

The tools of cognitive neuroscience offer various possibilities to education, including the early diagnosis of special educational needs, the monitoring and comparison of the effects of different kinds of educational input on learning, and an increased understanding of individual differences in learning and the best ways to suit input to learner. I will now describe briefly some recent neuroscience studies in certain areas of cognitive development, and give a flavour of how their methods could contribute to more specifically educational questions.

Language

Despite sharing 98.5% of our genome with chimpanzees, we humans can talk and chimps cannot. Interestingly, genes expressed in the developing brain may hold part of the answer. For example, a gene called FOXP2 differs in mouse and man by three amino acid differences, two of which occurred after separation from the common humanchimp ancestor about 200,000 years ago (Marcus & Fisher, 2003). This gene is implicated in a severe developmental disorder of speech and language that affects the control of face and mouth movements, impeding speech. Neurally, accurate vocal imitation appears to be critical for the development of speech (Fitch, 2000). Hence when linguistic input is degraded or absent for various reasons (e.g., being hearing impaired, being orally impaired), speech and language are affected. Studies of normal adults show that grammatical processing relies more on frontal regions of the left hemisphere, whereas semantic processing and vocabulary learning activate posterior lateral regions of both hemispheres. For reasons that are not yet well understood, the brain systems important for syntactic and grammatical processing are more vulnerable to altered language input than the brain systems responsible for semantic and lexical functions. ERP studies show that when English is acquired late due to auditory deprivation or late immigration to an English-speaking country, syntactic abilities do not develop at the same rate or to the same extent (Neville et al., 1997). Late learners do not rely on left hemisphere systems for grammatical processing, but use both hemispheres (Weber-Fox & Neville, 1996). ERP studies also show that congenitally blind people show bilateral representation of language functions (Röder et al., 2000). Blind people also process speech more efficiently (Hollins, 1989), for example, they speed up cassette tapes, finding them too slow, and still comprehend the speech even though the recording quality suffers.

Reading

Neuroimaging studies of both children and adults suggest that the major systems for reading alphabetic scripts are lateralised to the left hemisphere. These studies typically measure brain responses to single word reading using fMRI or ERPS. Reviews of such studies conclude that alphabetic/orthographic processing seems mainly associated with occipital, temporal and parietal areas (e.g., Pugh et al., 2001). The occipital-temporal areas are most active when processing visual features, letter shapes and orthography. The inferior occipital-temporal area shows electrophysiological dissociations between words and non-words at around 180 ms, suggesting that these representations are not purely visual but are linguistically structured. Activation in temporo-occipital areas increases with reading skill (e.g., Shaywitz et al., 2002), and is decreased in children with developmental dyslexia.

Phonological awareness (the ability to recognize and manipulate component sounds in words) predicts reading acquisition across languages, and phonological processing appears to be focused on the temporo-parietal junction. This may be the main site supporting letter-to-sound recoding and is also implicated in spelling disorders. Dyslexic children, who typically have phonological deficits, show reduced activation in the temporo-parietal junction during tasks such as deciding whether different letters rhyme (e.g., P, T = yes, P, K = no). Targeted reading remediation increases activation in this area (e.g., Simos et al., 2002). Finally, recordings of event-related magnetic fields (MEG) in dyslexic children suggest that there is atypical organisation of the right hemisphere (Heim et al., 2003). This is consistent with suggestions that compensation strategies adopted by the dyslexic brain require greater right hemisphere involvement in reading.

Although to date neuroimaging studies have largely confirmed what was already known about reading and its development from behavioural studies, neuroscience techniques also offer a way of distinguishing between different cognitive theories (e.g., whether dyslexia has a visual basis or linguistic basis in children). Neuroimaging techniques also offer a potential means for distinguishing between deviance and delay when studying developmental disorders. For example, our preliminary studies of basic auditory processing in dyslexic children using ERPs suggest that the phonological system of the dyslexic child is immature rather than deviant. Dyslexic children show remarkable similarity in N1 response to younger reading level controls, while showing much larger N1 amplitudes than age-matched controls. Finally, PET studies have shown that the functional organization of the brain differs in literate and illiterate adults (Castro-Caldas et al., 1998). Portuguese women in their sixties who had never learned to read because of lack of access to education were compared with literate Portuguese women from the same villages in word and non-word repetition tasks. It was found that totally different brain areas were activated during nonword repetition for the illiterate versus literate participants. Learning to read and write in childhood thus changes the functional organization of the adult brain.

Mathematics

For mathematics, cognitive neuroscience is beginning to go beyond existing cognitive models. It had been argued that there is more than one neural system for the representation of numbers. A phylogenetically old 'number sense' system, found in animals and infants as well as older participants, seems to underpin knowledge about numbers and their relations (Dehaene et al., 1998). This system, located bilaterally in the intraparietal areas, is activated when participants perform tasks such as number comparison, whether the comparisons involve Arabic numerals, sets of dots or number words. Because mode of presentation does not affect the location of the parietal ERP components, this system is thought to organize knowledge about number quantities. Developmental ERP studies have shown that young children use exactly the same parietal areas to perform number comparison tasks (Temple & Posner, 1998). A different type of numerical knowledge is thought to be stored verbally, in the language system (Dehaene et al., 1999). This neural system also stores knowledge about poetry and overlearned verbal sequences, such as the months of the year. Mathematically, it underpins counting and rote-acquired knowledge such as the multiplication tables. This linguistic system seems to store 'number facts' rather than compute calculations. Many simple arithmetical problems (e.g., $3 + 4$, 3×4) are so overlearned that they may be stored as declarative knowledge. More complex calculation seems to involve visuospatial regions (Zago et al., 2001), possibly attesting to the importance of visual mental imagery in multi-digit operations. […] Finally, a distinct parietal-premotor area is activated during finger counting and also calculation.

This last observation may suggest that the neural areas activated during finger-counting (a developmental strategy for the acquisition of calculation skills) eventually come to partially underpin numerical manipulation skills in adults. If this were the case, then perhaps finger counting has important consequences for the developing brain, and should be encouraged in school. In any event, neuroimaging techniques offer ways of exploring such questions. They can also be used to discover the basis of dyscalculia in children. For example, dyslexic children often seem to have associated mathematical difficulties. If dyslexia has a phonological basis, then it seems likely that the mathematical system affected in these children should be the verbal system underpinning counting and calculation. Dyslexic children with mathematical difficulties may show neural anomalies in the activation of this system, but not in the activation of the parietal and premotor number systems. Children with dyscalculia who do not have reading difficulties may show different patterns of impairment. Knowledge of the neural basis of their difficulties could then inform individual remedial curricula.

Direct effects of experience

Although it is frequently assumed that specific experiences have an effect on children, neuroimaging offers ways of investigating this assumption directly. The obvious prediction is that specific experiences will have specific effects, increasing neural representations in areas directly relevant to the skills involved. One area of specific experience that is frequent in childhood is musical experience. fMRI studies have shown that skilled pianists (adults) have enlarged cortical representations in auditory cortex, specific to piano tones. Enlargement was correlated with the age at which musicians began to practise, but did not differ between musicians with absolute versus relative pitch (Pantev *et al.*, 1998). Similarly, MEG studies show that skilled violinists have enlarged neural representations for their left fingers, those most important for playing the violin (Elbert *et al.*, 1996). Clearly, different sensory systems are affected by musical expertise depending on the nature of the musical instrument concerned. ERP studies have also shown use-dependent functional reorganization in readers of Braille. Skilled Braille readers are more sensitive to tactile information than controls, and this extends across all fingers, not just the index finger (Röder *et al.*, 1996). The neural representations of muscles engaged in Braille reading are also enlarged. Finally, it is interesting to note that London taxi drivers who possess 'The Knowledge' show enlarged hippocampus formations (Maguire *et al.*, 2000). The hippocampus is a small brain area thought to be involved in spatial representation and navigation. In London taxi drivers, the posterior hippocampi were significantly larger than those of controls who did not drive taxis. Furthermore, hippocampal volume was correlated with the amount of time spent as a taxi driver. Again, localised plasticity is found in the adult brain in response to specific environmental inputs.

Plasticity in children, of course, is likely to be even greater. Our growing understanding of plasticity offers a way of studying the impact of specialized remedial programmes on brain function. For example, on the basis of the cerebellar theory of dyslexia, remedial programmes are available that are designed to improve motor function. It is claimed that these programmes will also improve reading. Whether this is in fact the case can be measured directly via neuroimaging. If the effects of such remedial programmes are specific, then neuroimaging should reveal changes in motor representations but not in phonological and orthographic processing. If the effects generalize to literacy (for example, via improved automaticity), then changes in occipital, temporal and parietal areas should also be observed.

Sleep and cognition

The idea that sleep might serve a cognitive function dates from at least the time of Freud, with his analysis of dreams. Recent neuroimaging studies suggest indeed that Rapid Eye Movement (REM) sleep is not only associated with self-reports of dreaming but is important for learning and memory. Maquet and colleagues (Maquet *et al.*, 2000) used PET to study regional brain activity during REM sleep following training on a serial reaction time task. During task learning, volunteer students were trained to press one of six marked keys on a computer in response to associated visual signals on the computer screen. Training lasted for four hours, from 4 p.m. until 8 p.m. The participants were then scanned during sleep. Controls were either scanned when awake while receiving the training, or were scanned when asleep following no training. It was found that the brain areas most active in the trained awake group when performing the task were also most active during REM sleep in the trained participants. They were not active during sleep in the untrained participants. Hence certain regions of the brain (in occipital and premotor cortex) were actually *reactivated* during sleep. It seems that REM sleep either allows the consolidation of memories or the forgetting of unnecessary material (or both together). When tested again on the computer task on the following day, significant improvement in performance was found to have occurred. Although the cellular mechanisms underlying this are not understood, it seems likely that memory consolidation relies on augmented synaptic transmission and eventually on increased synaptic density – the same mechanisms that structure the developing brain. Again, this suggests substantial plasticity even in adulthood, supporting educational emphases on life-long learning.

Emotion and cognition

It is increasingly recognized that efficient learning does not take place when the learner is experiencing fear or stress. Stress can both help and harm the body. Stress responses can provide the extra strength and attention needed to cope with a sudden emergency, but inappropriate stress has a significant effect on both physiological and cognitive functioning. The main emotional system within the brain is the limbic system, a set of structures incorporating the amygdala and hippocampus. The 'emotional brain' (LeDoux, 1996) has strong connections with frontal cortex (the major site for reasoning and problem solving). When a learner is stressed or fearful, connections with frontal cortex become impaired, with a negative impact on learning. Stress and fear also affect social judgments, and responses to reward and risk. One important function of the emotional brain is assessing the value of information being received. When the amygdala is strongly activated, it interrupts action and thought, and triggers rapid bodily responses critical for survival. It is suggested by LeDoux that classroom fear or stress might reduce children's ability to pay attention to the learning task because of this automatic interruption mechanism. To date, however, neuroimaging studies of the developmental effects of stress on cognitive function are sparse or non-existent. In the educational arena, studying the role of stress (and emotional affect generally) in classroom learning seems an area ripe for development. Simple ERP measures of attentional processes, such as those used by Seifert et al. (2003) to study children with ADHD receiving Ritalin, could easily be adapted for such purposes.

Neuromyths

The engaging term 'neuromyths', coined by the OECD report on understanding the brain (OECD, 2002), suggests the ease and rapidity with which scientific findings can be translated into misinformation regarding what neuroscience can offer education. The three myths given most attention in the OECD report are (1) the lay belief in hemispheric differences ('left brain' versus 'right brain' learning etc.), (2) the notion that the brain is only plastic for certain kinds of information during certain 'critical periods', and that therefore education in these areas must occur during the critical periods, and (3) the idea that the most effective educational interventions need to be timed with periods of synaptogenesis.

Regarding neuromyth (1), the left brain/right brain claims probably have their basis in the fact that there is some hemispheric specialization in terms of the localisation of different skills. For example, many aspects of language processing are left-lateralised (although not, as we have seen, in blind people or in those who emigrate in later childhood to a new linguistic community). Some aspects of face recognition, in contrast, are lateralised to the right hemisphere. Nevertheless, there are massive cross-hemisphere connections in the normal brain, and both hemispheres work together in every cognitive task so far explored with neuroimaging, including language and face recognition tasks.

Regarding neuromyth (2), optimal periods for certain types of learning clearly exist in development, but they are sensitive periods rather than critical ones. The term 'critical period' implies that the opportunity to learn is lost forever if the biological window is missed. In fact, there seem to be almost no cognitive capacities that can be 'lost' at an early age. As discussed earlier, some aspects of complex processing suffer more than others from deprivation of early environmental input (e.g., depth perception in vision, grammar learning in language), but nevertheless learning is still possible. It is probably better for the final performance levels achieved to educate children in, for example, other languages during the sensitive period for language acquisition. Nevertheless, the existence of a sensitive period does not mean that adults are unable to acquire competent foreign language skills later in life.

Neuromyth (3) concerning synaptogenesis may have arisen from influential work on learning in rats. This research showed that rodent brains form more connections in enriched and stimulating environments (e.g., Greenough *et al.*, 1987). As discussed earlier, any kind of specific environmental stimulation causes the brain to form new connections (recall the enlarged cortical representations of professional musicians and the enlarged hippocampi of London taxi drivers). These demonstrations do not mean that greater synaptic density *predicts* a greater capacity to learn, however.

Other neuromyths can also be identified. One is the idea that a person can either have a 'male brain' or a 'female brain'. The terms 'male brain' and 'female brain' were coined to refer to differences in *cognitive* style rather than biological differences (Baron-Cohen, 2003). Baron-Cohen argued that men were better 'systemizers' (good at understanding mechanical systems) and women were better 'empathisers' (good at communication and understanding others). He did not argue that male and female brains were radically different, but used the terms male and female brain as a psychological shorthand for (overlapping) cognitive profiles.

Another neuromyth is the idea that 'implicit' learning could open new avenues educationally. Much human learning is 'implicit', in the sense that learning takes place in the brain despite lack of attention to/conscious awareness of what is being learned (e.g., Berns *et al.*, 1997, but see Johnstone & Shanks, 2001). Almost all studies of implicit learning use *perceptual* tasks as their behavioural measures (e.g., the participant gets better at responding appropriately to 'random' letter strings in a computer task when the 'random' strings are actually generated according to an underlying 'grammar' or rule system which can be learned). There are no studies showing implicit learning of the *cognitive* skills underpinning educational achievement. These skills most likely require effortful learning and direct teaching.

Conclusions

Clearly, the potential for neuroscience to make contributions to educational research is great. Nevertheless, bridges need to be built between neuroscience and basic research in education. Bruer (1997) suggested that cognitive psychologists are admirably placed to erect these bridges, although he also cautioned that while neuroscience has learned a lot about neurons and synapses, it has not learned nearly enough to guide educational practice in any meaningful way. This view is perhaps too pessimistic. Cognitive developmental neuroscience has established a number of neural 'markers' that can be used to assess development, for example, of the language system. These markers may be useful for investigating educational questions. Taking [event related potential] (ERP) signatures of language processing as a case in point, different parameters are robustly associated with semantic processing (e.g., N400), phonetic processing (e.g., mis-match negativity or MMN), and syntactic processing (e.g., P600). These parameters need to be investigated longitudinally in children. [...] Educational and cognitive psychologists need to take the initiative, and think 'outside the box' about how current neuroscience techniques can help to answer outstanding educational questions.

References

Baron-Cohen, S. (2003). *The essential difference: Men, women and the extreme male brain*. London: Penguin/Allen Lane.

Berns, G.S., Cohen, J.D., & Mintun, M.A. (1997). Brain regions responsive to novelty in the absence of awareness. *Science, 276*, 1272–1275.

Bruer, J.T. (1997). Education and the brain: A bridge too far. *Educational Researcher, 26(8)*, 4–16.

Castro-Caldas, A., Petersson, K.M., Reis, A., Stone-Elander S., & Ingvar, M. (1998). The illiterate brain. Learning to read and write during childhood influences the functional organization of the adult brain. *Brain, 121*, 1053–1063.

Dehaene, S., Dehaene-Lambertz, G., & Cohen, L. (1998). Abstract representations of numbers in the animal and human brain. *Trends in Neuroscience, 21(8)*, 355–611.

Dehaene, S., Spelke, E., Pinel, P., Sranescu, R., & Tsirkin, S. (1999). Sources of mathematical thinking: Behavioural and brain-imaging evidence. *Science, 284*, 970–974.

Elbert, T., Pantev, C., Wienburch, C., Rockstroh, B., & Taub, E. (1996). Increased cortical representation of the fingers of the left hand in string players. *Science, 270*, 305–307.

Fagiolini, M., & Hensch, R.K. (2000). Inhibitory threshold for critical-period activation in primary visual cortex. *Nature, 404*, 183–186.

Fitch, W.T. (2000). The evolution of speech: A comparative review. *Trends in Cognitive Sciences, 4(7)*, 258–267.

Greenough, W.T., Black, J. E., & Wallace, C.S. (1987). Experience and brain development. *Child Development, 58*, 539–559.

Heim, S., Eulitz, C., & Elbert, T. (2003). Altered hemispheric asymmetry of auditory P100m in dyslexia. *European Journal of Neuroscience, 17*, 1715–1722.

Hollins, M. (1989). *Understanding blindness*. Hillsdale, NJ: Lawrence Erlbaum.

Jackson, S. (2000). Seeing what you feel. *Trends in Cognitive Sciences, 4*, 257.

Johnstone, T., & Shanks D.R. (2001). Abstractionist and processing accounts of implicit learning. *Cognitive Psychology, 42*, 61–112.

LeDoux, J. (1996). *The emotional brain*. New York: Simon Schuster.

Maguire, E.A., Gadian, D.S., Johnsrude, I.S., Good, C.D., Ashburner, J., Frackowiak, R.S., & Frith, C.D. (2000). Navigation related structural change in the hippocampi of taxi drivers. *Proceedings of the National Academy of Sciences of the United States of America, 97(8)*, 4398–4403.

Maquet, P., Laureys, S., Peigneux, P., Fuchs, S., Petiau, C., Phillips, C., Aerts, J., DelFiore, G., Degueldre, C., Meulemans, T., Luxen, A., Franck, G., Van Der Linden, M., Smith, C., & Cleeremans, A. (2000). Experience-dependent changes in cerebral activation during human REM sleep. *Nature Neuroscience, 3(8)*, 831–836.

Marcus, G.F., & Fisher, S.E. (2003). FOXP2 in focus: What can genes tell us about speech and language? *Trends in Cognitive Sciences, 7(6)*, 257–262.

Maurer, D., Lewis, T.L., & Brent, H. (1989). The effects of deprivation on human visual development: Studies in children treated with cataracts. In F.J. Morrison, C. Lord & D.P. Keating (Eds.), *Applied developmental psychology* (pp. 139–227). San Diego, CA: Academic Press.

Neville, H. J. (1995). Developmental specificity in neurocognitive development in humans. In M.S. Gazzaniga (Ed.), *The cognitive neurosciences* (pp. 219–231). Cambridge, MA: MIT Press.

Neville, H.J., & Bavelier, D. (2000). Specificity and plasticity in neurocognitive development in humans. In M.S. Gazzaniga (Ed.), *The cognitive neurosciences* (pp. 83–98). Cambridge, MA: MIT Press.

Neville, H.J., Schmidt, A., & Kutas, M. (1983). Altered visual-evoked potentials in congenitally deaf adults. *Brain Research, 266,* 127–132.

Neville, H.J., Coffey, S.A., Lawson, D.S., Fischer, A., Emmorey, K., & Bellugi, U. (1997). Neural systems mediating American Sign Language: Effects of sensory experience and age of acquisition. *Brain & Language, 57,* 285–308.

Neville, H.J., Bavelier, D., Corina, D., Rauschecker, J., Karni, A., Lalwani, A., Braun, A., Clark, V., Jezzard, P., & Turner, R. (1998). Cerebral organisation for language in deaf and hearing subjects: Biological constraints and effects of experience. *Proceedings of the National Academy of Sciences of the United States of America, 95* (Feb), 922–929.

OECD (2002). *Understanding the brain: Towards a new learning science.* Available online from oecd.org

Pantev, C., Oostenveld, R., Engelien, A., Ross, B., Roberts, L.E., & Hike, M. (1998). Increased auditory cortical representation in musicians. *Nature, 393,* 811–814.

Pugh, K.R., Mencl, W.E., Jenner, A.R., Katz, L., Frost, S.J., Lee, J.R., Shaywitz, S.E., & Shaywitz, B.A. (2001). Neurobiological studies of reading and reading disability. *Journal of Communication Disorders, 34,* 479–492.

Röder, B., & Neville, H. (2003). Developmental functional plasticity. In J. Grafman & I.H. Robertson (Eds.), *Handbook of neuropsychology* (2nd ed., Vol. 9, pp. 231–270). Oxford: Elsevier Science.

Röder, G., Rösler, F., & Neville, H.J. (1999). Effects of interstimulus interval on auditory event-related potentials in congenitally blind and normally sighted humans. *Neuroscience Letters, 264,* 53–56.

Röder, G., Rösler, F., & Neville, H.J. (2000). Event-related potentials during language processing in congenitally blind and sighted people. *Neuropsychologia, 38,* 182–1502.

Röder, G., Rösler, F., Hennighausen, E., & Nacker, F. (1996). Event related potentials during auditory and somatosensory discrimination in sighted and blind human subjects. *Cognitive Brain Research, 4,* 77–93.

Seifert, J., Scheuerpflug, P., Zillessen, K.E., Fallgater, A., & Warnke, A. (2003). Electrophysiological investigation of the effectiveness of methylphenidate in children with and without ADHD. *Journal of Neural Transmission, 110(7),* 821–829.

Shaywitz, B., Shaywitz, S., Pugh, K., Mencl, W., Fulbright, R., Skudlarski, P., Constable, T., Marchione, K., Fletcher, J., Lyon, G., & Gore, J. (2002). Disruption of posterior brain systems for reading in children with developmental dyslexia. *Biological Psychiatry,* 101–110.

Simos, P.G., Fletcher, J. M., Bergman, E., Breier, J.I., Foorman, B.R., Castillo, E.M., Davis, R.N., Fitzgerald, M., & Papanicolaou (2002). Dyslexia-specific brain activation profile becomes normal following successful remedial training. *Neurology, 58,* 1203–1213.

Strauss, S. (2003). Teaching as a natural cognition and its implications for teacher education. In D. Pillemer & S. White (Eds.), *Developmental psychology and the social changes of our time.* New York: Cambridge University Press.

Strauss, S., Ziv, M. & Stein, A. (2002). Teaching as a natural cognition and its relations to preschoolers' developing theory of mind. *Cognitive Development, 17,* 1473–1787.

Temple, E., & Posner, M.I. (1998). Brain mechanisms of quantity are similar in 5-year-old children and adults. *Proceedings of the National Academy of Sciences of the United States of America, 95* (June), 7836–7841.

Weber-Fox, C.M., & Neville, H.J. (1996). Maturational constraints on functional specialisation for language processing: ERP and behavioural evidence in bilingual speakers. *Journal of Cognitive Neuroscience, 8,* 231–256.

Zago, L., Pesenti, M., Mellet, E., Crivello, F., Mazoyer, B., & Tzourio-Mazoyer, N. (2001). Neural correlates of simple and complex mental calculation. *NeuroImage, 13,* 314–327.

3

Meaning

Etienne Wenger

Our attempts to understand human life open a vast space of relevant questions – from the origin of the universe to the workings of the brain, from the details of every thought to the purpose of life. In this vast space of questions, the concept of practice is useful for addressing a specific slice: a focus on the experience of meaningfulness. Practice is, first and foremost, a process by which we can experience the world and our engagement with it as meaningful.

Of course, in order to engage in practice, we must be alive in a world in which we can act and interact. We must have a body with a brain that is functioning well enough to participate in social communities. We must have ways to communicate with one another. But a focus on practice is not merely a functional perspective on human activities, even activities involving multiple individuals. It does not address simply the mechanics of getting something done, individually or in groups; it is not a mechanical perspective. It includes not just bodies (or even coordinated bodies) and not just brains (even coordinated ones), but moreover that which gives *meaning* to the motions of bodies and the workings of brains.

Let me illustrate this point by analogy to a work of art. There are all sorts of mechanics involved in producing a painting: a canvas, brushes, color pigments, and sophisticated techniques. The image itself is but a thin veneer. Yet in the end, for the painter and for the viewer, it is the painting as an experience of meaning that counts. Similarly, in the pursuit of our enterprises, we engage in all sorts of activities with complex bodies that are the result of millennia of evolution. Still, in the end, it is the meanings we produce that matter.

This focus on meaningfulness is therefore not primarily on the technicalities of "meaning." It is not on meaning as it sits locked up in dictionaries. It is not just on meaning as a relation between a sign and a reference. But neither is it on meaning as a grand question – on the meaning of life as a philosophical issue. *Practice is about meaning as an experience of everyday life.*

If the kind of meaning I am interested in is an experience, and if it is not the kind we can find in dictionary definitions or in philosophical discussions, then I need to address the questions of where it is located and how it is constituted. In this chapter, I will first argue that:

1   meaning is located in a process I will call the *negotiation of meaning*
2   the negotiation of meaning involves the interaction of two constituent processes, which I will call *participation* and *reification*
3   participation and reification form a duality that is fundamental to the human experience of meaning and thus to the nature of practice.

[This is the first chapter from *Communities of Practice* (1998) and draws on ethnographic fieldwork in a medical insurance claims processing centre (Alinsu) in the U.S.]

From: Chapter 1 in Wenger, E., *Communities of Practice Learning, Meaning and Identity* (Cambridge: Cambridge University Press, 1998). © Cambridge University Press 1998, reproduced with permission.

These concepts are essential to my argument, and I will start by explaining in some detail what I mean by them and just why they are important.

Negotiation of meaning

The experience of meaning is not produced out of thin air, but neither is it simply a mechanical realization of a routine or a procedure. For Ariel, [a claims processor working in a medical insurance centre] no two claims are the same, even though she has learned to coerce these claims into manageable categories. Indeed, medical claims processing is largely a classificatory activity. Its purpose is to impose standards of sameness and difference in the midst of a flow of change so that claims can be recognized as belonging to categories amenable to well-understood treatment. But for Ariel, this routinization must constantly be achieved anew, claim after claim.

Our engagement in practice may have patterns, but it is the production of such patterns anew that gives rise to an experience of meaning. When we sit down for lunch for the thousandth time with the same colleagues in the same cafeteria, we have seen it all before. We know all the steps. We may even know today's menu by heart; we may love it or we may dread it. And yet we eat again, we taste again. We may know our colleagues very well, and yet we repeatedly engage in conversations. All that we do and say may refer to what has been done and said in the past, and yet we produce again a new situation, an impression, an experience: we produce meanings that extend, redirect, dismiss, reinterpret, modify or confirm – in a word, negotiate anew – the histories of meanings of which they are part. In this sense, living is a constant process of *negotiation of meaning*.

I will use the concept of negotiation of meaning very generally to characterize the process by which we experience the world and our engagement in it as meaningful. Whether we are talking, acting, thinking, solving problems, or daydreaming, we are concerned with meanings. I have argued that even routine activities like claims processing or eating in a cafeteria involve the negotiation of meaning, but it is all the more true when we are involved in activities that we care about or that present us with challenges: when we look in wonder at a beautiful landscape, when we close a delicate deal, when we go on a special date, when we solve a difficult mystery, when we listen to a moving piece of music, when we read a good book, or when we mourn a dear friend. In such cases, the intensity of the process is obvious, but the same process is at work even if what we end up negotiating turns out to be an experience of meaninglessness. Human engagement in the world is first and foremost a process of negotiating meaning.

The negotiation of meaning may involve language, but it is not limited to it. It includes our social relations as factors in the negotiation, but it does not necessarily involve a conversation or even direct interaction with other human beings. The concept of negotiation often denotes reaching an agreement between people, as in "negotiating a price," but it is not limited to that usage. It is also used to suggest an accomplishment that requires sustained attention and readjustment, as in "negotiating a sharp curve." I want to capture both aspects at once, in order to suggest that living meaningfully implies:

1   an active process of producing meaning that is both dynamic and historical
2   a world of both resistance and malleability
3   the mutual ability to affect and to be affected

4   the engagement of a multiplicity of factors and perspectives
5   the production of a new resolution to the convergence of these factors and perspectives
6   the incompleteness of this resolution, which can be partial, tentative, ephemeral, and specific to a situation.

I intend the term *negotiation* to convey a flavor of continuous interaction, of gradual achievement, and of give-and-take. By living in the world we do not just make meanings up independently of the world, but neither does the world simply impose meanings on us. The negotiation of meaning is a productive process, but negotiating meaning is not constructing it from scratch. Meaning is not pre-existing, but neither is it simply made up. Negotiated meaning is at once both historical and dynamic, contextual and unique.

The negotiation of meaning is a process that is shaped by multiple elements and that affects these elements. As a result, this negotiation constantly changes the situations to which it gives meaning and affects all participants. In this process, negotiating meaning entails both interpretation and action. In fact, this perspective does not imply a fundamental distinction between interpreting and acting, doing and thinking, or understanding and responding. All are part of the ongoing process of negotiating meaning. This process always generates new circumstances for further negotiation and further meanings. It constantly produces new relations with and in the world. The meaningfulness of our engagement in the world is not a state of affairs, but a continual process of renewed negotiation.

From this perspective, meaning is always the product of its negotiation, by which I mean that it exists in this process of negotiation. Meaning exists neither in us, nor in the world, but in the dynamic relation of living in the world.

The dynamics of negotiated meaning

The processing of a given claim form by a processor like Ariel is an example of the negotiation of meaning. It takes place in a context that combines a vast array of factors, including the organization of the insurance industry, the official and unofficial training the processor underwent, the way the particular claim looks, past experiences with similar claims, the way the day is going, who else is around, what else is happening, and so on. The contexts that contribute to shaping the experience of a claim reach far and wide in time and space.

When Ariel grabs a new claim, she may not know exactly what to do, but she is in familiar territory. Even if there is a problem, she may be annoyed but she is not surprised; it will be resolved eventually. In fact, she can hardly recall the tentativeness of that first day, the unsettling mysteriousness of those training weeks, the reaching out during her first months on the floor, when just about every claim she was processing presented one problem or another. It had seemed so big then – claims processing, Alinsu, the medical establishment. But now it is familiar. It is her job, and she is reasonably good at it.

The claim too comes with a history. It started out as a blank form designed by technical specialists at Alinsu. It was approved by various professional associations before it was printed. It was sent to a client company where a benefit representative distributed it to an employee. It was partially filled out by that employee and submitted to medical professionals who completed it. Then it was sent back to Alinsu, where it was first sorted by clerical personnel to be routed in a bundle to Ariel's processing unit. And now it is on her desk, to be coerced somehow into the confines of the processible.

Processing claims requires a very specific way of looking at a claim form. The ability to interpret a claim form reflects the relations that both the claim and Ariel have to particular practices. Ariel contributes to the negotiation of meaning by being a member of a community and bringing to bear her history of participation in its practice. Similarly, the claim contributes to this process by reflecting aspects of practice that have been congealed in it and fixed in its shape. I would say that the processor as a member of a community of practice embodies a long and diverse process of what I will call *participation*. Similarly, the claim as an artifact of certain practices embodies a long and diverse process of what I will call *reification*. It is in the convergence of these two processes in the act of processing the claim that the negotiation of meaning takes place.

As a pair, participation and reification refer to a duality fundamental to the negotiation of meaning. In order to clarify why this is so, I will first discuss each term separately before turning to the duality that their complementarity forms.

Participation

My use of the term *participation* falls within common usage. It is therefore helpful to start with Webster's definition: "To have or take a part or share with others (in some activity, enterprise, etc.)." Participation refers to a process of taking part and also to the relations with others that reflect this process. It suggests both action and connection.

I will use the term participation to describe the social experience of living in the world in terms of membership in social communities and active involvement in social enterprises. Participation in this sense is both personal and social. It is a complex process that combines doing, talking, thinking, feeling, and belonging. It involves our whole person, including our bodies, minds, emotions, and social relations.

Participation is an active process, but I will reserve the term for actors who are members of social communities. For instance, I will not say that a computer "participates" in a community of practice, even though it may be part of that practice and play an active role in getting certain things done. Neither will I say that a fish in its bowl in the living room participates in a family. But I would be open to considering that a family dog, for instance, participates in some peripheral but real way in that family. In this regard, what I take to characterize participation is the possibility of mutual recognition. When we shave a piece of wood or mold a piece of clay, we do not construe our shaping these objects as contributing to their experience of meaning. But when we engage in a conversation, we somehow recognize in each other something of ourselves, which we address. What we recognize has to do with our mutual ability to negotiate meaning. This mutuality does not, however, entail equality or respect. The relations between parents and children or between workers and their direct supervisor are mutual in the sense that participants shape each other's experiences of meaning. In doing so, they can recognize something of themselves in each other. But these are not relations of equality. In practice, even the meanings of inequality are negotiated in the context of this process of mutual recognition.

In this experience of mutuality, participation is a source of identity. By recognizing the mutuality of our participation, we become part of each other. [...]. [A] defining characteristic of participation is the possibility of developing an "identity of participation," this is, an identity constituted through relations of participation.

Before I proceed, it is worth clarifying a few more points about my use of the term participation.

- First, participation as I will use the term is not tantamount to collaboration. It can involve all kinds of relations, conflictual as well as harmonious, intimate as well as political, competitive as well as cooperative.
- Second, participation in social communities shapes our experience, and it also shapes those communities; the transformative potential goes both ways. Indeed, our ability (or inability) to shape the practice of our communities is an important aspect of our experience of participation.
- Finally, as a constituent of meaning, participation is broader than mere engagement in practice. Claims processors are not claims processors just while they work in the office. Of course, that time of intense engagement with their work and with one another is especially significant. But they do not cease to be claims processors at five o'clock. Their participation is not something they simply turn off when they leave. Its effects on their experience are not restricted to the specific context of their engagement. It is a part of who they are that they always carry with them and that will surface if, for instance, they themselves happen to go to the doctor, fill out an insurance form, or call a customer service center. In this sense, participation goes beyond direct engagement in specific activities with specific people. It places the negotiation of meaning in the context of our forms of membership in various communities. It is a constituent of our identities. As such, participation is not something we turn on and off.

From this perspective, our engagement with the world is social, even when it does not clearly involve interactions with others. Being in a hotel room by yourself preparing a set of slides for a presentation the next morning may not seem like a particularly social event, yet its meaning is fundamentally social. Not only is the audience there with you as you attempt to make your points understandable to them, but your colleagues are there too, looking over your shoulder, as it were, representing for you your sense of accountability to the professional standards of your community. A child doing homework, a doctor making a decision, a traveler reading a book – all these activities implicitly involve other people who may not be present. The meanings of what we do are always social. By "social" I do not refer just to family dinners, company picnics, school dances, and church socials. Even drastic isolation – as in solitary confinement, monastic seclusion, or writing – is given meaning through social participation. The concept of participation is meant to capture this profoundly social character of our experience of life.

Reification

The term *reification* is less common than participation. But I hope to show that, in conjunction with participation, reification is a very useful concept to describe our engagement with the world as productive of meaning. Again, it will help to start with Webster's definition of reification: "To treat (an abstraction) as substantially existing, or as a concrete material object."

Etymologically, the term reification means "making into a thing." Its usage in English has a significant twist, however: it is used to convey the idea that what is turned into a concrete, material object is not properly a concrete, material object. For instance, we make representations of "justice" as a blindfolded maid holding a scale, or use expressions such as "the hand of fate."

In everyday discourse, abstractions like "democracy" or "the economy" are often talked about as though they were active agents. When a newscast reports that "democracy took a blow during a military coup," or that "the economy reacted slowly to the government's action," the process of reification provides a shortcut to communication.

This succinctness derives from a slight illusion of excessive reality, but it is useful because it focuses the negotiation of meaning. This is the subtle idea I want to capture by using the term reification. We project our meanings into the world and then we perceive them as existing in the world, as having a reality of their own. For example, my own use of the term reification in the context of this book is itself a case in point. The term is a projection of what I mean. It is an abstraction. It does not do the work by itself. But after a while, as I use it to think with, it starts talking to me as though it were alive. Whereas in participation we recognize ourselves in each other, in reification we project ourselves onto the world, and not having to recognize ourselves in those projections, we attribute to our meanings an independent existence. This contrast between mutuality and projection is an important difference between participation and reification.

The concept of reification

I will use the concept of reification very generally to refer to the process of giving form to our experience by producing objects that congeal this experience into "thingness." In so doing, we create points of focus around which the negotiation of meaning becomes organized. Again, my use of the term reification is its own example. I am introducing it into the discourse because I want to create a new distinction to serve as a point of focus around which to organize my discussion. Writing down a law, creating a procedure, or producing a tool is a similar process. A certain understanding is given form. This form then becomes a focus for the negotiation of meaning, as people use the law to argue a point, use the procedure to know what to do, or use the tool to perform an action.

I would claim that the process of reification so construed is central to every practice. Any community of practice produces abstractions, tools, symbols, stories, terms, and concepts that reify something of that practice in a congealed form. Clearly, I want to use the concept of reification in a much broader sense than its dictionary definition. But I want to preserve the connotations of excessive concreteness and projected reality that are suggested by the dictionary definition. Indeed, no abstraction, tool, or symbol actually captures in its form the practices in the context of which it contributes to an experience of meaning. A medical claim, for instance, reifies in its form a complex web of conventions, agreements, expectations, commitments, and obligations, including (on the part of medical professionals) the right to bill for certain services and the obligation to do so in a standardized way and (on the part of the insurance company) the right to decide if the claim is legitimate and duly filled out, together with the obligation to honor the claim if it is.

With the term reification, I mean to cover a wide range of processes that include making, designing, representing, naming, encoding, and describing, as well as perceiving, interpreting, using, reusing, decoding, and recasting. Reification occupies much of our collective energy: from entries in a journal to historical records, from poems to encyclopedias, from names to classification systems, from dolmens to space probes, from the Constitution to a signature on a credit card slip, from gourmet recipes to medical procedures, from flashy advertisements to census data, from single concepts to entire theories, from the evening news to national archives, from lesson plans to the compilation of textbooks, from private address lists to sophisticated credit reporting databases, aspects of human experience and practice are congealed into fixed forms and given the status of object.

Reification shapes our experience. It can do so in very concrete ways. Having a tool to perform an activity changes the nature of that activity. A word processor, for instance, reifies a view of the activity of writing, but also changes how one goes about writing. The effects of reification can also be less obvious. Reifying the concept of gravity may not change its effect on our bodies, but it does change our experience of the world by focusing our attention in a particular way and enabling new kinds of understanding. Similarly, reifying the concept of body weight as a measure of self-worth does not make us heavier but can weigh heavily on our sense of self. […]

Again, I should clarify a few points about my use of the concept of reification before proceeding.

- Reification can refer both to a process and its product, and I will use the term in both senses. This liberty is not just a lack of rigor, but part of the point. If meaning exists only in its negotiation then, at the level of meaning, the process and the product are not distinct. Reification is not just objectification; it does not end in an object. It does not simply translate meaning into an object. On the contrary, my use of the concept is meant to suggest that such translation is never possible, and that the process and the product always imply each other.
- Claims processors are not the designers of the rules and forms they use, yet they must absorb them into their practice. In an institutional environment such as a claims processing site, a very large portion of the reification involved in work practices comes from outside the communities of workers. Even so, however, reification must be reappropriated into a local process in order to become meaningful.
- The process of reification does not necessarily originate in design. A detective may spend much time studying fingerprints on a doorknob; an archaeologist is fascinated by traces of ancient life in a cave. Most human activities produce marks in the physical world. These marks are vestiges. They freeze fleeting moments of engagement in practice into monuments, which persist and disappear in their own time. Whether intentionally produced or not, they can then be reintegrated as reification into new moments of negotiation of meaning.
- Reification can take a great variety of forms: a fleeting smoke signal or an age-old pyramid, an abstract formula or a concrete truck, a small logo or a huge information-processing system, a simple word jotted on a page or a complex argument developed in a whole book, a telling glance or a long silence, a private knot on a handkerchief or a controversial statue on a public square, an impressionist painting of a butterfly or a scientific specimen in an entomological collection.

What is important about all these objects is that they are only the tip of an iceberg, which indicates larger contexts of significance realized in human practices. Their character as reification is not only in their form but also in the processes by which they are integrated into these practices. Properly speaking, the products of reification are not simply concrete, material objects. Rather, they are reflections of these practices, tokens of vast expanses of human meanings.

The double edge of reification

As an evocative shortcut, the process of reification can be very powerful. A politician can reify voters' inarticulate longings in one phrase that galvanizes support. A good tool can reify an activity so as to amplify its effects while making the activity effortless. A procedure can reify a concept so that its application is automatic. A formula can express in a few terms a regularity that pervades the universe.

But the power of reification – its succinctness, its portability, its potential physical persistence, its focusing effect – is also its danger. The politician's slogan can become a substitute for a deep understanding of and commitment to what it stands for. The tool can ossify activity around its inertness. Procedures can hide broader meanings in blind sequences of operations. And the knowledge of a formula can lead to the illusion that one fully understands the processes it describes.

The evocative power of reification is thus double-edged. Classifying people under broad categories can focus attention on a kind of diversity, but the reification can give differences and similarities a concreteness they do not actually possess. Similarly, if an organization displays a statement of values in its lobby, it has created a reification of something that does or should pervade the organization. Though this "something" is probably much more diffuse and intangible in practice, it gains a new concreteness once framed in the lobby. It becomes something people can point to, refer to, strive for, appeal to, and use or misuse in arguments. Yet, as a reification, it may seem disconnected, frozen into a text that does not capture the richness of lived experience and that can be appropriated in misleading ways. As a focus of attention that can be detached from practice, the reification may even be seen with cynicism, as an ironic substitute for what it was intended to reflect.

Indeed, my use of the term reification does not assume an inherent correspondence between a symbol and a referent, a tool and a function, or a phenomenon and an interpretation. On the contrary, the concept of reification suggests that forms can take a life of their own, beyond their context of origin. They gain a degree of autonomy from the occasion and purposes of their production. Their meaningfulness is always potentially expanded and potentially lost. Reification as a constituent of meaning is always incomplete, ongoing, potentially enriching, and potentially misleading. The notion of assigning the status of object to something that really is not an object conveys a sense of mistaken solidity, of projected concreteness. It conveys a sense of useful illusion. The use of the term reification stands both as a tribute to the generative power of the process and as a gentle reminder of its delusory perils.

The duality of meaning

In their interplay, participation and reification are both distinct and complementary, as suggested by the illustration in Figure 3.1. The reification of a Constitution is just a form; it is not equivalent to a citizenry. Yet it is empty without the participation of the citizens

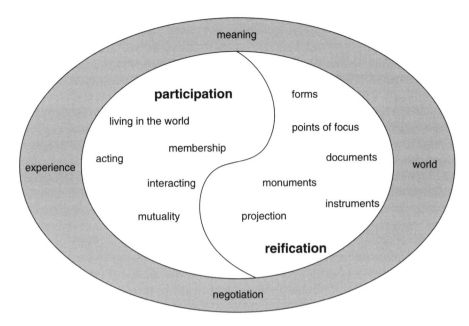

Figure 3.1   The duality of participation and reification

involved. Conversely, the production of such a reification is crucial to the kind of negotiation that is necessary for them to act as citizens and to bring together the multiple perspectives, interests, and interpretations that participation entails.

   As the figure suggests, participation and reification cannot be considered in isolation:
they come as a pair. They form a unity in their duality. Given one, it is a useful heuristic
to wonder where the other is. To understand one, it is necessary to understand the other.
To enable one, it is necessary to enable the other. They come about through each other, but
they cannot replace each other. It is through their various combinations that they give rise
to a variety of experiences of meaning.

   We don't usually think of the experience of meaning as a duality because the interplay
of participation and reification remains largely unproblematic. Processes of reification and
participation can be woven so tightly that the distinction between them seems almost
blurred. The use of language in face-to-face interactions is a good example. Words as projections of human meaning are certainly a form of reification. In face-to-face interactions,
however, speech is extremely evanescent; words affect the negotiation of meaning through
a process that seems like pure participation. As a consequence, words can take advantage
of shared participation among interlocutors to create shortcuts to communication. It is this
tight interweaving of reification and participation that makes conversations such a powerful form of communication.

   More generally, the negotiation of meaning weaves participation and reification so
seamlessly that meaning seems to have its own unitary, self-contained existence: a medical claim is a medical claim; a smile is a smile; a joke is a joke. Of course, it is often con-
venient to act as though meanings are in actions or artifacts themselves. So a medical claim
is indeed a medical claim; it was produced to be a medical claim; it exists for us in a civ-
ilization where everything concurs to make it a medical claim. And yet what it is to be a

medical claim is always defined with respect to specific forms of participation that con-textualize meaning. It cannot be assumed to be intrinsic or universal.

The complementarity of participation and reification

Although seamlessly woven into our practices, the complementarity of participation and reification is something familiar. We use it as a matter of course in order to secure some continuity of meaning across time and space. Indeed, in their complementarity, participa-tion and reification can make up for their respective limitations. They can compensate for each other's shortcomings, so to speak.

- On the one hand, participation makes up for the inherent limitations of reification. We send ambassadors with our treaties and hire judges to interpret our laws; we offer 800 numbers as customer service for our products in addition to our careful docu-mentation; we convene a meeting to introduce a new policy in order to avoid mis-understandings; we discuss what we read in order to compare and enrich our interpretations. Participation is essential to repairing the potential misalignments inherent in reification. When the stiffness of its form renders reification obsolete, when its mute ambiguity is misleading, or when its purpose is lost in the distance, then it is participation that comes to the rescue.
- On the other hand, reification also makes up for the inherent limitations of partici-pation. We create monuments to remember the dead; we take notes to remind our-selves of decisions made in the past; we share our notes with colleagues who could not attend a meeting; we are surprised by the way someone else describes a common event or object; we clarify our intentions with explanations and representational devices; we coordinate our coming and going with clocks. Mirroring the role of par-ticipation, reification is essential to repairing the potential misalignments inherent in participation: when the informality of participation is confusingly loose, when the fluidity of its implicitness impedes coordination, when its locality is too confining or its partiality too narrow, then it is reification that comes to the rescue.

One advantage of viewing the negotiation of meaning as constituted by a dual process is that we can consider the various trade-offs involved in the complementarity of participation and reification. Indeed, given an action or an artifact, it becomes a relevant question to ask how the production of meaning is distributed, that is, what is reified and what is left to participation.

- A computer program, for instance, could be described as an extreme kind of reifica-tion, which can be interpreted by a machine incapable of any participation in its meaning.
- A poem, by contrast, is designed to rely on participation, that is, to maximize the work that the ambiguity inherent in its form can do in the negotiation of meaning.

From such a perspective, communication is not just a quantitative issue. Indeed, what says more: the few lines of a tightly written poem or a volume of analytical comments on it?

The communicative ability of artifacts depends on how the work of negotiating meaning is distributed between reification and participation. Different mixes become differentially productive of meaning.

The complementarity of participation and reification yields an obvious but profound principle for endeavors that rely on some degree of continuity of meaning – communication, design, instruction, or collaboration. Participation and reification must be in such proportion and relation as to compensate for their respective shortcomings. When too much reliance is placed on one at the expense of the other, the continuity of meaning is likely to become problematic in practice.

- If participation prevails – if most of what matters is left unreified – then there may not be enough material to anchor the specificities of coordination and to uncover diverging assumptions. This is why lawyers always want everything in writing.
- If reification prevails – if everything is reified, but with little opportunity for shared experience and interactive negotiation – then there may not be enough overlap in participation to recover a coordinated, relevant, or generative meaning. This helps explain why putting everything in writing does not seem to solve all our problems.

In cases of mismatches, it is necessary to analyze the situation in terms of the duality and to redress any imbalance. […]

A fundamental duality

The duality of participation and reification […] is a fundamental aspect of the constitution of communities of practice, of their evolution over time, of the relations among practices, of the identities of participants, and of the broader organizations in which communities of practice exist.

In this context, as I tried to emphasize with the diagram of Figure 3.1, it is important *not* to interpret the duality of participation and reification in terms of a simple opposition. I will end this chapter by expanding this point. […]

As suggested by Figure 3.1, a duality is a single conceptual unit that is formed by two inseparable and mutually constitutive elements whose inherent tension and complementarity give the concept richness and dynamism. In what follows, I will clarify this idea by contrasting the duality of participation and reification with related, more traditional dichotomies of opposites – for example, tacit versus explicit, formal versus informal, individual versus collective, private versus public, conscious versus unconscious, or people versus things. I will do so via a list of statements, in each case saying both what the duality of participation and reification is and what it is not.

• Participation and reification are a duality, not opposites

Participation and reification are not defined merely by opposition to each other. The tacit is that which is not made explicit; the informal that which is not formalized; the unconscious that which is not conscious. But participation is not merely what is not reified. Both participation and reification are processes defined each in their own terms. As a result, they are not mutually exclusive. On the contrary, they take place together; they are two constituents intrinsic to the process of negotiation of meaning, and their complementarity reflects the inherent duality of this process.

Participation and reification both require and enable each other. On the one hand, it takes our participation to produce, interpret, and use reification; so there is no reification without participation. On the other hand, our participation requires interaction and thus generates shortcuts to coordinated meanings that reflect our enterprises and our takes on the world; so there is no participation without reification.

- **Participation and reification are two dimensions that interact; they do not define a spectrum**

One way to avoid thinking starkly in terms of opposites is to consider a spectrum. Knowledge can be more or less explicit; learning can be more or less formal; an impression can be more or less conscious; a meaning can be more or less individual. While a continuum does allow more nuanced distinctions, it is still a relation between opposites. Moving to one side implies leaving the other. More of one implies less of the other.

With an interacting duality, by contrast, both elements are always involved, and both can take different forms and degrees. In particular, there can be both intense participation and intense reification. In fact, the creative genius of great scientists and artists can be construed as stemming from their ability to bring the two together: on the one hand, an intense involvement with the reificative formalisms of their discipline; and on the other, a deep participative intuition of what those formalisms are about. This is true of a scientist like Albert Einstein, who insisted on the importance of exploring ideas intuitively as well as being able to give them mathematical expression. It is as true of a musician like Johann Sebastian Bach, who combined intricate forms of musical structure with melodic inspiration.

Such a perspective has pedagogical implications for teaching complex knowledge: an excessive emphasis on formalism without corresponding levels of participation, or conversely a neglect of explanations and formal structure, can easily result in an experience of meaninglessness.

- **Participation and reification imply each other; they do not substitute for each other**

Increasing the level of participation or reification does not dispense with the other. On the contrary, it will tend to increase the requirements for the other.

Indeed, reification always rests on participation: what is said, represented, or otherwise brought into focus always assumes a history of participation as a context for its interpretation. In turn, participation always organizes itself around reification because it always involves artifacts, words, and concepts that allow it to proceed.

Explicit knowledge is thus not freed from the tacit. Formal processes are not freed from the informal. In fact, in terms of meaningfulness, the opposite is more likely. To be understood meaningfully as a representation of a piece of physics knowledge, an abstract reification like $E = mc^2$ does not obviate a close connection to the physics community but, on the contrary, requires it. In general, viewed as a reification, a more abstract formulation will require more intense and specific participation to remain meaningful, not less.

From such a perspective, it is not possible to make everything explicit and thus get rid of the tacit, or to make everything formal and thus get rid of the informal. It is possible only to change their relation.

- **Participation and reification transform their relation; they do not translate into each other**

A dichotomy tends to suggest that there must be a process by which one can move from one to the other by translation into a different but equivalent state. We can transform tacit knowledge into explicit knowledge or vice versa; we can formalize a learning process; we can share our thoughts; we can make our emotions more conscious. By contrast, a change in the relations of participation and reification is never neutral; it always transforms the possibilities for negotiating meaning.

  - Participation is never simply the realization of a description or a prescription. Participating in an activity that has been described is not just translating the description into embodied experience, but renegotiating its meaning in a new context.
  - Reification is not a mere articulation of something that already exists. Writing down a statement of values, expressing an idea, painting a picture, recounting an event, articulating an emotion, or building a tool is not merely giving expression to existing meanings, but in fact creating the conditions for new meanings.

As a consequence, such processes as making something explicit, formalizing, or sharing are not merely translations; they are indeed transformations – the production of a new context of both participation and reification, in which the relations between the tacit and the explicit, the formal and the informal, the individual and the collective, are to be renegotiated.

- **Participation and reification describe an interplay; they are not classificatory categories**

There is a fundamental difference between using a distinction to classify things (e.g., meanings, thoughts, knowledge, learning) as one pole or the other and using a distinction to describe an inherent interplay.

In a duality, what is of interest is understanding the interplay, not classifying. The duality of participation and reification is not a classificatory scheme. It does not classify meanings, thoughts, knowledge, or learning as tacit or explicit, formal or informal, conscious or unconscious, individual or collective. Rather, it provides a framework to analyze the various ways in which they are always both at once.

Traditional dichotomies are useful distinctions when they are used to highlight an aspect of a process that has not received enough attention. But when it comes to issues like meaning, knowing, or learning, dichotomies cannot provide clean classificatory categories because they focus on surface features rather than on fundamental processes. For instance, the contrast between explicit and tacit knowledge is quite useful because it is important to recognize the existence of aspects of knowledge that we cannot easily articulate; hence, being able to *tell* and being able to *do* are not equivalent.

Classifying knowledge as explicit or tacit runs into difficulties, however, because both aspects are always present to some degree. For example, people who know how to ride a bicycle often cannot articulate how they keep their balance. In particular, they cannot say which way they steer in order to avoid falling, even though they do it right. To classify riding a bicycle as tacit knowledge is tricky because people are not exactly speechless about the process. They can tell you, for instance, that you must pedal and steer, hold the bar, and not wiggle too much or sit backward unless you're a pro. Classifying knowledge then becomes a matter of deciding what counts as explicit, and that depends on the enterprise we are involved in.

Walking is a very embodied knowledge, but if someone tells me to walk, I can do it. Requiring only this yields a good enough relation between the explicit and the tacit for certain purposes, though probably not good enough for an orthopedist who needs to know which muscles I use to keep my balance and move my legs – but that is a different enterprise altogether. Conversely, I'd bet that physicists, whose knowledge many of us would consider very explicit, would have as hard a time articulating exactly how they make sense of concepts such as force and space–time as we have explaining how we ride a bicycle. When it comes to meaningful knowing in the context of any enterprise, the explicit must always stop somewhere. It is always possible to find aspects that are not explicit, and this is exactly what a duality of participation and reification would predict: we produce precisely the reification we need in order to proceed with the practices in which we participate.

The duality of participation and reification is more fundamental than our ability to put things in words, create formalisms, articulate our feelings, or share our thoughts. It is therefore important not to reduce participation and reification to any of the dichotomies I have mentioned.

- For instance, participation is not just tacit, informal, or unconscious, because our participation includes actions like having a conversation, teaching a formalized curriculum, or reflecting on our motives.
- Reification is not just explicit, because there are many ways of reifying that are not simply putting things into words. A painting, for instance, reifies a perception of the world, an understanding. It is an expression that makes a statement and focuses our attention in specific ways. But it is difficult to say whether this expression is explicit or tacit. Similarly, building a tool or systematically ignoring people to let them know they are outsiders are acts of reification that cannot easily be classified as tacit or explicit.
- Neither participation nor reification can be easily thought of in terms of contrasts of individual versus collective, or private versus public. Participation is clearly a social process, but it is also a personal experience. Reification allows us to coordinate our actions and is therefore of a collective character, but it shapes our own perceptions of the world and ourselves.
- Reification can be public to the extent that it produces tangible objects, but participation can also be public to the extent that our actions are observable. Moreover, the effects of both on our experience are not so visible or easily classified as public or private.

Finally, the duality of participation and reification is not just a distinction between people and things. It is true that participation is something we do as persons, and reification has to do with objects. But the duality of participation and reification suggests precisely that, in terms of meaning, people and things cannot be defined independently of each other.

- On the one hand, we experience the world as we make it amenable to our practices. I remember being awed by the complex system of distinctions and nuances that wine tasters have developed to describe what to most people is merely a better or worse glass of wine.
- On the other hand, our sense of ourselves includes the objects with which we identify because they furnish our practices. Mastering the wine-tasting vocabulary and being able to appreciate and discuss all the nuances of a good wine can become a source of distinction, pride, and identity.

What it means to be a person and what it means to be a thing both involve an interplay of participation and reification. From this perspective, people and things do not have to be posited as a point of departure. They need not be assumed as given to start with. It is engagement in social practice that provides the baseline. Through the negotiation of meaning, it is the interplay of participation and reification that makes people and things what they are.

In this interplay, our experience and our world shape each other through a reciprocal relation that goes to the very essence of who we are. The world as we shape it, and our experience as the world shapes it, are like the mountain and the river. They shape each other, but they have their own shape. They are reflections of each other, but they have their own existence, in their own realms. They fit around each other, but they remain distinct from each other. They cannot be transformed into each other, yet they transform each other. The river only carves and the mountain only guides, yet in their interaction, the carving becomes the guiding and the guiding becomes the carving.

   [...]

Bibliography

Anderson J. R. (1983). *The Architecture of Cognition.* Cambridge, MA: Harvard University Press.

Clancey, W. (1997). *Situated Cognition: On Human Knowledge and Computer Representations.* Cambridge University Press.

Dewey, J. (1992). *Human Nature and Conduct. An Introduction to Social Psychology.* London: Allen and Unwin.

Dreyfus, H. L. (1991). *Being-in-the-World, A Commentary on Heidegger's Being and Time, Division I.* Cambridge, MA: MIT Press.

Edelman, G. (1993). *Bright Air, Brilliant Fire: On the Matter of the Mind.* New York: Basic Books.

Giddens, A. (1979). *Central Problems in Social Theory. Action, Structure, and Contradiction in Social Analysis Berkeley:* University of California Press.

Giddens, A. (1984). *The Constitution of Society.* Berkeley: University of California Press.

Giddens, A. (1990). *The Consequences of Modernity.* Stanford University Press.

Giddens, A. (1991). *Modernity and Self Identity: Self and Society in the Late Modern Age.* Stanford University Press.

Heidegger, M. (1927, translated 1962). *Being and Time.* New York: Harper & Row.

Hutchins, E. (1995). *Cognition in the Wild.* Cambridge, MA: MIT Press.

Johnson, M. (1987). *The Body in the Mind. The Bodily Basis of Meaning, Imagination and Reason.* Chicago University Press.

Leont'ev, A. N. (1981). The problem of activity in psychology. In J. Wertsch (ed.), *The Concept of Activity in Soviet Psychology.* Armonk, NY: M. E. Sharpe.

Lukács, G. (1992, translated 1971). *History and Class Consciousness: Studies in Marxist Dialectics.* Cambridge, MA: MIT Press.

Marx, K. (1867) *Capital: A Critique of Political Economy.* New York: International.

Polanyi, M. (1983). *The Tacit Dimension.* Magnolia, MA: Peter Smith.

Wertsch, J. (1985). *Vygotsky and the Social Formation of Mind.* Cambridge, MA: Harvard University Press.

Section 2

Culture, Tools and Learning

4

Thinking with the Tools and Institutions of Culture

Barbara Rogoff

Although thinking is often regarded as a private, solo activity, cultural research has brought to light many ways that thinking involves interpersonal and community processes in addition to individual processes. The study of cognitive development now attends to more than the unfolding of children's understanding through childhood. It includes attention to how people come to understand their world through active participation in shared endeavors with other people as they engage in sociocultural activities.

[…]

Scholars searched for theoretical guidance that would help them understand how people's thinking relates closely to their cultural experience, to replace the idea that cognition was a general process that could be "influenced" by culture. Many found inspiration in Vygotsky's cultural-historical theory, which posited that individual cognitive skills derived from people's engagement in sociocultural activities. According to this theory, cognitive development occurs as people learn to use cultural tools for thinking (such as literacy and mathematics) with the help of others more experienced with such tools and cultural institutions.

The sociocultural approach also offers an integrated approach to human development. Cognitive, social, perceptual, motivational, physical, emotional, and other processes are regarded as aspects of sociocultural activity rather than as separate, free-standing capabilities or "faculties," as has been traditional in psychology. An integrated approach makes it easier to understand how thinking involves social relations and cultural experience, without an artificial separation into isolated parts.

This perspective has shifted our understanding of cognition from a focus solely on the thoughts of supposedly solitary individuals to a focus on the active processes of individuals, whether momentarily solo or in ensembles, as they engage in shared endeavors in cultural communities. From this perspective, cognitive development is not the acquisition of knowledge or of skills; rather, it takes a more active form. Cognitive development consists of individuals changing their ways of understanding, perceiving, noticing, thinking, remembering, classifying, reflecting, problem setting and solving, planning, and so on—in shared

---

[This is an edited excerpt from an extensive, illustrated chapter in *The Cultural Nature of Human Development*, 2003]

From: Chapter 7 in Rogoff, B., *The Cultural Nature of Human Development* (Oxford: Oxford University Press, 2003). By permission of Oxford University Press, Inc.

endeavors with other people building on the cultural practices and traditions of communities. Cognitive development is an aspect of the transformation of people's participation in sociocultural activities.

[...]

Cultural values of intelligence and maturity

For many years, cognitive testing procedures were regarded as context-free, supposedly allowing observation of people's cognitive skills in some sort of pure fashion, unrelated to their life experiences. Along with noticing the importance of familiarity of language, concepts, and materials in test performance, researchers began to consider the familiarity of the values and everyday experience connected with the test format.

Of course, the values embedded in some widely used tests can be part of their role as selection devices for ensuring that certain children get access to opportunities. They can also be political tools to influence public policies:

> In 1912, when racism in America swelled on a rising tide of immigration, the U.S. Public Health Service hired psychologist H. H. Goddard to help screen out the imagined menace of inferior minds that were poised to contaminate the (equally imagined) pellucid American gene pool. Goddard, who invented the term "moron," created his own test for mental deficiency. Gould's *Mismeasure of Man* gives a remarkable account of how Goddard's test questions were fired at immigrants as they stepped bewildered and exhausted off the boat at Ellis Island. (Many had never before held a pencil, and had no possible frame of reference for understanding what was being asked of them.) Goddard arrived at these staggering results: 83 percent of Jews, 87 percent of Russians, 80 percent of Hungarians, and 79 percent of Italians were diagnosed as morons. ... Ethnic quotas on U.S. immigration were in place with the decade. (Kingsolver, 1995, p. 77)

Even without such motives, value systems are built into the procedures and interpretation of tests. This section examines how cognitive testing is a kind of cultural practice involving academic institutions and forms of communication between a tester and the person being tested. Then it turns to how communities vary in their definitions of intelligence and maturity.

Familiarity with the interpersonal relations used in tests

Cognitive tests rely on particular conversational forms that are often central in schools. Schooled people are familiar with an interview or a testing situation in which a high-status adult, who already knows the answer to a question, requests information from a lower-status person, such as a child (Mehan, 1979).

Even before attending school, children in some communities where schooling is central begin to participate with their family in the sort of discourse that often occurs in tests and schools. Middle-class European American parents often play language games with their toddlers that involve test questions in the same format as the known-answer questions used by teachers and testers (such as "Where is your belly button?"). Familiarity with questions that serve as directives to perform in specific ways can make a difference in whether children respond as expected by the tester, creatively play with the materials or warily try to figure out what is going on (Massey et al., 1982; Moreno, 1991).

In some cultural settings where schooling is not a central practice, culturally appropriate behavior may depart from what a researcher expects. The situation may call for showing respect to the questioner, or it may call for attempting to avoid being made a fool of by giving an obvious answer to what must be a trick question—otherwise why would a knowledgeable person ask it?

Judith Irvine suggested that Wolof (North African) research participants' interpretation of an experimenter's purpose may have conflicted with giving straightforward answers to Piagetian questions. In a prior study, Wolof adolescents had responded that the quantity of water in a conservation test had changed because the researcher had poured it (Greenfield, 1966). Irvine (1978) reported that, except in school interrogation, Wolof people seldom ask questions to which they already know the answers: "Where this kind of questioning does occur it suggests an aggressive challenge, or a riddle with a trick answer". When Irvine presented the task as language-learning questions about the meaning of quantity terms such as *more* and *the same*, using water and beakers for illustration, her informants' responses reflected understanding of conservation.

Values about social relationships influence people's responses to cognitive questions. For example, rather than performing and competing as individuals, children in some communities avoid distinguishing themselves from the group by volunteering an answer (Philips, 1972; Whiting & Whiting, 1975). In tests, as in many Western schools, reliance on a companion for help may be considered cheating, whereas in many cultural settings, not to employ a companion's assistance may be regarded as folly or egoism.

Similarly, ideals about relationships between children and others may lead children to place primacy on appropriate social relations rather than to focus on a cognitive puzzle. In many communities, for instance, the role of children may be to observe and carry out directives but not to initiate conversation or talk back to a person of higher status (Blount, 1972; Harkness & Super, 1977; Ward, 1971). In some communities, displaying a skill before it is well learned (as in a test) is considered an important part of the learning process. However, it is regarded as premature and inappropriate in others, where careful, thoughtful problem solving is prioritised (Cazden & John, 1971; S. Ellis, 1997; Swisher and Deyhle, 1989).

Cultural models of social relations, which implicitly or explicitly provide rationales for children's and adults' appropriate behavior and ways of relating (Harkness & Super, 1977), are not held in abeyance in cognitive tests. Indeed, they are centrally involved in each community's definitions of intelligence and maturity.

Varying definitions of intelligence and maturity

Many differences among cultural communities in performance on cognitive tasks may be due to varying interpretations of what problem is to be solved and different values defining "proper" methods of solution (Goodnow, 1976). For example, the appropriateness of treating a cognitive task as a self-contained intellectual puzzle independent of the social context varies across communities. Likewise, speed of problem solving may be regarded either favorably or negatively. Ugandan villagers associated intelligence with adjectives such as *slow, careful,* and *active,* whereas Ugandan teachers and Westernized groups associated intelligence with the word *speed* (Wober, 1972). The reflective pace valued among the Navajo may account for the greater planning and fewer errors by Navajo children, compared with Anglo children, in determining routes in a maze game (Ellis & Siegler, 1997).

Some groups define children's intelligence in terms of both capability in specific situations and social responsibility (Serpell, 1977, 1982). For example, Mexican American ideas of intelligence are reflected in being *educado,* which has a broader meaning than the English term *educated.* It refers to attaining, through orientation by the family, a sense of moral and personal responsibility and respect for the dignity of others that serves as the foundation for all other learning (Munoz, personal communication, February 2000).

Popular conceptions of intelligence held by middle-class European American groups differ from those of some other groups in valuing technical intelligence as distinct from social and emotional skills. The Ifaluk of the western Pacific regard intelligence as not only having knowledge of good social behavior, but also performing it (Lutz & LeVine, 1982). Kipsigis (Kenyan) parents interpret intelligence as including trustworthy, responsible participation in family and social life (Super & Harkness, 1983; see also Ogunnaike & Houser, 2002).

To study what is meant by intelligence in a rural community in Zambia, Robert Serpell asked adults to identify particular children in their village whom they would select for a series of imaginary tasks and asked them to explain why.
[...]

The adults often justified their choice of a particular child with the concept of *nzelu,* which resembles the English *intelligence.* However, whereas the English term has a primarily cognitive meaning, *nzelu* seems to correspond with the areas that in English are called *wisdom, cleverness,* and *responsibility.* The concept of *nzelu* does not apply to people who use their intelligence for selfish purposes (such as the mischievous and manipulative cunning of the character Brer Rabbit), only to those who use their intelligence in a socially productive way (Serpell, 1993).

A central meaning of the socially responsible dimension of *nzelu* is the idea of being trusted to carry out something for others, from toddlers who are frequently asked to bring an adult something they cannot reach without standing up, to friends commissioned to make small purchases on a trip. To be sent on such errands is recognition of being both a responsible person and a comrade. It requires understanding of the demands of the task as well as a cooperative attitude.

Serpell summarized similar concepts of intelligence in other African communities, which also include the idea of social responsibility. For example, the concept of *o ti kpa* (from the Baoulé of the Ivory Coast) involves

> the performance of tasks which contribute to the family's welfare ... with the connotation of responsibility and a touch of initiative as well as know-how. ... What is important is that the child should help out, pull his weight in domestic and agricultural work. But it is not just a matter of performing these tasks: the child is more *o ti kpa* the more he performs them well, spontaneously, and responsibly. (Dasen et al., 1985, pp. 303–304; translated and cited by Serpell, 1993, p. 44)

In the United States, the term *intelligence* also seems to be used more broadly among laypeople than by psychologists. Psychologists from around the United States and the general public in New Haven, Connecticut, differed in how they rated behaviors as characterizing an intelligent person (Sternberg et al., 1981). Both psychologists and laypeople included problem-solving ability and verbal ability in their concept of intelligence; laypeople also included social competence, comprised by characteristics such as admitting mistakes, having a social conscience, and thinking before speaking and doing.

Ideas of developmental maturity, precocity, and retardation are tied to judgments regarding what aspects of human intelligence and behavior are valued in the community. Among the Abaluyia (in Kenya),

> mothers use evidence that a child has the ability to give and receive social support, and assist others, as markers of a child's more general developmental level, much as an American parent might use literacy skills such as knowing the alphabet, or verbal facility, to show how grown-up or precocious his or her child is. (Weisner, 1989, p. 86)

An indicator of intelligence and social acuity among Chamulas (Mayan Indians of Mexico) is boys' and young men's virtuosity in highly structured, improvisational verbal dueling (Gossen, 1976). Pairs of youths trade rapid-fire insults that must echo the prior turn with only small changes in the sounds of a phrase, at the same time giving a clever response to the partner's turn. The fellow who can keep the game going longest (sometimes hundreds of turns), returning lewd original puns that follow very exacting rules, is regarded as superior. Boys of 5 or 6 routinely beat small boys of 2 or 3, but truly good players do not emerge until adolescence. By engaging in verbal duelling, boys and young men develop the locally valued form of intelligence–eloquence. Grace and power in the use of language, shown in the arena of verbal dueling, are key in evaluating young men for adult careers:

> Virtuosity [in this form of talk] bodes well for a boy's political and social future. With the reservoir of social rules and thorough knowledge of language which the genre inculcates, a consistent winner in verbal dueling is well equipped to begin the genuine play for rank and prestige which is an important aspect of adulthood. (p. 144)

Value judgments regarding which skills are desirable in young children include considerations of the meaning of the skill to the larger community, not just precocity or virtuosity itself. For example, recent policies in China have caused concern that very young children may be becoming *too* skilled in adapting their behavior to the circumstances:

> The single-child policy has constructed families ... where the children are often treated as the "center of the universe" at home, while at the day-care center they are but one among many. The rules of conduct are strictly enforced in day care but are often ignored at home. These mixed messages have created toddlers who ... have a heightened awareness of the appropriate verbiage and conduct for a particular context. They learn at an early age how to deal with events in appropriate ways and know what "face" to put forward at what time. This ability may appear to the Westerners as a great achievement for toddlers of 2 and 3 years of age; in fact, it is an impressive achievement. Nevertheless, it is of concern to many Chinese adults because these

children's behaviors are often void of honesty and sincerity. These behaviors are often opportunistic and are used to placate adults, particularly teachers. Thus, to some extent, the goal of educating children to become moral beings is in jeopardy. (Lee, 1992, p. 391)

Each community's goals or endpoints of development, methods of facilitating development, and assessments of progress toward an endpoint involve value judgments (Goodnow, 1980). The designation of certain goals or certain ways of solving problems as more sophisticated or important than others is itself a cultural process worthy of study (S. Ellis, 1997; Wertsch, 1991).

Research on culture and cognition has come to include recognition of the appropriateness of different approaches to tasks, depending on the ways that maturity and intelligence are conceived in different communities. Thus, over a few decades, the conception of cognitive development has changed dramatically from the assumption that thinking ability is a general characteristic of individuals. Cultural research has called attention to the specific nature of thinking as situated in the practices of cultural communities. Not only does it matter how familiar people are with the conservation or classification or memory task they are given, but cultural definitions of intelligent behavior and formats for social interaction come into play in any observation of thinking.

With the realization that cognitive tests examine specific skills, often ones that were practiced in school, the puzzle of how people apply what they have learned across situations is not yet resolved. The problem remains of accounting for how people generalize from their experience in one situation to another.

Generalizing experience from one situation to another

Since it became clear that generality could not be assumed across situations, scholars have continued to struggle with the question of how to handle the specificity of thinking. Is every situation different from every other, resulting in total specificity? Clearly not, or people would never be able to handle anything new or even to use language. There must be some ways in which understanding gained in one situation relates to a new situation.

Researchers sometimes write as though broad generalization of thinking processes is the goal of learning. However, generalization is not necessarily a good thing. Automatically doing the same thing in a new situation may or may not fit the new situation. For example, the Salt Lake City children who rehearsed the names of objects when asked to reconstruct a scene inappropriately generalized a familiar strategy for memorizing lists to a new problem (Rogoff & Waddell, 1982). Rather than needing to apply strategies broadly, they needed to know which strategies are helpful in what circumstances. The goal is *appropriate* generalization.

The likelihood of appropriately using understanding developed in one situation when faced with a new but related situation is based partly on achievement of conceptual understanding (Hatano, 1988). People do not appropriately generalize procedures across relevant circumstances without having some understanding of the procedures. For example, people familiar with mathematical procedures from school or from everyday nonschool experience may not appropriately apply the procedures in relevant new situations unless they understand the principles involved (Schliemann et al., 1997).

However, understanding the principles in a certain situation does not automatically lead to applying them in another one for which they are relevant (Nunes, 1995). This has puzzled scholars who assume that people treat problems with the same structure similarly or are automatically able to apply their knowledge to new problems within the same domain (such as within the domain of biology or of cooking or of addition).

In a sense, these scholars regard the process of generalization as residing within the problem structure or domain of knowledge. Such a stance falls short of considering the need to *discern relevance* to the new situation. This requires relating the goals of the new situation to those of prior situations, not just access to "pieces" of knowledge or the principles underlying them. Once we abandon the idea of generalization being automatic (within similar problems or domains), the question of the extent of generalization is open to investigation rather than assumed to be mechanically driven by characteristics of the "problems."

For a person to discern relevance of prior understanding to a new situation requires considering how the purposes of each are related. The unit of analysis used in sociocultural theory—the whole activity—helps researchers to focus on the goals that people pursue by thinking and to understand how people's participation in one activity relates to their participation in another. The idea is that individuals handle later situations according to how they relate to prior ones in which they have participated (Rogoff, 1998).

This view of cognition moves beyond the idea that development consists of *acquiring* knowledge and skills. Rather, a person develops through *participation in* an activity, *changing* to be involved in the situation at hand in ways that contribute both to the ongoing event and to the person's preparation for involvement in other similar events.

[…]

For individuals and groups to generalize appropriately across experiences involves what Giyoo Hatano (1988) has called *adaptive expertise*. Development of adaptive expertise is supported by the extent to which people understand the goals and principles of relevant activities and gain experience with varying means to achieve them. Cultural practices and social interaction support learning which circumstances relate to each other and which approaches fit different circumstances.

Learning to fit approaches flexibly to circumstances

Learning to fit approaches flexibly to circumstances is itself an important aspect of cognitive development. It is needed for making decisions in the various realms of intelligence that are prioritized in different communities, whether technical or social. Consistent with a sociocultural approach to cognitive development, some of the most relevant research on fitting approaches to circumstances comes from research on social relations, not just in more narrowly cognitive problem-solving situations.

In some communities, learning to distinguish appropriate circumstances is an explicit goal in child development. Takie Lebra (1994) referred to this goal in Japanese child rearing as *boundary training*, in which children learn to conduct themselves according to their various roles: as a school-child, as a neighbor, as the child of a doctor, and so on.

The Japanese educational system encourages children to learn the circumstances in which they should act one way or another (Ben-Ari, 1996). For example, in the preschool years, rather than trying to achieve consistency across mother-child and teacher-child relations, children are helped by parents and teachers to distinguish the contexts and the approach that is appropriate to each. In middle childhood, children are immersed in an elementary school system that promotes harmonious learning in the group with little emphasis on competition or individuals standing out; by junior high school age, many of the children also attend private afterschool *juku* lessons that are organized competitively (White, 1987). In this way, Japanese children learn to participate in both harmonious group relations and individual competition in different contexts and to distinguish the contexts in which these approaches apply.

Similarly, working-class African American families emphasize helping children learn flexible ways of acting and speaking, adapted to shifting roles and situations. Shirley Brice Heath (1983) noted that adults in this community often asked questions that encouraged children to seek appropriate relationships between situations based on the children's experience. The adults thus gave importance to flexibility as well as to metaphorical thinking and speaking.

Marquesan toddlers from Polynesia learn to observe contextual cues to determine when to be obedient and when to be demanding and mischievous (Martini & Kirkpatrick, 1992). Caregivers enjoy toddlers' teasing, as in the case of a toddler who responded to a mother's request for a kiss, "No, Mama, you smell." Parents talk proudly about times their toddler stood up to adult authority. Teasing may give toddlers lessons in how to handle inconsistency, helping them learn under what circumstances somebody is treating them in a truthful, straightforward fashion and under what circumstances somebody is pretending in a way that they should not treat as the truth.

In contrast, middle-class European American child-rearing experts' advice to parents often includes suggestions to "be consistent," treating a child in the same fashion at all times. College-educated European American mothers stressed the importance of providing consistency when asked what they think is important for child rearing (Chao, 1995).

[...]

Differences in acting appropriately at home and at school are faced by children everywhere, but especially by children whose community ways differ from the ways of Western schooling. For example, American Indian children are often expected to be respectfully silent when learning at home, but their non-Indian teachers may regard their silence as disinterest or even resistance (Plank, 1994). Similarly, a collaborative mode at home may be inconsistent with an expectation at school that students compete with each other and try to show off their knowledge.

Showing respect to an adult at school may require looking him or her in the eye; at home it may require averting one's gaze (e.g., for Navajo, Puerto Rican, and African American children; Byers & Byers, 1972; Chisholm, 1996; Hale-Benson, 1986). However, many European American teachers expect eye contact and infer lack of respect or attention without it ("I don't know if you're paying attention if you don't look at me"). This is problematic if the children have been taught that looking an adult in the eye is an affront that challenges adult authority and shows arrogance. Dolores Mena, a Mexican American graduate student, reflected on this conflict:

I remember growing up and many times feeling conflicted because what my parents told me to do and what other people told me to do was not always consistent. [My parents] would tell us not to look at older people in the eyes because it was disrespectful but, yet, at school we were told by the teachers to look at them when we spoke or were spoken to. And so at school, averting eye contact was misinterpreted as not being attentive in class. I remember one time when I actually stared my father straight in the eyes when he was asking me to do something for him. Just the look in his eyes sent a chill up my spine and I never again stared him straight in the eyes. (personal communication, October 1999)

To avoid communication problems when home and school practices differ, children must learn to distinguish the appropriate approach for the setting. In the home community, children may be expected to answer a question immediately, whereas in school they may be expected to wait to speak until they are called on by the teacher. At home, several people may be expected to talk at once, whereas at school there may be a rule of one person speaking at a time. Alternatively, at home, people may provide a respectful pause between turns at speaking, but at school, children from a background requiring a respectful pause may never get a chance to speak. At home, children may be expected to show respect for others by not contradicting them, but in school, they may be expected to argue ideas in ways that seem like contradiction.

Learning to distinguish the appropriate ways to act in different situations is a very important accomplishment in all communities, for children as well as for their elders. Learning which approach to use at school and home, along with determining which strategy to use in cognitive tests and other problem solving situations, amount to learning to generalize appropriately from one situation to another.

Sociocultural theories have built on the realization that thinking is closely tied to particular situations. As this section has demonstrated, the connection between thinking and situations is not mechanical. Rather, individuals determine their approaches to particular situations with reference to cultural practices in which they have previously participated. The creative role of individuals in relating one situation to another is supported by social interaction in which social partners suggest connections. In addition, individuals and social groups build on connections made for them by previous generations, often mediated by cultural tools that they inherit. As people use cultural tools such as literacy and number systems to handle cognitive problems, in the process they often extend or modify the use of such tools for themselves and future generations.

Cultural tools for thinking

In early cross-cultural research, there were many indications that schooling and literacy relates to performance on cognitive tests. It became clear that the relation was rather specific to particular aspects of performance on cognitive tests and had to do with specific uses of literacy or particular schooling formats. These findings, along with the inspiration provided by Vygotskian theory, contributed to the transformation of cultural cognitive research to a focus on how one learns to use the cognitive tools of one's cultural community. In this section, I examine the use of several cultural tools for thinking that have received considered research attention: literacy, mathematics, and other conceptual systems.

Literacy

The invention of literacy has been argued to have had profound historical effects on how societies handle cognitive challenges. With the availability of written records, the importance of memory for preserving chronicles in the form of oral narrative diminished. At the same time, the concept of remembering information word for word (rather than for its gist) may also have arisen with the possibility of checking recall against written records (Cole & Scribner, 1977).

Literacy, it has been argued, fosters the examination of propositions for their internal logic (Goody & Watt, 1968; Olson, 1976). Written statements may more easily be examined for consistency and can be treated *as* if meaning were contained in the text itself, as in solving logical syllogisms or story problems. Of course, as cultural research has demonstrated, the social context of the writer and reader are very much a part of treating text in this manner. The reader's familiarity with such genres and prior knowledge of the specific topic play pivotal roles in making sense of written text.

One of the early claims about the importance of literacy assumed it had a broad, general influence on individuals' cognitive abilities. To examine these claims, Sylvia Scribner and Michael Cole (1981) studied the relation between cognitive skills and literacy of various types. They pointed out that most speculations about literacy focus on the use of essayist text (expository writing). In their research, they worked with Via people from Liberia who employed several different types of literacy:

> *Vai script* is used for the majority of personal and public needs (such as letter writing) in the villages and is transmitted informally by nonprofessional literates who teach friends and relatives over a period of up to two months. Vai script is an independently developed phonetic writing system, consisting of a syllabary of 200 characters with 20 to 40 commonly used characters.
>
> In addition, some Vai individuals are literate in *Arabic* from their study of religious texts in traditional Qur'anic schools, which emphasize memorizing or reading aloud, often without understanding the language.
>
> And some Vai are literate in *English* from their study in Western-style official schools.

The Vai script has many important uses, but it does not involve writing essays to examine ideas. Hence, Scribner and Cole (1981) predicted that Vai literacy would not have the intellectual consequences that have been suggested to result from high levels of school-based literacy, such as those reviewed above. Indeed, they found little difference between individuals literate and not literate in Vai on logic and classification tasks.

However, specific cognitive skills correlated with particular aspects of the different systems of literacy. For example, in communication tasks requiring the description of a board game in its absence, Vai literates excelled, compared with nonliterates and with Arabic literates. Scribner and Cole expected this relationship, because Vai literates frequently write letters, a practice requiring communication to be carried largely in the text, with relatively diminished support from other aspects of context. Vai literates were also more skilled in comprehending sentences presented syllable-by-syllable at a slow rate. This resembles the necessity in Vai literacy to integrate syllables into words, as Vai script is written without word division. Arabic literacy was associated with skill in remembering a string of words in order, with one word added to the list on each trial. This test resembles the method for learning the Qur'an by those literate in Arabic.

Scribner and Cole's (1981) results indicate that literacy relates to cognitive skills through specific practices involved in the use of literacy. Different forms of written script (such as alphabetic or phonemic writing, with or without word divisions) and different uses of literacy (such as essayist prose, letters, story problems, lists, chants) promoted distinct cognitive skills. Variations in the purposes and practices of literacy appear to be closely related to the skills that individuals using a technology gain from its use. Such variations are embedded in the social institutions in which skill with technologies is practiced and developed.

Variation in the societal uses of literacy is clear in shifts in recent U.S. history in the definition of functional literacy (Myers, 1984, 1996; Resnick & Resnick, 1977; Wolf, 1988). In the United States of the 1700s, literacy was defined as being able to sign one's name or an X to legal documents. In the late 1800s, literacy became the ability to read and recite memorized passages, not necessarily with comprehension, as the United States sought order in recovering from a civil war and incorporating influxes of immigrants, and the machinery of industry warmed up. In the early 1900s, being able to read began to require literal understanding of unfamiliar passages. At this time, Army testers sought recruits for World War I who could read instructions for operating equipment, and the efficiency goals of increasingly centralized industry required workers who could extract information from text. By the late 1900s, "higher" levels of literacy (making inferences and developing ideas through written material) were expected on a mass basis for the first time. This latest definition of literacy was prompted in part by widespread use of information technology in the workplace.

Such historical shifts in the use of a cultural technology underscore the relation between individual cognitive practices and the specific institutions, technologies, and goals of society.

[…]

Mathematics

Similar to the findings for literacy, performance on mathematical tests relates to familiarity with particular numerical practices. For example, experience with schooling was related to Liberian tailors' skill in handling arithmetic problems in the format used in school, whereas tailoring experience was related to skill in solving arithmetic problems in the format used in tailoring (Lave, 1977). Neither schooling nor tailoring provided "general" skill in numeric operations.

[…]

Likewise, Japanese abacus experts showed specific consequences of skill in using the abacus. They mentally calculated without an abacus as accurately as with one, and often faster, imagining problems of many digits on an abacus (Hatano, 1982; Stigler *et al.*, 1982). Visualizing problems on an abacus apparently facilitated specific skill in remembering: abacus experts recalled a series of 15 digits either forward or backward. However, their memory span for the Roman alphabet and for fruit names was not different from the usual 7 plus or minus 2 units found for most adults in memory-span tasks. The processes involved in their impressive mental abacus operations are tailored to the activities in which they were practiced, and are applied specifically to related activities.

Similar to the research on literacy, research on mathematics has indicated the central role of cultural tools of thought. Such tools include the abacus, school forms of calculation, the pricing structure of candy to be sold on the street, the metric system, and the use of body parts or clay tokens to represent numbers (S. Ellis, 1997; Nicolopoulou, 1997; Saxe, 1981, 1991; Ueno & Saito, 1995). People's strategies for handling mathematical problems relate closely to the purpose of the calculation and the available and familiar tools.

Mathematical tools and skills are not all-purpose; rather, they are adapted to the circumstances. The adaptations made by individuals, as well as institutions, often prioritize simplification of work and reduction of mental effort, with the use of specialized strategies to deal with routine situations (Cole, 1996; Lave, 1988; Scribner, 1984).

When mathematics is used for practical purposes—such as by vendors, carpenters, farmers, and dieters—people seldom came up with nonsense results in their calculations. However, calculations in the context of schooling regularly produce some absurd errors, with results that are impossible if the meaning of the problem being solved is considered:

> The rule-bound solutions traditionally taught in schools seem to provide [people] with procedures that are not always understood and become useless in generating appropriate solutions to problems out of school contexts. In contrast, the strategies developed by individuals as tools to solve problems out of school are characterized by their flexibility and by constant monitoring of the meaning of the situation, the problem questions, and the quantities involved.
>
> As summarized by Nunes (1993), the two most important differences between the two types of mathematics are that, (1) while outside of schools mathematics is used as a tool to achieve some other goals, in schools mathematics is an aim in itself, and (2) the situations where mathematics is used out of schools give meaning to computations, while mathematics, as it is traditionally taught in schools, becomes mainly a process of manipulation of numbers. (Schliemann et al., 1997, pp. 197–198)

National differences in skill on international mathematics tests have aroused a great deal of public debate regarding the role of schools and cultural practices in fostering mathematical understanding. The differences are striking: The best-performing U.S. fifth-grade classrooms (in Minnesota) scored lower on the mathematics test than the worst-performing Japanese classrooms and all but one Chinese classroom (Stevenson et al., 1986). Only 1 U.S. fifth-grader scored in the top 100 (out of 720 children), but 67 of them appeared in the group of 100 children who scored lowest on the test.

Some of the differences may relate to differences in how numbers are represented in different languages, yielding different cognitive tools for thinking. Some languages represent numbers such as 12 in a base-10 system ("ten-two"), whereas others have a nonbase-10 label ("twelve"). Languages with systematic use of base-10 may facilitate learning of the place value of numbers.

This was confirmed in a study in which children represented numbers using blocks in units of ten or units of one. Middle-class first-graders whose language systematically represents numbers in a base-10 system (Japanese, Chinese, and Korean) showed facility in representing place value. In comparison, middle-class first-graders from France, Sweden, and the United States, whose languages do not systematically represent base-10 numbers in the number labels, had much more difficulty (Miura et al., 1994). Similarly, Chinese 4- and 5-year-olds had less difficulty reciting the numbers and counting objects above 10 than did middle-class U.S. preschoolers, but there were not differences below 10 (Miller et al., 1995).

Efforts to understand the differences in the fifth-graders' mathematical performances have also focused attention on variations in the structure of schooling (Stevenson et al., 1986). U.S. children spent about half as much classroom time devoted to academic activities as children in Japan and China. U.S. teachers spent a much smaller proportion of their time imparting information than did Japanese or Chinese teachers; the U.S. teachers spent more time giving directions than imparting information. These differences are compounded by the fact that the school year is much shorter for the U.S. children (178 days) than for the Japanese and Chinese children (240 days). The U.S. school day is also shorter and U.S. children spent less time on homework than did Japanese or Chinese children.

The impressive achievements of Japanese children in mathematics are accompanied by other differences in values and community organization surrounding academic achievement and group relations (Lewis, 1995; Stevenson et al., 1986; White, 1987). Attitudes toward achievement emphasize that success comes from hard work (not from innate ability). In classes averaging 42 students, Japanese teachers focused on the children's engagement in their work rather than on discipline; classes were noisy but spent more time focused on learning. Japanese teachers also delegated more classroom responsibility to children and supported the development of peer group structures as part of the learning environment. Classmates served as resources in examining mathematical concepts rather than solely as competitors for the teacher's attention. Teachers examined a few problems in depth rather than covering many problems superficially; children's errors were used as learning tools for the group.

[…]

Very few Japanese parents emphasize academic goals as reasons for children to attend preschool; they emphasize social goals such as developing empathy for others. U.S. parents, on the other hand, usually emphasize academic goals for preschool. Japanese kindergartners spend four times as much time in free play as in the United States, and Japanese elementary schools emphasize children supporting each other in learning together, not test scores. Lewis suggested that the Japanese children's impressive test performance grows from the attention given in preschool and early elementary school to developing a sense of community in the classroom, so that the children feel a part of the group and are responsible to it, allowing a deeper and more focused attention to the subjects taught.

U.S. awareness of national differences in mathematical performance sparked intense interest in the Japanese system of elementary schooling (especially during Japan's economic boom). However, often it was one or two specific techniques that attracted U.S. attention, rather than how the system fits together, integrating mathematics learning, school structure and practices, and family and community practices and values. As Giyoo Hatano and Kayoko Inagaki (1996) pointed out, adoption of specific techniques (such as focusing class attention on individuals' errors) may not help and could be counterproductive without examining how specific procedures fit together in cultural systems of values and practices.

[…]

Skilled use of cultural tools such as mathematics is intimately connected with many aspects of the practices and values of the communities in which they are used. The use of cultural tools such as mathematical systems relates to properties of the tools themselves (such as whether a number system uses base-10 systematically), community values regarding uses of the tools and how they can be learned, and interpersonal and intercommunity relations in uses of the tools.

Other conceptual systems

In addition to literacy and number systems, other conceptual tools provide cultural technologies that support and constrain thinking. The following complex cultural knowledge systems help their users organize information and facilitate decision making:

- Scientific systems such as classification of animals and plants in the folk biology of various cultural communities provide extensive codification of local knowledge (Berlin, 1992).
- The tools available in star maps and spatial metaphors provide navigational systems that guide impressive seafaring expertise in Polynesia (Gladwin, 1971).
- Narrative and schematic maps along with a strategy of continual updating of orientation support extremely accurate wayfinding on land among aboriginal groups in Australia (Chatwin, 1987; Levinson, 1997).
- Linguistic distinctions regarding location and shape along with geographic narratives may support Inuit skill in spatial cognition and wayfinding in the Arctic (Kleinfeld, 1973).
- Folk psychology provides systems of assumptions for organizing beliefs about other people's understanding, desires, and intentionality (Lillard, 1997).

[…]

Linguistic labels for concepts also serve as cultural tools for thinking. The relation between thought and language has long been debated, and from numerous angles. The early hypothesis derived from Benjamin Whorf, that language systems determine thought, appears overly deterministic. At the same time, the idea that language systems simply derive from thought that is unrelated to language is also oversimplified. Recent work suggests that children more easily learn classification systems that are supported by concepts that receive labels in their community's language (Lucy & Gaskins, 1994).

Language systems are tools of thinking that both channel and result from community-wide ways of thinking and acting. Concepts that are easily expressed in the language system of a community provide a tool for thinking. At the same time, important community practices and traditions often find expression in words, to facilitate communication among people. That is, through participation in community practices as well as in communication about them, both thinking and language develop in ways that support each other […].

Cultural preferences in use of language go beyond the words that are used to express concepts. The narrative structure that is valued in each community gives form to the ways that people express ideas in conversation and writing […].

For example, Japanese narrative structure often follows a succinct three-part scheme resembling the Japanese poetry form *haiku*. The narrative omits information that the listener is judged to be able to easily infer if the listener were to take the narrator's perspective, consistent with Japanese valuing of empathy and collaboration (Minami & McCabe, 1995, 1996). To European American teachers, Japanese children are encouraged in this cultural form, regarded as elegantly compressed. They are very familiar with hearing haiku-like, succinct storytelling, and their mothers encourage them to narrate everyday events in this format through the kind of conversational accompaniment the mothers provide.

In contrast, European American narrative formats are more descriptive of settings and emotions, elaborating on a single experience, often with a high point resolving a problem (Minami & McCabe, 1995). European American children's narratives were much longer than those of Japanese children. The preferred narrative structure was encouraged by mothers, who often asked the children questions that encouraged them to elaborate on details, even those that a listener might readily infer.

Distinct narrative structures may contribute to habits of thought that relate to such cognitive domains as how one examines evidence to support a claim and how one specifies ideas to oneself and others. For example, the formats for writing scientific articles have a narrative structure that both guides and constrains a scientist's thinking, embodying the structure of thought and communication termed "the scientific method." As is well-known, the scientific method may not be followed in the research process, but eventually the scientist recasts the process in terms that fit with this culturally valued format for others to understand the work.

Individuals' and generations' uses of cognitive tools—such as narrative structures, words, and systems of numbers and writing—make it clear that thinking is a process involving interpersonal and community processes, in addition to the usual focus on individual processes. The next section focuses on the idea that thinking is widely distributed across people and tools, as people use cultural tools for thinking together.

Distributed cognition in the use of cultural tools for thinking

The cognitive development of individuals occurs within communities of thinkers in which more than one person is working on a particular topic. [...]

> As civilized human beings, we are the inheritors, neither of an inquiry about ourselves and the world, nor of an accumulating body of information, but of a conversation, begun in the primeval forests and extended and made more articulate in the course of centuries. It is a conversation which goes on both in public and within each of ourselves. ... [Each new generation enters] an initiation into the skill and partnership of this conversation. And it is this conversation which, in the end, gives place and character to every human activity and utterance. (Oakeshott, 1962, p. 199)

As Ed Hutchins (1991) pointed out in his studies of how sailors collaborate in the calculations and planning required for navigating large ships, cognition is *distributed* across people as they collaborate with each other and with tools designed to aid in cognitive work. Figuring out how to turn a massive vessel progressing at a certain speed to come to dock in a small harbor is done through the coordination of many people. They work with cognitive devices developed by predecessors to handle some aspects of the necessary data gathering, calculations, and interpersonal problem solving. Similarly:

> An ethnographer studying a group of machine technicians came to a blunt rethinking of what expertise means in the context of the workplace. His analysis was that expert knowledge among technicians is less a matter of what each individual knows than of their joint ability to produce the right information when and where it's needed. ... In other words, expertise is a social affair. (Schrage, 1990, p. 49)

[...]

Cognition beyond the skull

The idea that cognition is distributed across individuals, other people, and cultural tools and institutions may be difficult to consider if one assumes that cognition resides wholly inside individual heads. From the perspective that human development is a process of transformation of participation in sociocultural activities, the assumption that thinking occurs completely inside the skull is rejected.

The assumption that there is an arbitrary boundary between the individual and the rest of the world has created unnecessary complications in understanding development and thinking. It had also gotten in the way of understanding the relation among individual, interpersonal, and community processes.

[...]

In learning to use language and literacy, children also learn the use of physical movements and objects as mental tools. Arbitrary sounds, and their relative positions to one another, come to have such meaning that, for skilled speakers, the tools and the process of learning become almost invisible. Likewise, for a skilled reader, the process of moving from ink spots on a page to meaningful ideas is so automatic that the role of the tools of literacy and the author's and other people's contribution of process of reading may be easily overlooked. For novices, however, the distributed roles of the material tool, other people, and themselves are much more obvious as they learn to use a cognitive tool such as spoken language or literacy. Especially with such mental tools, cognition is distributed not only across individuals and material objects but also across ideas and communication with other people.

[...]

Collaboration hidden in the design of cognitive tools and procedures

Some cultural tools—such as computers, literacy, workbooks, and diagrams—are particularly designed to foster collaboration and interaction in thinking among people participating in shared activity at a distance (Bruffee, 1993; Crook, 1994; Ochs et al., 1994; Pea & Gomez, 1992; Schrage, 1990). The role of such tools in thinking may be easily overlooked.

For example, it would be easy to overlook the role of the problem setup as a tool for learning in the Japanese science education method in which students are presented with a question along with three or four possible answers to discuss. The question and the alternatives guide how students verify their predictions simply in the way the questions are asked and the alternatives worded, providing a range of possibilities that encompass common misconceptions (Kobayashi, 1994). This aids students in discerning both which opinions are plausible and which predictions test out, providing them with clues for restructuring their naïve understanding into scientific concepts. Without considering the collaborative role of those who devise such cognitive tools and the structure of the tools themselves, the students' learning process would be incompletely understood.

The computer plays such an important cultural role an a cognitive tool that it is sometimes regarded as an interactive partner itself (Hawkins, 1987; Schrage, 1990). Of course, thinking with the aid of a computer also involves remote collaboration with the people who designed the hardware, the software, and the computer setting that is being used. For example, in classrooms, some forms of guidance can be provided by either a computer or a human partner. Both options involve collaboration with human partners acting either indirectly through a device or directly in face-to-face interaction (Zellermayer et al., 1991).

Roy Pea provided an apt illustration of including other people and cognitive tools in notions of intelligence and its development. He recounted a presentation by Seymour Papert of a computer program for building toy machines at a National Science Foundation meeting:

> Papert described what marvelous machines the students had built, with very little "interference" from teachers. ... On reflection, I felt this argument missed the key point about the "invisible" human intervention in this example—what the designers of Lego and Logo crafted in creating just the interlockable component parts of Lego machines or just the Logo primitive commands for controlling these machines. For there are only so many ways in which these components can be combined. Considerable intelligence has been *built into* these interpart relations as a means of constraining what actions are possible with the parts in combination. What I realized was that, although Papert could "see" teachers' interventions (a kind of social distri- bution of intelligence contributing to the child's achievement of activity), the designer's interventions (a kind of artifact-based intelligence contributing to the child's achievement of activity) were not seen.... [The child] could be scaffolded in the achievement of activity either explicitly by the intelligence of the teacher, or *implicitly* by that of the designers, now embedded in the constraints of the artifacts with which the child was playing. (1993, pp. 64–65)

Artifacts such as books, orthographies, computers, languages, and hammers are essentially social, historical objects, transforming with the ideas of both their designers and their later users. They form and are formed by the practices of their use and by related practices, in historical and anticipated communities (Brown & Duguid, 1994; Gauvain, 1993; Nicolopoulou, 1997; Rogoff et al., 1994). Artifacts serve to amplify as well as constrain the possibilities of human activity as the artifacts participate in the practices in which they are employed (Cole & Griffin, 1980; Wertsch, 1991). They are representatives of earlier solutions to similar problems by other people, which later generations modify and apply to new problems, extending and transforming their use.
[…]

Crediting the cultural tools and practices we think with

Although cognitive tools, and the social roles that they carry with them across history, are easily overlooked, their contribution to thinking is central. James Wertsch provided a com- pelling example:

> Consider the following multiplication problem:

$$343$$
$$\underline{\times822}$$

If asked to solve this problem, you could probably come up with the answer of 281,946. If asked how you arrived at this solution, you might say, "I just multiplied 343 by 822!" and you might show me your calculations, which might look like this:

$$
\begin{array}{r}
343 \\
\underline{822} \\
686 \\
686 \\
\underline{27\ 44} \\
281946
\end{array}
$$

... Was it really you (i.e., the isolated agent) who solved the problem? (After all, you said "I multiplied ...") To see the force of this question ... consider what you would do in response to the request to multiply 343 by 822, but without placing the numbers in the vertical array used above. Most of us would be stumped at this point. ... A seemingly slight change in how the problem is written out seems to make our ability to multiply disappear ...

The spatial organization, or syntax, of the numbers in this case is an essential part of a cultural tool without which we cannot solve this problem. In an important sense, then, this syntax is doing some of the thinking involved. We might be unaware of how or why this syntax should work, and we might have no idea about how it emerged in the history of mathematical thought. In this sense, we are unreflective, if not ignorant, consumers of a cultural tool. The extent to which our performance relies on it, however, quickly becomes clear when it is not available. This leads me to suggest that when asked who carried out such a problem, the more appropriate answer might be, "I and the cultural tool I employed did." (1998, pp. 24–25)

The importance of cultural tools for mathematical thinking has been noted in passing for centuries. For example, Shakespeare frequently referred to the use of "counters" (Swetz, 1987). The clown from *The Winter's Tale* struggled to calculate the amount of money that the wool of 1,500 sheep ("wethers") would cost, if 11 sheep provide one tod (28 pounds):

Let me see. Every 'leven wether tods, every tod yields pound and odd shilling; fifteen hundred shorn, what comes the wool to?...

I cannot do't without counters. (quoted in Swetz, 1987, p. 181)

[...]

Eventually, the successors to Shakespeare's clown made use of the pencil-and-paper cognitive tools referred to by Wertsch, usually without thinking of this as a controversial method or even thinking of it as part of their calculation at all. However, neither the clown, nor modern-day solvers of Wertsch's multiplication problem could calculate without relying on the cultural tools (conceptual as well as material) available to them from prior generations and faraway places. And current generations continue to transform the tools used.

This abbreviated account makes clear how cognitive processes develop together with cultural processes across centuries and continents. The developments involve the contributions and collaborations of individuals of renown and those whose names are not remembered, in inventing, borrowing, and modifying cultural tools of thought. Cultural-historical research has pointed to the importance of including cultural tools in the analysis of cognitive processes and led the way to understanding that thinking is collaborative and distributed among people in shared endeavors.

This line of research has also drawn attention to the importance of understanding thinking as a purposeful effort to accomplish something, often with other people. Cultural tools of thought are generally used for purposes that involve other people engaged in shared endeavors—whether in person or across time and space.

[…]

References

Ben-Ari, E. (1996). From mothering to othering: Organization, culture, and nap time in a Japanese day-care center. *Ethos, 24,* 136–164.

Berlin, B. (1992). *Ethnobiological classification: Principles of categorization of plants and animals in traditional societies.* Princeton: Princeton University Press.

Blount, B. G. (1972). Parental speech and language acquisition: Some Luo and Samoan examples. *Anthropological Linguistics, 14,* 119–130.

Brown, J. S., & Duguid, P. (1994). Borderline issues: Social and material aspects of design. *Human-Computer Interaction, 9,* 3–36.

Bruffee, K. A. (1993). *Collaborative learning. Higher education, interdependence, and the authority of knowledge.* Baltimore: Johns Hopkins University Press.

Byers, P., & Byers, H. (1972). Nonverbal communication and the education of children. In C. B. Cazden, V. P. John, & D. Hymes (Eds.), *Functions of language in the classroom.* New York: Academic.

Cazden, C. B., & John, V. P. (1971). Learning in American Indian children. In M. L. Wax, S. Diamond, & F. O. Gearing (Eds.), *Anthropological perspectives on education* (pp. 252–272). New York: Basic Books.

Chao, R. K. (1995). Chinese and European American cultural models of the self reflected in mothers' childrearing beliefs. *Ethos, 23,* 328–354.

Chatwin, B. (1987). *The songlines.* New York: Penguin Books.

Chisholm, J. S. (1996). Learning "respect for everything": Navajo images of development. In C. P. Hwang, M. E. Lamb, & I. E. Sigel (Eds.), *Images of childhood* (pp. 167–183). Mahwah, NJ: Erlbaum.

Cole, M. (1996). *Cultural psychology: A once and future discipline.* Cambridge, MA: Harvard University Press.

Cole, M., & Griffin, P. (1980). Cultural amplifiers reconsidered. In D. R. Olson (Ed.), *The social foundations of language and thought* (pp. 343–364). New York: Norton.

Cole, M., & Scribner, S. (1977). Cross-cultural studies of memory and cognition. In R. V. Kail Jr., & J. W. Hagen (Eds.), *Perspectives on the development of memory and cognition.* Hillsdale, NJ: Erlbaum.

Crook, C. (1994). *Computers and the collaborative experience of learning.* London: Routledge.

Ellis, S. (1997). Strategy choice in sociocultural context. *Developmental Review, 17,* 490–524.

Ellis, S., & Siegler, R. S. (1997). Planning as a strategy choice, or why don't children plan when they should? In S. L. Friedman & E. K. Scholnick (Eds.), *The developmental psychology of planning: Why, how, and when do we plan?* (pp. 183–208). Mahwah, NJ: Erlbaum.

Gauvain, M. (1993). Spatial thinking and its development in sociocultural context. *Annals of Child Development, 9,* 67–102.

Gladwin, T. (1971). *East is a big bird.* Cambridge, MA: Harvard University Press.

Goodnow, J. J. (1976). The nature of intelligent behavior: Questions raised by cross-cultural studies. In L. B. Resnick (Ed.), *The nature of intelligence.* Hillsdale, NJ: Erlbaum.

Goodnow, J. J. (1980). Everyday concepts of intelligence and its development. In N. Warren (Ed.), *Studies in cross-cultural psychology* (Vol. 2, pp. 191–219). London: Academic Press.

Goody, J., & Watt, I. (1968). The consequences of literacy. In J. R. Goody (Ed.), *Literacy in traditional societies.* Cambridge, England: Cambridge University Press.

Gossen, G. H. (1976). Verbal dueling in Chamula. In B. Krishenblatt-Gimblett (Ed.), *Speech play* (pp. 121–146). Philadelphia: University of Pennsylvania Press.

Greenfield, P. M. (1966). On culture and conservation. In J. S. Bruner, R. R. Olver, & P. M. Greenfield (Eds.), *Studies in cognitive growth*. New York: Wiley.

Hale-Benson, J. E. (1986). *Black children: Their roots, culture, and learning styles*. Baltimore, MD: Johns Hopkins University Press.

Harkness, S., & Super, C. M. (1977). Why African children are so hard to test. In L. L. Adler (Ed.), *Issues in cross-cultural research. Annals of the New York Academy of Sciences, 285,* 326–331.

Hatano, G. (1982). Cognitive consequences of practice in culture specific procedural skills. *Quarterly Newsletter of the Laboratory of Comparative Human Cognition, 4,* 15–17.

Hatano, G. (1988). Social and motivational bases for mathematical understanding. In G. B. Saxe & M. Gearhart (Eds.), *Children's mathematics* (pp. 55–70). San Francisco: Jossey-Bass.

Hatano, G., & Inagaki, K. (1996, May). *Cultural contexts of schooling revisited*. Paper presented at the conference "Global prospects for education: Development, culture, and schooling," Ann Arbor, MI.

Hawkins, J. (1987, April). *Collaboration and dissent*. Paper presented at the meetings of the Society for Research in Child Development, Baltimore, MD.

Heath, S. B. (1983). *Ways with words: Language, life, and work in communities and classrooms*. Cambridge, England: Cambridge University Press.

Hutchins, E. (1991). The social organization of distributed cognition. In L. B. Resnick, J. M. Levine, & S. D. Teasley (Eds.), *Perspectives on socially shared cognition*. Washington, DC: American Psychological Association.

Irvine, J. T. (1978). Wolof "magical thinking": Culture and conservation revisited. *Journal of Cross-Cultural Psychology, 9,* 300–310.

Kingsolver, B. (1995). *High tide in Tucson*. New York: Harper-Collins.

Kleinfeld, J. S. (1973). Intellectual strengths in culturally different groups: An Eskimo illustration. *Review of Educational Research, 43,* 341–359.

Kobayashi, Y. (1994). Conceptual acquisition and change through social interaction. *Human Development, 37,* 233–241.

Lave, J. (1977). Tailor-made experiments and evaluating the intellectual consequences of apprenticeship training. *Quarterly Newsletter of the Institute for Comparative Human Development, 1,* 1–3.

Lave, J. (1988). *Cognition in practice: Mind, mathematics and culture in everyday life*. Cambridge, England: Cambridge University Press.

Lebra, T. S. (1994). Mother and child in Japanese socialization: A Japan-U.S. comparison. In P. M. Greenfield & R. R. Cocking (Eds.), *Cross-cultural roots of minority child development* (pp. 259–274). Hillsdale, NJ: Erlbaum.

Lee, L. C. (1992). Day care in the People's Republic of China. In M. E. Lamb, K. J. Sternberg, C. -P. Hwang, & A. G. Broberg (Eds.), *Child care in context* (pp. 355–392). Hillsdale, NJ: Erlbaum.

Levinson, S. C. (1997). Language and cognition: The cognitive consequences of spatial description in Guugu Yimithirr. *Journal of Linguistic Anthropology, 7,* 98–131.

Lewis, C. C. (1995). *Educating hearts and minds: Reflections on Japanese preschool and elementary education*. Cambridge, England: Cambridge University Press.

Lillard, A. S. (1997). Other folks' theories of mind and behavior. *Psychological Science, 8,* 268–274.

Lucy, J. A., & Gaskins, S. (1994, December). *The role of language in shaping the child's transition from perceptual to conceptual classification*. Paper presented at the meetings of the American Anthropological Association, Atlanta, GA.

Lutz, C., & LeVine, R. A. (1982). Culture and intelligence in infancy: An ethnopsychological view. In M. Lewis (Ed.), *Origins of intelligence: Infancy and early childhood* (pp. 1–28). New York: Plenum.

Martini, M., & Kirkpatrick, J. (1992). Parenting in Polynesia: A view from the Marquesas. In J. L. Roopnarine & D. B. Carter (Eds.), *Parent-child socialization in diverse cultures: Vol. S. Annual advances in applied developmental psychology* (pp. 199–222). Norwood, NJ: Ablex.

Massey, G. C., Hilliard, A. G., & Carew, J. (1982). Test-taking behaviors of Black toddlers: An interactive analysis. In L. Feagans & D. C. Farran (Eds.), *The language of children reared in poverty* (pp. 163–179). New York: Academic.

Mehan, H. (1979). *Learning lessons: Social organization in the classroom.* Cambridge, MA: Harvard University Press.

Miller, K. F., Smith, C. M., Zhu, J., & Zhang, H. (1995). Preschool origins of cross-national differences in mathematical competence: The role of number-naming systems. *Psychological Science, 6,* 56–60.

Minami, M., & McCabe, A. (1995). Rice balls and bear hunts: Japanese and North American family narrative patterns. *Journal of Child Language, 22,* 423–445.

Minami, M., & McCabe, A. (1996). Compressed collections of experiences: Some Asian American traditions. In A. McCabe (Ed.), *Chameleon readers: Some problems cultural differences in narrative structure pose for multicultural literacy programs* (pp. 72–97). New York: McGraw-Hill.

Miura, I. T., Okamoto, Y., Kim, C. C., Chang, C. -M., Steere, M., & Fayol, M. (1994). Comparisons of children's cognitive representation of number: China, France, Japan, Korea, Sweden, and the United States. *International Journal of Behavioral Development, 17,* 401–411.

Moreno, R. P. (1991). Maternal teaching of preschool children in minority and low-status families: A critical review. *Early Childhood Research Quarterly, 6,* 395–410.

Myers, M. (1984). Shifting standards of literacy—the teacher's catch-22. *English Journal, 73,* 26–32.

Myers, M. (1996). *Changing our minds: Negotiating English and literacy.* Urbana, IL: National Council of Teachers of English.

Nicolopoulou, A. (1997). The invention of writing and the development of numerical concepts in Sumeria: Some implications for developmental psychology. In M. Cole, Y. Engeström, & O. Vasquez (Eds.), *Mind, culture, and activity: Seminal papers from the Laboratory of Comparative Human Cognition* (pp. 205–225). New York: Cambridge University Press.

Nunes, T. (1995). Cultural practices and the conception of individual differences: Theoretical and empirical considerations. In J. J. Goodnow, P. J. Miller, & F. Kessel (Eds.), *Cultural practices as contexts for development* (pp. 91–103). San Francisco: Jossey-Bass.

Oakeshott, M. J. (1962). *Rationalism in politics, and other essays.* New York: Basic Books.

Ochs, E., Jacoby, S., & Gonzales, P. (1994). Interpretive journeys: How physicists talk and travel through graphic space. *Configurations, 1,* 151–171.

Ogunnaike, O. A., & Houser, R. F., Jr. (2002). Yoruba toddlers' engagement in errands and cognitive performance on the Yoruba Mental Subscale. *International Journal of Behavioral Development, 26,* 145–153.

Olson, D. R. (1976). Culture, technology, and intellect. In L. B. Resnick (Ed.), *The nature of intelligence.* Hillsdale, NJ: Erlbaum.

Pea, R. D. (1993). Practices of distributed intelligence and designs for education. In G. Salomon (Ed.), *Distributed cognitions* (pp. 47–87). Cambridge, England: Cambridge University Press.

Pea, R. D., & Gomez, L. M. (1992). Distributed multimedia learning environments: Why and how? *Interactive Learning Environments, 2,* 73–109.

Philips, S. U. (1972). Participant structure and communicative competence: Warm Springs children in community and classroom. In C. B. Cazden, V. P. John & D. Hymes (Eds.), *Functions of language in the classroom* (pp. 370–394). New York: Teachers College Press.

Plank, G. A. (1994). What silence means for educators of American Indian children. *Journal of American Indian Education, 34,* 3–19.

Resnick, D. P., & Resnick, L. B. (1977). The nature of literacy: An historical exploration. *Harvard Educational Review, 47,* 370–385.

Rogoff, B. (1998). Cognition as a collaborative process. In W. Damon (Series Ed.) & D. Kuhn & R. S. Siegler (Vol. Eds.), *Cognition, perception and language: Vol. 2. Handbook of Child Psychology* (5th ed.). New York: Wiley.

Rogoff, B., Baker-Sennett, J., & Matusov, E. (1994). Considering the concept of planning. In M. M. Haith, J. B. Benson, R. J. Roberts, Jr., & B. F. Pennington (Eds.), *The development of future-oriented processes* (pp. 353–373). Chicago: University of Chicago Press.

Rogoff, B., & Waddell, K. J. (1982). Memory for information organized in a scene by children from two cultures. *Child Development, U53,* 1224–1228.

Saxe, G. B. (1981). Body parts as numerals: A developmental analysis of numeration among the Oksapmin in Papua New Guinea. *Child Development, 52,* 306–316.

Saxe, G. B. (1991). *Culture and cognitive development: Studies in mathematical understanding.* Hillsdale, NJ: Erlbaum.

Schliemann, A. D., Carraher, D. W., & Ceci, S. J. (1997). Everyday cognition. In J. W. Berry, P. R. Dasen, & T. S. Saraswathi (Eds.), *Handbook of cross-cultural psychology: Vol. 2. Basic processes and human development* (pp. 188–216). Boston: Allyn and Bacon.

Schrage, M. (1990). *Shared minds.* New York: Random House.

Scribner, S. (1984). Studying working intelligence. In B. Rogoff & J. Lave (Eds.), *Everyday cognition: Its development in social context* (pp. 9–40). Cambridge, MA: Harvard University Press.

Scribner, S., & Cole, M. (1981). *The psychology of literacy.* Cambridge, MA: Harvard University Press.

Serpell, R. (1977). Strategies for investigating intelligence in its cultural context. *Quarterly Newsletter of the Institute for Comparative Human Development, 1,* 11–15.

Serpell, R. (1982). Measures of perception, skills and intelligence. In W. W. Hartup (Ed.), *Review of child development research* (Vol. 6, pp. 392–440). Chicago: University of Chicago Press.

Serpell, R. (1993). *The significance of schooling: Life-journeys in an African society.* Cambridge, England: Cambridge University Press.

Sternberg, R., Conway, B., Ketron, J., & Bernstein, M. (1981). People's conceptions of intelligence. *Journal of Personality and Social Psychology, 4,* 37–55.

Stevenson, H. W., Lee, S-Y., & Stigler, J. W. (1986). Mathematics achievement of Chinese, Japanese, and American children. *Science, 231,* 693–699.

Stigler, J. W., Barclay, C., & Aiello, P. (1982). Motor and mental abacus skill: A preliminary look at an expert. *Quarterly Newsletter of the Laboratory of Comparative Human Cognition, 4,* 12–14.

Super, C. M., & Harkness, S. (1983). *Looking across at growing up: The cultural expression of cognitive development in middle childhood.* Unpublished manuscript, Harvard University.

Swetz, F. (1987). *Capitalism and arithmetic: The new math of the 15th century.* La Salle, IL: Open Court.

Swisher, K., & Deyhle, D. (1989). The styles of learning are different, but the teaching is just the same: Suggestions for teachers of American Indian youth. *Journal of American Indian Education, 21,* 1–14.

Ueno, N., & Saito, S. (1995, April). *Historical transformations of math as artifacts for socio-economic distribution in a Nepalese bazaar.* Paper presented at the meetings of the American Educational Research Association, San Francisco.

Ward, M. C. (1971). *Them children: A study in language learning.* New York: Holt, Rinehart & Winston.

Weisner, T. S. (1989). Cultural and universal aspects of social support for children: Evidence from the Abaluyia of Kenya. In D. Belle (Ed.), *Children's social networks and social supports* (pp. 70–90). New York: Wiley.

Wertsch, J. V. (1991). *Voices of the mind: A sociocultural approach to mediated action.* Cambridge, MA: Harvard University Press.

Wertsch, J. V. (1998). *Mind as action.* New York: Oxford University Press.

White, M. (1987). *The Japanese educational challenge: A commitment to children.* New York: Free Press.

Whiting, B. B., & Whiting, J. W. M. (1975). *Children of six cultures: A psycho-cultural analysis.* Cambridge, MA: Harvard University Press.

Wober, M. (1972). Culture and the concept of intelligence: A case in Uganda. *Journal of Cross-Cultural Psychology, 3,* 327–328.

Wolf, D. P. (1988). Becoming literate; One reader reading. *Academic Connections* 1–4.

Zellermayer, M., Salomon, G., Globerson, T., & Givon, H. (1991). Enhancing writing-related metacognitions through a computerized writing partner. *American Educational Research Journal, 28,* 373-391.

5

A Sociocultural Analysis of Organisational Learning

Nick Boreham and Colin Morgan

Introduction

In recent years, the concept of organisational learning has attracted increasing attention from researchers in many disciplines, including specialists in the fields of adult learning, vocational education and training and school improvement. This reflects several dimensions of contemporary social and economic change, among them the growing recognition that the workplace is an important site for learning, the increasing number of public and private sector organisations committed to 'continuous improvement' (Boreham, 2002) and the government's adoption of an industrial policy of creating a 'learning economy' out of 'learning regions' and 'learning organisations' (Lundvall, 2001). There now exists an extensive literature on organisational learning, but as most of the research had been carried out within the separate disciplines of management, economics, sociology, psychology and education, the field has become rather fragmented. [...] Nevertheless, spanning this complex field of study it is possible to identify a core definition of organisational learning. Most contemporary researchers define *learning* as *organisational* to the extent that it is undertaken by members of an organisation to achieve organisational purposes, takes place in teams or other small groups, is distributed widely throughout the organisation and embeds its outcomes in the organisation's system, structures and culture (Snyder & Cummings, 1998). [...]

Organisational learning is a problematic concept for many educationalists. It has often been contested, sometimes on the grounds that it is a powerful emotive symbol which excites enthusiasm in devotees but has little substance in fact (Dunphy, 1997), and sometimes on the grounds that it denies individuals the autonomy deemed essential for learning to be authentic (Fenwick, 2001). Moreover, as Engeström (2001) has observed, current theories of organisational learning are 'typically weak in spelling out the specific processes or actions that make the learning process' (p. 150). Despite important studies by Engeström himself (1987), Lave and Wenger (1991), Brown and Duguid (1991), Chaiklin and Lave (1993) and Wenger et al. (2002), there is very little empirical evidence about what actually takes place in organisations when they 'learn'. Related to this is a lack of evidence about the pedagogy of organisational learning. In contrast to the traditional view of learning in the workplace as informal, incidental and natural (Eraut et al., 1998), many researchers in vocational education and training are finding that employees are now

From: *Oxford Review of Education*, 30 (3), 2004, pp.307–25. Reprinted by permission of the publisher (Taylor & Francis Ltd, http://www.informaworld.com).

expected to teach, show, coach or otherwise instruct their co-workers in explicit and relatively structured ways (Fuller & Unwin, 2002). This raises the question of what is specifically 'organisational' about this role. [...].

The sociocultural perspective

[...] From the sociocultural perspective, learning is perceived as being embedded in social and cultural contexts, and best understood as a form of participation in those contexts. This concept of learning implies the simultaneous transformation of social practices and the individuals who participate in them, and thus the social and individual dimensions of learning are mutually constitutive. The first researchers to write about organisational learning at length, Argyris and Schön (1996—first edition 1978) adopted a broadly sociocultural approach when they described it as the growth of a culture of open communication, in which members of an organisation collaborate in 'organisational enquiries' to discover better ways of achieving the organisation's purposes. In the course of these enquiries, they recognise, question and replace the hidden assumptions ('theories-in-use') that underpin their current practices. The originality of Argyris and Sohön's thesis—for a Western audience, at least—was to make the organisation itself the learning subject, and to identify culture change as the central process by which it learns. Organisational culture has been defined by Schein (1992) as 'a pattern of shared basic assumptions that the group learned as it solved its problems of external adaptation and internal integration, and which has worked well enough to be taught to new members as the correct way to perceive, think and feel in relation to these problems' (p. 12). Schein makes the crucial claim that an organisation's culture determines what it can and cannot do, and that the extent of individual members' socialisation into that culture determines what they can and cannot do. This takes the concept of learning out of the province of individually-focused psychology and opens it up to a collectivistic interpretation (cf. Fox, 2000; Boreham, 2004).

Argyris and Schön (1996) do not make explicit links between their theory of organisational learning and the Russian sociocultural learning theorists Vygotsky and Leont'ev, whose work spanned the period from the 1930s to the 1970s and is now being reinterpreted for Western audiences by scholars such as Wertsch (1991) and Engeström (1987). However, it is important to trace the connections between these two fields of theory because Vygotsky and Leont'ev provide a more rigorous account of organisational learning than Argyris and Schön (1996). The fundamental principle on which their work rests is Vygotsky's (1978) claim that psychological functions such as perception and memory appear first as elementary functions and then develop into 'higher' functions through assimilation into the sociocultural practices that occur when people live and work together. These practices include the use of symbolic tools (such as spoken language and cultural artefacts) and the formative activities by which communities develop and sustain their pursuit of common goals (such as apprenticeship and guided participation—cf. Rogoff, 1995). It then becomes permissible to speak of 'higher functions' such as problem solving in the workplace as socially constructed characteristics of people-in-communities, constituted at the level of the group, community or organisation. This provides a theoretical rationale for Argyris and Schön's claim that organisations are capable of learning *per se*, which might seem oxymoronic to educationalists working within the frame of individually-focused psychology. It also provides a conceptual bridge to Lave and Wenger's (1991) assertion that 'learning is not merely situated in practice—as if it were some independently reifiable process that just happened to be located somewhere—learning is an integral part of generative social practice in the lived-in world' (p. 35). From the sociocultural perspective, the knowledge generated by organisational learning can be represented as a collective resource, the dynamic product of interactions between people, artefacts and information (Boreham, 2000; Boreham et al., 2002).

Important aspects of organisational learning are crystallised in the concept of an 'activity system', developed by Engeström (1987; 2001) out of Leont'ev's (1978) work on the collective dimension of the higher psychological functions. An activity system is a group of people whose orientation to the object of their collective activity (such as building a ship) is mediated by a division of labour (such as a workforce segmented into different trades), rules (such as standard operating procedures) and cultural artefacts (such as blue prints, meetings, computers and rivet guns). According to Leont'ev, a major part of the knowledge and expertise of a work group is embodied in its artefacts, which are significant constituents of its culture and essentially a means of communication. Potentially, all these aspects of the work culture can enable people to work together, co-ordinate their activity and make sense of the problems that confront them. An important extension of the concept of an activity system is Engeström's notion of 'expansive learning'. This replaces Vygotsky's focus on the individual attainment of higher psychological functions by the idea that the activity system learns *as a whole* by sharing experiences across the boundaries imposed by the division of labour. The stimulus to expansive learning is typically a perceived failure of the activity system to achieve the object of its activity. Expansive learning occurs when the group constructs new working practices by reflecting collectively on the historically-determined contradictions in the activity system that led to the failure, and by expanding its collective understanding of both the object of its activity and the means of attaining it.

The project

The research on which this chapter is based was carried out over three years in an oil refinery and petrochemicals manufacturing complex in the UK. This enterprise (hereafter, 'the company') is owned by a multinational oil corporation, employs about 850 people and occupies a 1,800 acre site on which 10 chemical plants are connected by a network of pipe tracks, roads and railways. In response to the challenges of international competition, over the last decade the company has undergone major organisational change. Formerly a monolithic, hierarchical organisation in which a segmented workforce followed fixed procedures laid down by management, it has adopted more flexible structures and has explicitly committed itself to continuous improvement. In an attempt to create a culture of collaborative enquiry and knowledge-sharing, the top-down management system has been replaced by a more participatory form of decision making. Several layers of middle and line management have been removed, and self-directed teams have been adopted as the basis for an increasing number of operations. Working in teams, employees are now encouraged to find ways of improving performance and to share their expertise throughout the organisation.

Viewing this company as an activity system, the common object of its activity is stated in a glossy booklet issued annually to all employees—to become the best small oil refinery in Europe. The booklet identifies 'learning as an organisation' as one of the 'core values' that will help the company achieve this goal, and makes a commitment to 'learn as a company from past mistakes and successes' and 'openly share knowledge and learning within the company'. The booklet continues: 'We are living in a volatile and challenging business environment ... In your teams, you have to decide what is achievable, then "deliver results with speed and excellence"'. The booklet sets out an action plan for the next five years and gives performance targets for the different dimensions of the business, covering *inter alia* health and safety, strategic cost reduction, labour costs, plant reliability, open and honest communication, learning from site power failures, diversity and inclusiveness, respect for people irrespective of backgrounds and environmental protection. These targets are agreed with the workforce in an 'all-to-the-table' process of negotiation. The technical targets are quantified by standard petrochemical measurements, whilst the 'softer' targets are quantified by Investors in People benchmarks.

Against this background, a succession of initiatives has been implemented to promote organisational learning. These involve employees in a range of activities which correspond to the definition of organisational learning given earlier—they are undertaken to achieve organisational purposes, they take place in teams or other small groups, they are distributed throughout the organisation and the outcomes are embedded in the organisation's system, structures and culture. To develop the workforce's capacity to engage in these activities, all employees have attended residential courses on techniques of group problem solving, active listening, the supportive development of shared ideas, managing disagreement and conflict, delegation, the exercise of authority and peer leadership.

The research was conducted in regular visits to the site, beginning with a series of exploratory interviews with key informants and desk research on the state of the chemical industry in the UK and globally. Further information on manpower issues in the industry was obtained in a meeting with the Chemicals Directorate of the Department of Trade and Industry. After this preparatory work, we visited a range of plants, control rooms and departments on the site to observe the work of all grades of employee, including process operators, maintenance technicians, office employees, training staff, refinery analysts, refinery technologists and various categories of manager. Then we conducted a series of 25 one-hour semi-structured interviews with a wide range of these employees, eliciting personal accounts of their involvement in the company's organisational learning initiatives. [...]

The procedures and competence development methodology

[...] Due to space limitations, the present analysis concentrates on the initiative known as the *Procedures and Competence Development Methodology*. The essence of this initiative was to involve all grades of employee in rewriting the company's standard operating procedures and to share the knowledge generated in this way throughout the company. In the petrochemicals industry, a 'standard operating procedure' is a specification of how a difficult or hazardous procedure should be carried out, such as bringing a pump on line, isolating a piece of apparatus or shutting down a distillation column. A company's standard operating procedures are a major part of its 'organisational memory', and from a sociocultural perspective, may be regarded as a significant constituent of its culture. Within the interpretative framework of activity theory, standard operating procedures are rules that mediate interaction between the members of the activity system, and between them and the object of their activity. As we will argue later, standard operating procedures written in the collaborative way required by the Procedures and Competence Development Methodology were important mediators of organisational learning.

Before the company was reorganised, the standard operating procedures were written by refinery technologists. The staff concerned were graduate chemical engineers, usually fresh from university with no experience of performing the operations they were proceduralising. This reflects the Taylorist principle that the knowledge base of an industrial organisation is concentrated in the minds of its scientifically qualified staff, the role of the manual workers being to follow instructions issued from above. However, the introduction of the Procedures and Competence Development Methodology has ended this practice, for now the responsibility for writing the procedures is placed in the hands of the process operators who have to carry them out. Analysis of company documents reveals that this reflects changed epistemological assumptions about the company's knowledge base, which is now explicitly recognised as including the contextualised and experiential know-how of the operators as well as the scientific knowledge of the chemical engineers.

The way in which the Procedures and Competence Development Methodology was introduced is a clear example of the company's policy of decentralising control over day-to-day operations. Following one of the residential courses on organisational learning described earlier, at which participants were asked to carry out an organisational enquiry when they returned to work, a group of technicians set themselves the task of revising and systematising the manuals which contained the existing standard operating procedures. To support them in this, the company hired an external consultancy to design a methodology for rewriting procedures, which the technicians adapted for their own purposes. As one of them told us:

We basically picked the bones out of it, said what was good, what was bad and changed it, and came up with the final format … so it's a good process and it does work.

Significantly, the technicians changed the name from 'Procedures Development Methodology' to 'Procedures *and Competence* Development Methodology' because they realised that they needed a way of creating new knowledge and sharing it through the organisation, not just a way of writing bureaucratic procedures. The methodology they devised was officially adopted by the company and is now being used for a systematic rewriting of all the standard operating procedures. The first stage is to select an operation by formal risk analysis or by taking suggestions from individual employees. Then a meeting is convened of all the workers who perform the operation in question, usually one member from each of the five shifts. They convene in an office armed with worksheets and follow a structured procedure which one interviewee described as follows:

There's a representative from each of the shifts that sit round that are going to look at this compressor that's blown up, and they're going to stop it happening, and what they do, they all sit round and say, 'Well, how do you do it?' The first person says, 'Well, what I do, I go out and I check these 15 bells and I do this and I do the other'. Then the next person says to him, 'Well, I do that but I don't necessarily do this' and they start talking about that, and then the third person chips in and he says, 'Well yes, I can see what you're doing there, but I actually do this as well'. The idea is, you're trying to get a consensus, and then you thrash out what the best practice is.

There is a close correspondence between this description of the Procedures and Competence Development Methodology and Argyris and Schön's (1996) account of organisational enquiry, in which workers investigate how operations are carried out, seek better ways of performing them and change the organisation's theories-in-use accordingly (p. 191). The description also shares the characteristics of expansive learning which Engeström (2001) found in meetings between the families of sick children, family doctors and hospital specialists. In all these instances, through collective activity, co-workers transcend the boundaries which separate them from their colleagues, establish a common (and expanded) understanding of the object of their joint activity and make a collective decision on how to achieve it.

Having completed their series of meetings and held extensive consultations with other workers affected by the operation under scrutiny, the Procedures and Competence Development team writes a 'reference task analysis'—a detailed specification of how the operation ought to be performed. This goes through an authorisation process in which it is reviewed by a refinery technologist, the head of operations in the plant and the plant manager, who check it for safety. Then it is placed on the company intranet for everybody to consult when performing their day-to-day work, effectively embedding the results of the organisational enquiry within the organisation's collective memory. This is another major change in the work process, as eventually each operator gains access to a codified version of a significant part of every other operator's expertise. In a very strong sense, collective understanding has replaced individually-contained understanding as the location of the company's operational knowledge base. Individual learning in this context is culturally mediated in the sense that it involves participating in the collaborative writing of procedures and drawing upon this collective knowledge base when carrying out operations. Individual and collective learning are thus mutually constitutive. The final stage of the methodology is the production of job aids such as flow charts and checklists which are distributed around workstations. Together with the reference task analyses, these artifacts play a crucial role in mediating learning.

A model of organisational learning: dialogue embedded in relational practices

It would be easy to underestimate the impact of the Procedures and Competence Development Methodology on working relations in the company, especially where basic-grade employees are concerned. Previously, each shift had its own way of running its plant, and under the hierarchical management system then prevailing it was common for employees to work in relative isolation. Typically, an employee would come into work, report to a charge hand and be assigned a task. If the employee encountered a problem, he or she would refer back to the charge hand, who would take over while the worker looked on, or give further instructions. This work system tended to isolate individuals from the wider community of employees. Most operators kept a 'Little Black Book' in which they compiled notes over the years on how to perform the operations for which they were responsible. They used these in preference to the company's standard operating procedures, partly because the latter were imposed from above, and partly because they tended to ignore contextual constraints—the result of being written by graduate chemical engineers who did not perform the work themselves. The Little Black Books and the knowledge they contained were private property, and as employees working different shifts hardly ever met each other, the know-how recorded in them was rarely shared. As one interviewee said:

> If you went out and did an operation on a column, ... in the old days you wouldn't necessarily tell anyone what you'd done, or how you'd done it, or whatever.

However, the introduction of the Procedures and Competence Development Methodology, alongside organisational changes such as the abolition of the grade of charge hand and the delegation of authority to self-directing teams, has radically altered this way of working. Dialogue in the workplace with peers is now commonplace:

> Where people are more likely to talk now is: 'Hey, I went out and did this, and I followed the procedure, but that's not the way we should be doing it' ... And then talking to their mates and saying 'Well, what do *you* think of it?'

The model of organisational learning proposed in this paper identifies *dialogue*—the structured exchange of messages, both verbal and non-verbal—as the foundational process by which organisations learn, and the adoption of a particular set of *relational practices* as the creation of a social structure to sustain such learning. Dialogue occupies a central position in the managerially-oriented American theories of organisational learning (e.g. Senge, 1990) and also in the sociocultural theories of collective learning which have emerged from the Russian school of psychology (e.g. Bokeno & Gantt, 2000). Nevertheless, there is a difference in the way these traditions interpret dialogue. Most of the American managerialists see it as a technique which a group can use for pooling information during problem solving: 'In dialogue a group accesses a larger "pool of common meaning" which cannot be accessed individually' (Senge, 1990, pp. 240–241). But the Russian sociocultural theorists take a broader view, seeing dialogue as a set of cultural practices which constitute a common world by creating shared meanings. Of course, even within the Russian school there are alternative accounts of dialogue. In this chapter, we draw on the writings of Bakhtin (1981) who describes the social world as a plurality held together by dialogue conducted according to principles such as willingness to listen, respect for others and openness to alternative interpretations. Bakhtin argues that social order is constituted through dialogue and makes the crucial point that dialogue can tear communities apart as well as bind them together. From this it follows that the capacity to constitute a shared world depends critically on the collective capacity to enact dialogical transactions appropriately.

Our model of organisational learning therefore emphasises that the effectiveness of the dialogue through which organisations learn depends on a shared developmental history in which certain *practices* have been adopted as the accepted way of behaving in that community. A practice may be defined as a recurrent pattern of activity embodying explicit rules, precepts and instructions (Schatzki, 1996). The idea that social order is constituted by the enactment of social practices is central to the work of theorists such as Garfinkel (1967), Bourdieu (1977) and Giddens (1979). Social practices are 'carried' by members of a community, both individually and collectively, and a particular social order—such as an organisation that learns—is established when people living together in communities reproduce particular types of practice in their everyday interactions.

Our research indicates that the Procedures and Competence Development Methodology promotes organisational learning by instituting a particular set of social practices. These embed the dialogue through which the organisation learns and counteract the tendency of a decentralised and potentially conflictual workplace to disintegrate socially. Essentially, they are *relational* practices, the kind of practice by which people connect with other people in their world, and which direct them to interact in particular ways (Holmberg, 2000). The company learns as an organisation because engaging in these practices enables co-workers to co-ordinate different subjectivities with different perspectives and experiences in relation to what then becomes, for the participants, the common object of their activity. Thematic analysis of the interview transcripts, guided by our observations on the site, identified at least three relational practices as the basis for organisational learning in this context. These were:

- opening space for the creation of shared meaning
- reconstituting power relations
- providing cultural tools to mediate learning.

Opening space for the creation of shared meaning

> If you have got five shifts, you have got five different ways of doing things, if you have got 15, you have got 15 different ways of doing things. The most amount of time [in the Procedures and Competence Development Methodology] is spent on get[ting] the common ground out, and then once you have got the common ground, say, 'Well the consequences of this, that and the other are …' and then develop the best practice for it. And once you have done that you can then write the final operating procedure. [Interviewer: Does it change the way people work?] Yes, it does change. You might find that myself at one shift had a certain element of incidents all the time, and another shift didn't. Well, obviously that other shift has got a better way of doing it. And it might be one shift pushing the feed up too quickly, for example, yes. But then again it might be the guys haven't got that good a handle on what was happening … and that brings together, get better at your activities.

As this interviewee reveals, the Procedures and Competence Development Methodology has established a pattern of interaction whose essence is to open space for the creation of shared meaning. In this space, each individual's orientation to the common object becomes a resource for co-workers to reflect on whether they share the same understanding. The practice is constituted in a pattern of doings, sayings and instructions introduced by the Procedures and Competence Development Methodology. It is carried by all members of the organisation, in the sense that they reproduce the same pattern of interaction every time they write procedures for new operations. By reaching agreement on their interpretations of common experiences, the workforce develops a collective knowledge base:

> We are able to seep back a lot of information. We have found little holes in some of the systems, and this sort of thing … We have got a good common knowledge now.

Many interviewees stressed that the collective nature of the Procedures and Competence Development Methodology was crucial in bringing this about:

> The important aspect of [the Procedures and Competence Development Methodology] is that it's done by consensus, by the whole of the group that's going to be involved.

Previously, when procedures were written by graduate chemical engineers and handed down, operators would resist them. But now this knowledge is apparently an integral part of the work culture:

> By getting [the operators] to take ownership of everything, it sort of gets into the culture of things …

The Procedures and Competence Development Methodology creates personal as well as social space. Gergen (1999a), for example, challenges the longstanding tradition of conceptualising the self as individually-contained, tracing its origins to the time of the Enlightenment and arguing that it is now disintegrating in the face of social change, especially the decline of the old industrial culture. In the contemporary world, the need Gergen perceives is 'to generate an alternative mode of constructing self and other, with the ultimate aim of wedding such discursive moves to ongoing social practice … To position ourselves in a way that we can ask providential questions about out collective lives' (Gergen, 1999b, p. 114). His alternative to the concept of the individually-contained self is the relational self (1999a, p. 115). This is derived in part from Bakhtin's (1973, 1981) theory of dialogue, according to which individuals exist primarily in their relationships with others. Whilst the individually-contained self is an independent entity with fixed qualities, the relational self is a process of dialogic self-construction. The self develops as individuals make sense of lived experienced by engaging in Bakhtinian dialogue, identifying with categories and discourses and using these to position and construct themselves in successive situations.

The concept of the relational self demands a revision of long-established assumptions about the autonomy of the adult learner. Sherwin (1998), for example, has argued that the concept of autonomous agents as people cut loose from all ties is unconvincing, and that it would be preferable to represent the autonomous person as one who is embedded in complex networks of personal and organisational relationships. Autonomous learning depends on relationships because it is only through relationships that we can engage in cultural activity, and hence on Vygotsky's view, develop higher psychological functions. So if dialogue—embedded in relational practices—is the essence of organisational learning, as our model proposes, then organisational learning can be regarded as constitutive of an autonomous self.

Ultimately, whether one theorises the self as individually-contained or relational is a matter of choice. But the employees interviewed in the course of this research often expressed the view that organisational learning had enhanced their autonomy by expanding their working relationships. They did not perceive knowledge-sharing in negative terms, but as something that improved the quality of their working lives by spreading the burden of operating hazardous plants. Several of them described the stress of working in isolation, and told us that sharing know-how in a context of collaborative activity could reduce this. Above all, the new ways of working entailed by the company's commitment to organisational learning had reduced the power of the grades most likely to oppress the average process operator—middle management, charge hands and older workers.

Reconstituting power relationships

> The world of the Head of Operations has changed dramatically. When I first started here at [Name of Company] you were the sergeant major, marched round with your chest out, and for want of a better word, probably a bit of a bully. They're not like that now … the people who are doing the job are not like that.

In his essay on the state of organisational learning theory, Vince (2001) notes that taking a political perspective widens understanding of the processes of learning in organisations, and the above interviewee is quoted in that connection. Vince points out that power relations are crucial for organisational learning because they 'directly mediate interpretative processes within organisations' (2001, p. 1329). As interpreted in the present paper, organisational learning depends on employees relating to each other in ways that enable all points of view to be expressed, and which give everybody access to a common knowledge base. Examination of the company's policy documents reveals that the management believed that the pattern of power relations that existed when the company was organised hierarchically had prevented the kind of learningful dialogue they hoped would develop when they introduced self-directing teams. It also reveals that they saw the Procedures and Competence Development Methodology as a way of reconstituting relationships more productively. Thus one company document represents the Methodology as an antidote to what it describes as 'the Little Black Book syndrome' in which 'knowledge [is] seen as power'. The Little Black Books enabled individuals to corner crucial knowledge, and this could lead to the domination of one worker by another. It had clearly been resented, as one former process operator made clear when he described the days of the Little Black Books with considerable strength of feeling:

> You got some fairly strong characters in there saying 'I am controlling this!' Well it's got nothing to do with [their] technology skill. [Raises his voice:] *'I am doing this!!!'*

The policy document states that the Procedures and Competence Development Methodology is intended to create what it calls 'a culture of shared knowledge for the common good'. On our analysis, it achieves this by instituting the practice of relating to others in ways that reconstitute power relations in more egalitarian ways. By reproducing this pattern of interaction every time they write new procedures for operations, the workforce neutralises the tendency for individuals and groups to dominate others by cornering knowledge and using their rank to assert their own views. For example, a major source of conflict in the workplace had always been the relations between older and younger employees, the older trying to dominate the younger by keeping operational know-how to themselves. (One interviewee told us that when he was following a traditional apprenticeship and trying to learn from an older employee how to perform a certain technical operation, the latter always waited till he was 'on the toilet' before rushing off to carry out the crucial operation unobserved). In contrast to this traditional restrictive practice, rewriting operating procedures by the Procedures and Competence Development Methodology requires participants to enact the practice of according each other equal opportunity to construct and access the collective knowledge base.

The day-to-day exercise of the scheme is not controlled by managers but by designated facilitators known as 'Procedures and Competence Development Methodology Focal Points', employees who work normal shifts and organise the writing of the standard operating procedures in their own plants. The extent of the redistribution of power in the refinery is reflected in the fact that basic-grade workers can now select which aspects of their work are redesigned by bringing their concerns to the attention of the facilitator. As one of them said:

> If you had an incident, for example, you are going to try and extract learning from it and take that to the Procedures and Competence Development Methodology meeting yourself.

Senior staff participated willingly in the reconstitution of power relationships. One of them, a university-educated refinery technologist, told us:

> I found it strange when I came here that I was writing operating procedures, because I'm not the guy who actually goes and turns the valve back … You should get someone who does the job to write it. I like this much better.

An example of how the Procedures and Competence Development Methodology promotes this relational practice, and how the practice itself enables learningful dialogue, can be found in the authorisation process by which newly-written procedures are submitted to senior staff for safety checks. By following this part of the Methodology, process operators and refinery technologists—situated at the bottom and top of the organisational hierarchy respectively—jointly reconstitute their unequal power relationship in a more egalitarian way. In one case we investigated, a team of operators wrote procedures for gaining better control of the refining process at 'critical control points' (stages which critically affect the quality of the product). When the procedures went through for authorisation, the operators discussed the data they had collected with the head of operations and the refinery technologists. This revealed that one section of the process went into alarm for a variety of reasons on a large number of occasions, indicating the presence of a design fault. This led to a dialogue between the process operators and the refinery technologists about the need to re-engineer that part of the plant, which the latter took forward. Such an open dialogue would hardly have taken place in the days of hierarchical management. But by implementing the Procedures and Competence Development Methodology, process operators and refinery technologists overrode formal rank in the interest of sharing information in pursuit of a common objective.

Providing cultural tools to mediate learning

> The … thing with the Procedures and Competence Development Methodology, it provides detail but it can also provide simplified check lists, task aids if you like, which can be put in key positions; control panels outside on the units to assist operators … It's a good tool for deciding what information you need and where you need it, so it does improve things in that respect.

Leont'ev (1978) regarded a tool as a product of human culture, a social object and a means by which human thought is developed and expressed. In the present context, it is significant how readily interviewees, such as the one quoted above, referred to the Procedures and Competence Development Methodology as a 'tool'. Other examples are legion:

> It is one of the tools [Name of Company] has given me to enable me to do my job. We've had a lot of successes with the Procedures and Competence Development Methodology … I think [it is] a very useful tool.

Sitting in the company intranet in the form of reference task analyses, and affixed to equipment in the form of job aids such as flow charts, the standard operating procedures are symbolic tools which embody the collective knowledge that emerges from the dialogues we have described. According to Vygotsky (1978), learning by cultural mediation occurs when people use symbolic tools to regulate their activity, and this is exactly how the standard operating procedures are used. Vygotsky explains that as people engage in joint activity in pursuit of a goal, the ways in which they think and act accommodate themselves to the functions and limitations of the tools in use. The development and transmission of knowledge and skill in a community can then be explained by the progressive acquisition of socially constructed capacities which result from carrying out operations with these tools. The Procedures and Competence Development Methodology provides crucial underpinning for the process: employees accommodate themselves to the standard operating procedures, and the standard operating procedures are accommodated to the ongoing activity of the teams who write them.

Designating an object 'a tool' implies that the user has a degree of discretion in the way he or she deploys it. There has been a tendency among industrial sociologists to depict the proceduralisation of work as a form of deskilling which eliminates operator discretion, as occurs in the Taylorist reduction of work to mindless rule-following (Noon & Blyton, 1997). Such practices could hardly serve the purposes of mediation described by socio-cultural learning theorists. However, our investigation revealed that the Procedures and Competence Development Methodology was not implemented in such a narrow way. Pentland and Reuter (1994) draw a distinction between procedures which fully determine the operator's actions and those which define a pattern of activity which may be enacted differently on different occasions. The standard operating procedures generated by the Procedures and Competence Development Methodology are the latter kind: as a manager told us, 'We try to go with, what we call, generic procedures'.

It is important to recall Leont'ev's (1978) insistence that tools are not just physical artifacts—they incorporate a 'social utilisation scheme'. By this is meant the complex of social practices that are 'attached' to the tool, in the sense that they are how the tool is perceived within the culture in which it is used (cf. Lammont & Boreham, 2002). The concept of a utilisation scheme is crucial for explaining organisational learning—it is not the physical artifact, but the culture of its use that is assimilated by a new member of the workforce who learns to use it in the workplace. This process is revealed in the interviews which made it clear that the standard operating procedures were not perceived solely as physical operations (turn this valve then switch on this pump, etc.) but as symbols of the new culture of continuous improvement and cross-boundary collaboration:

> Procedures and Competence Development Methodology, I feel, is more of a culture thing, it's not a cold process thing. It's a culture thing, you've got to believe in it and you've got to believe that without this you ain't gonna perform ...
>
> I don't think it's just a case of getting a consensus on the procedure .... It's a change in attitudes, attitudes to working practices. A lot of these sound like clichés, but it's things like in pride of ownership of the kit ... If something falls over, it's not a maintenance issue, it's also an operations issue and very often it affects process-production, which costs big bucks ... it's a general state of mind.

Conclusion

For many educationalists, organisational learning is a challenging concept. When first encountered, the notion of learning collectively in order to achieve organisational purposes seems to compromise the autonomy of the individual learner. Moreover, whilst there is an extensive literature on the concept of organisational learning itself, there is a lack of empirical evidence about the practices through which it is brought about, especially its pedagogy. Perhaps in recognition of these problems, the use of the term 'learning' in the organisational sense has been contested. In reply, we have argued that it is possible to construe organisational learning in more favourable terms if the frame of individualistic psychology is abandoned for a sociocultural perspective in which individual and social learning are mutually constitutive. Discarding the concept of the individually-contained self for the concept of the relational self makes it possible to reconcile the apparently conflicting ideas of individual autonomy and learning collectively on behalf of the organisation. Moreover, the concept of organisational learning is more than an emotive slogan because it can be located within a rigorous theoretical framework centring on Vygotsky's principle that mind—manifested in the higher psychological functions—does not, and cannot, exist outside of social practice.

For an organisation to be able to learn *as an organisation*, there must be a common object of its collective activity, without which it would cease to be the kind of unitary entity that could be identified as a learning subject. In the case studied, the 850 company employees had adopted the common object of improving their collective performance against the targets in the site plan (this was genuinely a 'common object' because all levels of employee participated in setting the targets). To clarify the nature of organisational learning, we have proposed a model in which dialogue is the foundational process, but contrary to the American management theorists, who tend to represent dialogue as a tool for use on particular occasions, we follow Bakhtin (1981) in perceiving dialogue as both constitutive of social order and potentially disintegrative. We go beyond earlier studies by identifying relational practices as the social structure that embeds organisational learning and promotes collaboration. A social practice is a recurring pattern of activity that embodies explicit rules, precepts and instructions. The organisational learning initiative known as the Procedures and Competence Development Methodology instituted relational practices which generated learningful dialogue and which also counteracted the tendency of a decentralised and potentially conflictual workplace to disintegrate socially. The implication of these findings is that an organisation wishing to learn as an organisation is unlikely to succeed unless it brings about the kind of culture change implied by the adoption of practices of this kind. The three relational practices we identified as underpinning organisational learning in the case analysed were: opening space for the creation of shared meaning, reconstituting power relationships and providing cultural tools to mediate learning. Individually and collectively, members of the workforce were the carriers of these practices, and the culture needed to sustain a period of learning as an organisation was created when they reproduced them in their everyday interactions.

The investigation reported in this chapter adduces empirical evidence of what can be learned through participating in social practices. It also throws light on the pedagogy of organisational learning. We define this pedagogy in terms of participation in the relational practices we have described. Clearly, any complex organisation will provide many ways in which an employee can participate in such practices. One is by being a carrier of the practice—understanding it, internalising it and committing oneself to it, so that one reproduces it on successive occasions. The residential courses the company provided on techniques of group problem solving, active listening, the supportive development of shared ideas, managing disagreement and conflict, delegation, the exercise of authority and peer leadership, can be interpreted as an attempt to induct employees into appropriate relational practices. However, a short training course is unlikely to change an entrenched culture, so the company created roles to reinforce these practices in day-to-day activity. For example, the role of middle management is very different from the days of hierarchical command-and-control, now emphasising the facilitation of worker-led initiatives. This can be seen in the way managers supported the technicians who had the original idea for the Procedures and Competence Development Methodology, buying consultancy time for them and giving them freedom to develop it—in this way, they were enacting the practice of reconstituting power relations along more egalitarian lines, and the technicians themselves were enacting the practice of providing cultural tools to mediate learning. Another important pedagogic role is the Procedures and Competence Development Methodology Focal Point, the ordinary worker in a plant who keeps the process of writing new procedures moving forward by convening meetings and providing worksheets and intranet access. Incumbents in this role take the lead in opening space for the creation of shared meaning and in providing cultural tools to mediate learning. When everybody in the company participates in these kinds of relational practice, they are engaging in the pedagogy of organisational learning, which ultimately must be seen as one dimension of the organisation's culture.

References

Argyris, C. & Schön, D. (1996) *Organisational learning II* (Reading, Addison-Wesley).

Bakhtin, M. (1973) *Problems of Dostoevsky's poetics* (2nd edn) (R. W. Rotsel, trans.) (Ann Arbor, MI, Ardis).

Bakhtin, M. (1981) *The dialogic imagination* (Austin, TX, University of Austin Press).

Bokeno, R. M. & Gantt, V. W. (2000) Dialogic mentoring: core relationships for organisation learning, *Management Communication Quarterly*, 14, 237–270.

Boreham, N. C. (2000) Collective professional knowledge, *Medical Education*, 34, 505–506.

Boreham, N. (2002) Work process knowledge in technological and organisational development, in: N. Boreham, R. Samurçay & M. Fischer (Eds) *Work process knowledge* (London, Routledge), 1–14.

Boreham, N. (2004) A theory of collective competence: challenging the neo-liberal individualisation of performance at work, *British Journal of Educational Studies*, 52, 5–17.

Boreham, N., Samurçay, R. & Fischer, M. (Eds) (2002) *Work process knowledge* (London, Routledge).

Bourdieu, P. (1977) *Outline of a theory of practice* (Cambridge, Cambridge University Press).

Brown, J. S. & Duguid, P. (1991) Organisational learning and communities of practice: toward a unified view of working, learning and innovation, *Organisation Science*, 2, 40–57.

Chaiklin, S. & Lave, J. (1993) (Eds) *Understanding practice: perspectives on activity and context* (Cambridge, Cambridge University Press).

Dunphy, D. (1997) Organisational learning as the creation of corporate competencies: the use of reshaping competencies, *Journal of Management Development*, 16, 232–245.

Engeström, Y. (1987) *Learning by expanding: an activity-theoretical approach to developmental research* (Helsinki, Orienta-Konsultit).

Engeström, Y. (2001) Expansive learning at work: toward an activity theoretical reconceptualisation, *Journal of Education and Work*, 14, 133–156.

Eraut, M., Alderton, J., Cole, G. & Senker, P. (1998) Learning from other people at work, in: F. Coffield (Ed.) *Learning at work* (Bristol, The Policy Press).

Fenwick, T. (2001) Questioning the concept of the learning organisation, in: C. Paechter, M. Preedy, D. Scott & J. Soler (Eds) *Knowledge power and learning* (London, Paul Chapman), 74–88.

Fox, S. (2000) Communities of practice, Foucault and actor-network theory, *Journal of Management Studies*, 37, 853–867.

Fuller, A. & Unwin, L. (2002) Developing pedagogies for the contemporary workplace, in: K. Evans, P. Hodkinson & L. Unwin (eds) *Working to learn* (London, Kogan Page), 95–111.

Garfinkel, H. (1967) *Studies in ethnomethodology* (Englewood Cliffs, NJ, Prentice-Hall).

Gergen, K. J. (1999a) *An invitation to social construction* (London, Sage Publications).

Gergen, K. J. (1999b) Agency: social construction and relational action, *Theory & Psychology*, 9, 113–115.

Giddens, A. (1979) *Central problems in social theory* (London, Macmillan).

Holmberg, R. (2000) Organisational learning and participation: some critical reflections from a relational perspective, *European Journal of Work and Organisational Psychology*, 9, 177–188.

Lammont, N. & Boreham, N. (2002) Creating work process knowledge with new technology in a financial services workplace, in: N. Boreham, R. Samurçay & M. Fischer (Eds) *Work process knowledge* (London, Routledge), 94–105.

Lave, J. & Wenger, E. (1991) *Situated learning: legitimate peripheral participation* (Cambridge, Cambridge University Press).

Leont'ev, A. N. (1978) *Activity, consciousness and personality* (Englewood Cliffs, NJ, Prentice Hall).

Lundvall, B-A. (2001) Innovation policy in the globalising learning economy, in: D. Archibugi & B-A. Lundvall (Eds) *The globalising learning economy* (Oxford, Oxford University Press), 273–291.

Noon, M. & Blyton, P. (1997) *The realities of work* (Basingstoke, Palgrave).

Pentland, B. T. & Reuter, N. (1994) Organisational routines as grammars of action, *Administrative Science Quarterly*, 39, 484–510.

Rogoff, B. (1995) Observing sociocultural activity on three planes, in: J. Wertsch, P. Del Rio & A. Alvarez (eds) *Sociocultural studies of mind* (New York, Cambridge University Press), 139–164.

Schatzki, T. R. (1996) *Social practices* (Cambridge, Cambridge University Press).

Schein, E. (1992) *Organisational culture and leadership* (2nd edn) (San Francisco, CA, Jossey Bass).

Senge, P. (1990) *The fifth discipline* (New York, Doubleday).

Sherwin, S. (1998) A relational approach to autonomy in health care, in: S. Sherwin (ed.) *The politics of women's health: exploring agency and autonomy* (Philadelphia, PA, Temple University Press), 19–47.

Snyder, W. M. & Cummings, T. G. (1998) Organisational learning disorders: conceptual model and intervention hypotheses, *Human Relations*, 51, 873–895.

Vince, R. (2001) Power and emotion in organisational learning, *Human Relations*, 54, 1325–1351.

Vygotsky, L. S. (1978) *Mind in society: the development of higher psychological functions* (Cambridge, MA, Harvard University Press).

Wenger, E., McDermott, R. & Snyder, W. M. (2002) *Cultivating communities of practice* (Boston, MA, Harvard Business School Press).

Wertsch, J. V. (1991) *Voices of the mind: a sociocultural approach to mediated action* (Cambridge, MA, Harvard University Press).

6

Gender Issues in Testing and Assessment

Jannette Elwood

Introduction

Key areas of debate in the field of assessment and testing concern [a] 'paradigm shift' in how we view students' learning and how this learning should be assessed. These debates stem from research suggesting that more formative approaches to assessment will improve students learning (Black & Wiliam, 1998, 2005; Shepard, 2000; Hargreaves et al., 2002; CERI, 2005), and arguing that good, formative assessment (assessment done in classrooms, by teachers, with and for students' learning) will enhance student attainment and develop teachers' own assessment and pedagogical practice. However, these debates have generally ignored the social contexts of classrooms where formative assessment takes place and, to an even greater degree, have ignored the interaction of these different modes of assessment practice with gender and thus how they affect boys' and girls' performances.

While the 'assessment for learning' agenda gathers pace (Black & Wiliam, 2005), those of us concerned with the social consequences of assessment practices and who recognize that any form of assessment regime will have repercussions for boys' or girls' achievements, see very little attention given to the multiple contexts in which assessment for learning takes place. Moreover, the redefinition of the learner and the model of learning associated with formative assessment practices has major implications for teacher–student relationships, which are affected and mediated by gender and stereotypical perceptions of what boys and girls can achieve.

The aim of this chapter, therefore, is twofold: to consider research in relation to gender issues and testing and assessment, but also to offer new insights into the very complex relationship between learning, mind, and assessment that demands a different way of looking at gender and its role in understanding achievement. Understanding this relationship is fundamental if we wish to comprehend fully boys' and girls' achievements in school.

As a framework for the ideas discussed in the chapter, I present a continuum (Figure 6.1) along which differing views of learning, mind, assessment and gender are represented. As we move along from left to right, the ways in which we look at the four concepts (learning, mind, assessment and gender) shift considerably. Thus, in changing how we view mind and how we understand how students learn, we see there are major implications for how students should be assessed, how we view responses to assessment tasks and how we view gender in relation to these.

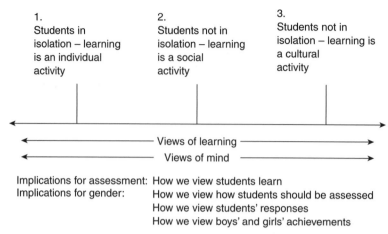

Figure 6.1   **Continuum of views of learning, mind, assessment and gender**

Linking assessment and models of learning

Very little research within the field of assessment concerns itself with the social consequences of assessment practice and policy (Broadfoot, 1996). Furthermore, many researchers in the field of assessment and testing more generally fail to articulate the model(s) of learning that support the assessment or testing system they promote. For example, the considerable growth of research in the field of computer-adaptive assessment rarely articulates the underpinning model of the learner or learning (Bennett et al., 2003). Most of the research in this area continues to be on the development of the computer tech-nology, the logistics of large-scale computer testing, and the way in which the student experience of the subject and of being tested will change (Baird, 2002). One cannot review systems of testing and assessment without acknowledging their relationship to the model of learning and of the learner underpinning the assessment or test. Moreover, this rela-tionship between the model of assessment and testing, and that of the learner and learning demands a consideration of gender in all its complexities. This is because an understand-ing of how gender mediates learning, achievement, and teachers' and students' experiences of assessment and testing is crucial to an understanding of the performances observed.

Theories of learning are many and are often contested, and the prominence of certain the-ories changes over time and in different contexts (Murphy, 1999). McDermott (1999, p16) argues that *learning traditionally gets measured on the assumption that it is a possession of individuals that can be found inside their heads [but] learning is not in heads but in the rela-tions between people.* He goes on to suggest that learning is in the conditions that bring people together and points of contact that allow particular pieces of information to take on relevance; without these points of contact, without the system of relevancies, there is no learning. In rela-tion to theories of learning, there are connected theories of mind, which, according to Murphy (1999), fall into two categories: symbolic cognition or processing (Bruner, 1999, Fordor, 2000) and situated cognition (Lave & Wenger, 1991). A symbolic processing view of mind is concerned with an individual's internal mental processing as the way to understand learning.

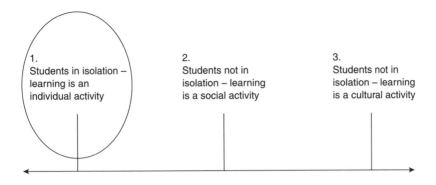

Traditional views of testing, assessment and gender:

(i)   assessment and testing systems and tasks are socially neutral
(ii) students learn in isolation and their ability can be checked up on
(iii) gender is static and a variable (i.e. sex of test taker) against which results are reported

Figure 6.2   Assessment and testing as isolated activities

The learner is seen as separate from the environment, and mind is symbolically represented as somewhere where learning can be stored and retrieved when required (like a computer). A situated view of mind is concerned with the interaction of human knowledge and the environment, the two being seen as inseparable. In this view of mind, learning is integral with the social world. Murphy (1999, p ix) goes on to argue that these are by no means the only two approaches to mind that exist, but that *the tension between these two 'families' of theories is giving rise to a great deal of productive thinking about learners, learning and assessment* from which considerations of gender can also develop.

One could further argue that these two categories of mind can also be considered as a local model of mind (mind in the head, intrinsic to the learner) and a non-local model of mind (mind outside the head, mind between individuals). The non-local model of mind extends the situated cognition model, as it suggests that nothing about mind or learning is located with the individual. Thus, if we can understand how learning happens at all, it does not take place in the head but between individuals. A non-local view of mind goes further to suggest that the learner and the teacher are entangled, that learning cannot be viewed in isolation, but only in relationship between the learner and the teacher (or other).

Testing and Assessment: As Isolated Activities

Stage 1 on the continuum (Figure 6.2) positions learning, mind, and gender as things that are fixed and isolated within the individual. Assessment is seen as something done to an individual to measure this fixed learning, and gender is a category against which the measurement of this learning can be reported. Here assessment and testing are located within the traditional psychometric model of testing (Goldstein, 1996a). This is a powerful model, as it underpins much of the world's testing systems and testing industry (Lemann, 2000) and influences the conduct of almost all forms of quantitative assessment

(Goldstein, 1996a). The psychometric model of testing and assessment has underlying assumptions about the existence of psychological attributes and that observed responses to test items can provide evidence about the state or value of these attributes (often ability is classified as such an attribute). This model also assumes that tests and assessments are activities that take place in isolation from the classroom, the teacher and other learners. Furthermore, this model advocates the use of summative assessments that are carried out *on* students under test conditions at the end of a course or period of learning, and that these tests or examinations are independently checking up on a student's ability, what students can do *on their own*.

The model of learning underpinning such testing practices sees learning as an individual activity that takes place in isolation and via transmission; it is a one-way process that goes from teacher to student. This view of learning is consistent with behaviourist psychology, which emphasizes a stimulus-response theory of learning:

> The test item is the stimulus and the answer the response, and a learner has to be 'conditioned' to the appropriate response to any given stimulus. Because the response is the only observable, attention is not paid to any model of the thinking process of the pupil which might intervene between stimulus and response. (Black, 1999, p120)

Furthermore, this model of testing and its associated theory of learning assumes that mind is located (and isolated) within the student (the local or symbolic view of mind). Thus learning is seen as being *stored* within the student. When given a test, students *retrieve* the information they need to answer the items on the test, and the test is checking up on the *stored* knowledge. Furthermore, assessment tasks are seen as neutral, and the testing system itself has no influence on the performances observed. So, students responding to test items are isolated from social influences and are thus separately analyzable through the test items used.

This traditional view of assessment and testing also assumes a traditional view of gender. Within this perspective, gender is seen as the same as sex group (male and female), and is a static variable against which differences in test data can be reported (Goldstein, 1996b). The publication of sex-group differences is only one variable among many by which test data can be reported. For example, in the UK differential performance data by males and females in public examinations and national curriculum tests are reported annually as a matter of course (JCGQ, 2004). This type of data, alongside research evidence from studies of large-scale international assessment programs (OECD, 2000; 2004) and research evidence from other studies focusing on sex differences in performance on tests (Willingham & Cole, 1997), show distinctly different patterns of performance between males and females, which are seen across different subjects, different ages and different testing situations. Some of these patterns of male and female performance in large-scale tests are outlined next.

International tests of achievement

In international tests of achievement, distinct patterns of performance for males and females across the subjects of English (or native language) maths and science have been identified. In the assessment of English, females consistently outperformed males in all main aspects of the subject, especially in reading and writing, across all assessment systems (NAEP, 2000; OECD, 2000, 2004). The gaps in performance between males and females are established early in primary school and continue to grow until females outperform males to a significant degree by the end of compulsory schooling. In maths, many international and cross-national surveys (Martin et al., 1999; OECD, 2000, 2004) show that, on average, males and females in the earlier stages of schooling perform similarly in maths, but, as age increases, males generally outperform females, and by age 15/16, males achieve better performances in virtually all aspects of mathematics tested. In science, evidence from large-scale assessment programs at both cross-national and international level show that males perform better than females in science, but that the gaps in science are the smallest across the three subject areas (Martin et al., 1999; NAEP, 2000; OECD, 2004).

National assessments

At more local levels, performance patterns of males and females paint a similar picture. Thus, on more syllabus-based examinations, females tend to perform better than males across a range of subjects and leave school better qualified than their male counterparts (JCGQ, 2004). For example, in the UK, on large-scale assessment programs at ages 16 (GCSE) and 18 (GCE A level), females are reported to have performed better than males across a range of subjects and at both stages of schooling. In the USA, recent studies show that females outperform males on state and national tests. They are also more likely to perform better on school-based measures of attainment, stay on at school longer and successfully graduate (Alperstein, 2005).

From sex group differences to gender differences

There are two aspects to the publication of results by sex group and the gendered discourse that surrounds them that are of interest in any consideration of gender and achievement.

First, published data on male and female achievement have improved over several years to the extent that we now have extensive datasets across various levels of testing and schooling that provide information on how males and females achieve on tests and examinations. Research in the field of gender and assessment and testing has greatly benefited from this data, especially as much of it is disaggregated at a number of levels – the examination as a whole, the examination or test paper, the test item, and the mode of assessment. Thus, we are better informed as to how males and females perform on various types of tests and assessments. These data have certainly enhanced our knowledge of differential performance, as we can monitor the results of different groups across a range of tests and assessments, and pursue questions of fairness and equity at a macrolevel.

Second, the routine publication of results by sex group has, however, brought associated gendered discourses that position boys and girls as opposites, and as competitors. Consequently, more popular interpretations of male and female patterns of performance have created debates about the underachievement of boys and the overachievement of girls. Thus, we have an annual circus of comparisons of boys' and girls' performances on examinations and associated gendered discourses that hve created new gendered stereotypes (Elwood, 2005). In these discourses, boys are positioned as problematic, troublesome, and lacking, and their underachievement is seen as extrinsic to boys themselves (Epstein et al., 1998). Girls, on the other hand, are positioned as a valuable commodity in

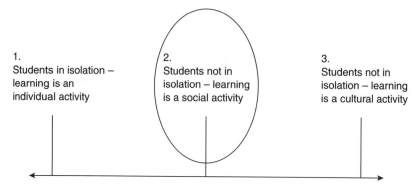

Less traditional views of assessment and gender:

(i)   rejects idea that students do things on their own
(ii) the social context influences learning/assesment
(iii) significant others (elders or peers) can support learning

But:

(i)   still treats students as individuals who once they have learned
      from others, can do things on their own
(ii) doesn't traditionally acknowledge gender – all children treated as
      individuals

Figure 6.3   Assessment and testing as social activities

the qualifications market place and their overachievement is seen as the result of the whole curriculum and examination system being feminized in their favour:

> Girls are doing better than boys in exams, but that does not mean they are brighter ...
> What has happened is that exams have been feminised – and so has the country.
> (Pirie, 2001, p1)

This traditional view of learning and assessment that considers gender as a static variable is reductionist and no longer helpful in understanding the complexities around gender and performance on tests and assessments. If we believe that learning does not take place in isolation and that examinations are not socially neutral, and if we observe that not all boys are underachieving and not all girls are overachieving, we are forced to look further along the continuum to different considerations of the learner, the mind, and assessment to help us understand gender differences in performance.

Testing and Assessment as Social Activities

Stage 2 on the continuum (Figure 6.3) positions learning, mind, gender and assessment as complex concepts and activities that are socially generated and mediated. If we understand assessment and testing as social activities, we reject the idea that students do things on their own (in isolation from their teacher and others) and that tests check up on what individuals know. Furthermore, gender is viewed less in terms of sex-group differences and more as a socially positioned concept that influences students' experiences of school. Moreover, there is an acknowledgement that gender interacts with assessment activities and structures, and that this interaction is manifested in the differences in performance observed (Elwood & Murphy, 2002; Francis et al., 2003; Read et al., 2004; Elwood, 2005); the social context and the gendered nature of learning, classrooms and schools influence assessment outcomes.

Here the view of learning and of the learner that underpins the models of assessment and testing is one of learners as active participants in their learning, and where learning from and with others is key:

> Human learning presupposes a specific social nature and a process by which children grow in to the intellectual life of those around them. (Vygotsky, 1978, p88)

This view of learning falls within social constructivist theories of learning (von Glasersfeld, 1987), in which attention is focused on the need for *models of mental processes to be involved when anyone responds to new information or to new problems* (Black, 1999, p120), and in which instruction is seen *not as direct transfer of knowledge but as an intervention in an ongoing knowledge construction process* (Gipps, 1999, p372). Thus, in social constructivist learning theories, students learn by *actively making sense of new knowledge, making meaning from it and mapping it into their existing knowledge map or schema* (ibid., p72). Even though social constructivists argue that learning is a social activity and that learners construct their own meaning, a symbolic view of cognition still prevails and mind is still located 'in the head' (Cobb, 1999, p135). Thus, learning and meaning are co-constructed but eventually this learning gets located back within the individual. Furthermore, formative or summative assessments are still measuring something that is the property of the individual. Learning is still about the internalization of external knowledge, and what the student can do alone after learning through social interaction (Vygotsky, 1978).

Researchers who advocate the benefits of formative assessment invoke social constructivist theories of learning to support arguments about assessment being something that should be done for and with the student rather than something that is done to them (Sadler, 1998; Gipps, 1999; Rust et al., 2005). Here assessment is seen as the best way in which to seek clarification of students' existing knowledge and understanding and to enable them to acquire new knowledge and understanding based on this (Black, 1999). New forms of summative assessment and tests (especially in the UK) now tend to reflect these shifting views of learning and achievement, and aim to bring examinations closer to classroom learning and students' experiences (Elwood, 1995). The introduction of performance assessments in the USA reflected similar considerations (Gipps, 1999). Thus, examination and test items reflect a more social emphasis on learning and knowing and broader definitions of achievement. Consequently, there has been a growth in the use of different assessment techniques (both formative and summative) in an attempt to articulate different achievements by boys and girls and to enable them to show their learning through different assessment activities and processes.

A view of assessment and learning from a social constructivist position sees *all* assessment tests and tasks as socially constructed, value-laden and highly problematic. Research into gender and performance from this perspective argues that tests and assessment themselves are contributing to the differences in performance observed (e.g. Stobart et al., 1992a, b; Willingham & Cole, 1997; Murphy & Elwood, 1998; Elwood, 2001; Elwood & Murphy, 2002). In understanding differential performance, we need to look at the actual tests themselves. The choices made as to which assessment technique is used (multiple-choice tests, coursework portfolios, performance assessments, mode of response and styles of examination) and the assessment techniques themselves all have a role to play in the creation of the gender differences observed.

Gendered consequences of choice of assessment technique

In the UK, two key research studies (Stobart et al., 1992b, Elwood & Comber, 1996) considered the impact of assessment and examining techniques on gender differences in performance. The critical focus of both these studies was how the social nature of public examinations shapes the experiences of students and teachers, their perceptions of subjects, the ways in which knowledge and understanding are assessed, and how these factors contribute to the differences observed.

Several factors in the design of examination systems and the assessment techniques used to assess students were identified as contributing significantly to gender differences in performance. For example, one key factor was the operational structure of examination systems at age 16. GCSE examination syllabuses in the UK are structured into different levels, or tiers of entry; each tier has a restricted set of grades that define the maximum and minimum achievement possible. For example, GCSE mathematics has three tiers of entry: foundation tier (grades D–G), intermediate tier (grades B–F) and higher tier (grades A*–C). Students are permitted to enter for one tier only at any one time, and any candidate not achieving the lowest restricted grade on any tier is unclassified.

Research found that one of the social consequences of the use of tiering is that gender significantly interacts with teachers' judgments on entry decisions; teachers use other considerations, not solely students' prior achievements, to allocate them to tiers (Stobart et al., 1992b; Elwood & Murphy, 2002). For example, in GCSE maths, more boys than girls are entered for the foundation tier with maximum grade D, more girls are entered for the intermediate tier with maximum grade B, and more boys are entered for the higher tier with maximum grade A*. Disaffection among students (notably boys) seems to be increased in the foundation tier with the limited range of grades available. The intermediate tier acts as a safety net where less confident students (notably girls) are entered if anxious about failure. More confident students (notably boys) are entered for the higher tier and perform well.

Thus, teachers' decisions about which tier to enter students are based on affective factors (perceived ability, and confidence or anxiety within subjects) as well as cognitive factors, and this seems unintentionally to limit the achievements of some boys and some girls (Murphy & Elwood, 1998). Thus, even before students sit the examination, decisions are made about the limits of boys' and girls' achievements. Although supported as a valid way of assessing students that enables them to show their learning to good effect, the legacy of such systems is that boys and girls have differential access to either the full curriculum in certain subjects and/or the full range of grades available within the examination.

Therefore, the interaction of gender and assessment technique suggests that not all boys and not all girls are equally and fairly affected by all types of testing and assessment. The research outlined above and other similar work has mainly concerned itself with large-scale summative assessment (Gipps & Murphy, 1994; Willingham & Cole, 1997). Any such attention to gender and its interaction with formative assessment tasks and practices is rare (Murphy, 1995) as are any perspectives that consider problematic issues in classroom assessment reform. Indeed, Hargreaves et al. (2002) seem to be lone voices in cautiously reminding us that not all classroom-based assessments are *humanistic and benign in their implications for supporting student learning and development* (2002, p70).

The assessment for learning movement promotes a view of learning within a social arena but tends to ignore gender. Proponents of this type of assessment tend to treat boys and girls as individuals and look only to within the individual to consider learning and achievement (Gipps, 1999; Black et al., 2003). As yet, there are few considerations of the position of gender in the changed teacher–student relationship necessary for success in this assessment practice, or of the social contexts of classrooms in which this type of assessment takes place. From our knowledge of the interaction of gender and teachers' decision making around tiered examination systems, it is possible to argue that when teachers turn from the role of coach of students (for summative assessment) to that of judge of students (for formative assessment), gender significantly influences their evaluation of boys' and girls' achievements and successes.

This view of learning, mind, assessment and gender is still problematic for those of us seeking to understand fully the complex interactions of gender with classroom-based assessment tasks and the practice of assessment in general. We are thus pushed further along the continuum as we observe that classrooms have cultural contexts; that teacher–student relationships are gendered, complex and problematic; and that such relationships and interactions have major implications for how we assess boys and girls. When classrooms are viewed as cultural settings in which students participate, we can no longer omit from our evaluation of students' achievements what they bring to the classroom setting as a consequence of their participation in a myriad of other cultural contexts.

Testing and assessment as cultural activities

Stage 3 on the continuum (Figure 6.4) positions learning, mind, gender and assessment as things that are culturally generated and mediated. Here we recognize the essential relationship and interaction between learning; the assessment of that learning; the social, cultural and historical lives of students and teachers; and the economic and political contexts in which assessment operates (Sutherland, 1996; Leathwood, 2005). Students and teachers bring social, cultural and historical experiences to assessment situations (Murphy & Ivinson, 2004), and to understand students' performances on assessment tasks we need to look into students' histories, into their *forms of life* (McGinn, 1997) and not into their heads. It is by looking into their forms of life that we can start to understand their learning and why they respond to tasks in different and gendered ways.

The model of learning at this stage is one underpinned by socio-cultural perspectives on learning. Socio-cultural theorists consider a view of learning that takes account of the socially constituted nature of individuals; they cannot be considered in isolation from their social and historical contexts (Rogoff, 2003; Murphy & Ivinson, 2004). Bruner and Haste (1987) further suggest that through

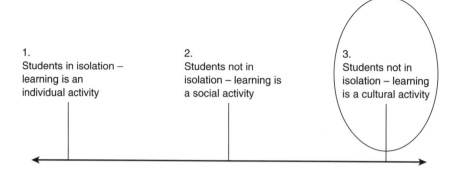

View of testing and assessment, learning, and mind that acknowledges the influence of students' 'form of life' – i.e. the social, cultural and historical lives of students:

(i)   students bring social, cultural and historical experiences to assessment and learning
(ii) gender is a social representation and found in students' 'forms' of life i.e. in the behaviour, assumptions, practices and lived-experiences that social beings share
(iii) students' gendered learning manifested through assessment tasks
(vi) teachers' gendered representations of achievement at the subject level

Figure 6.4   Assessment and testing as cultural activities

social life, the child acquires a framework for interpreting experience and learns how to negotiate meaning in a manner congruent with the requirements of the culture. Making sense is a social process; it is an activity that is always situated in a cultural and historical perspective. (1987, p1)

Aligned with a socio-cultural view of learning, there is a different view of mind. In this model, mind is considered situated between individuals *in social action* (Cobb, 1999, p135). Wertsch (1991, p6) describes a socio-cultural approach to mind as one that *creates an account of human mental processes that recognises the essential relationship between these processes and their cultural, historical and institutional settings.* Thus, mind is not local to the individual but situated in the cultural setting and within cultural relationships, and resides between individuals' interactions and reactions. A non-local view of mind suggests further that the learner and the teacher are entangled, and that learning (ability or achievement) is the product of the relationship between the teacher, the student and the test paper or assessment task.

The theoretical underpinning of a non-local view of mind comes also from considerations of Wittgenstein's philosophy, in relation to how he viewed meaning, understanding, and especially *form of life* (Bloor, 1983; McGinn, 1997; Grayling, 2001). Further, there is an analogue to this view of mind within quantum theory, which has entanglement at its heart (Herbert, 1985; Moore, 2001; Pinkerton, 2002; Morrison, 2005).

Grayling (2001) offers us an interpretation of Wittgenstein's 'forms of life'. He describes it as the

underlying consensus of linguistic and non-linguistic behaviour, assumptions, practices, traditions and natural propensities which humans as social beings share with
one another and which is therefore presupposed in the language they use. (2001, p97)

Form of life is the frame of reference we learn to work within when trained (or educated)
in the language of our community. Thus, meaning, knowledge and understanding reside
within communities (however defined) and can be understood only within this cultural
context. Gender, in this respect, is intricate to form of life. Girls and boys experience different, gendered forms of life and learn through a gendered mediating of the wider communities to which they belong (social, subject and gender).

The analogue of a non-local view of mind in quantum theory allows us to talk about
entanglement, influence, and action and reaction. Entanglement is defined as follows:

When two systems of which we know the states by their respective representation,
enter into a temporary physical interaction due to known forces between them and
when after a time of mutual influence the systems separate again, then they can no
longer be described as before, viz. by endowing each of them with a representative of
its own. (Schrödinger, 1935, in Aczel, 2003, p70)

If we take the analogy that teachers and students are like quantum systems, then once in
interaction, they can no longer be separately described or analyzed. They become part of
an indivisible whole; neither teacher nor student is separate, and the product of learning
(ability) is not separately analyzable. If we bring gender into this situation, we can see that
as with 'form of life', gender becomes something that is absolutely entangled with the
interactions of students and teachers – gender becomes part of the indivisible whole of the
teacher, the student, the assessment task and the ability represented in the response.

Thus, we can articulate gender, in a very profound way, as a fluid, social representation –
a set of ideas, social norms, conventions and associations within society that has definition
within our community (Ivinson & Murphy, 2003) rather than something that is fixed and
static. Boys and girls create and are created by their different forms of life, their entangled,
social interactions with teachers, and others, and the gendered appropriation of subject
knowledge, thought processes and lived-experiences. Viewing learning, mind and gender
in this way has profound implications for assessment practice and how we understand
assessment outcomes.

Gender differences in styles and approaches to the study of English

In using socio-cultural approaches to understand assessment data and the social representation of gender, Murphy and Ivinson (2004) argue that, within teachers' practice, there are
strong, gendered messages indirectly presented to students about what constitutes valued
subject knowledge and knowledge that is equated with success. Boys and girls interact
with these messages very differently by the way in which they respond to assessment tasks.
To illustrate these points further, Elwood (1998) considered teachers' evaluations of the
differences in boys' and girls' expression in writing and choices of writing styles in
advanced level English. These considerations highlighted interesting notions of what

teachers valued as 'good English writing' at this stage of schooling. Teachers articulated an ideal style of writing that again showed gender as a mediating factor.

> I think the boy's approach is much more effective at A level, far more effective. He will write you a side-and-a-half where others are writing four or five pages … it is like a knife through butter – almost notes but not quite, a very sparse style of writing. I have never seen a girl do that, never. (female English teacher, quoted in Elwood, 1998, p177).
>
> He combines a flair for literature with an analytical instinct, whereas she emphasises more but is less analytical and I would argue … that's what distinguishes the very best [students] from the rest. (male English teacher, quoted in Elwood, 1998, p 77)

These statements illustrate that certain styles of expression are expected and associated with success in this particular subject. Moreover, similar work suggests that such gendered expectations carry on into third-level study and within academic literacies more generally (Lillis, 2001; Francis et al., 2003; Read et al., 2004, 2005). Teachers give out messages, either knowingly or unknowingly, to students about what type of achievement aligns with success. Often the non-explicit nature of these messages means that some students (either boys or girls) either can or cannot meet teachers' criteria for success. Thus, how teachers view success in the community of the subject, with its conventions, forms, practices and cultural settings, significantly influences their judgments of boys' and girls' abilities. These definitions of success are entangled with teachers' and students' forms of life; it is only by looking into these forms of life that we begin to obtain a more humble understanding of gender and attainment.

Conclusion

This chapter has attempted to explore the very complex relationship between assessment, learning, mind, and gender. To support this exploration, I offered the reader a continuum as a framework along which to understand the differing notions of these fundamental and interrelated concepts and activities. In moving along the continuum in an attempt to get a more holistic and humble understanding of gender and achievement, I suggested the rejection of the traditional view of learning as something done in isolation, of mind as something that is located in the head, of gender as a static variable and the traditional psychometric view of assessment which sees it as checking up on what students know. Such a position, I have argued, gives us a very limited and distorted view of how boys and girls learn and how they achieve. Thus, to understand fully the highly complex relationship between gender and achievement, I have advocated the position along the far end of the continuum that views learning as a cultural activity, mind as between individuals, gender as a fluid, social representation, and assessment and testing as cultural activities that can describe students learning only in relationship to their teachers and their form of life. It is this position that offers a more humble approach to what we can actually say about boys' and girls' achievements in schools. The way in which we view learning, mind, gender and assessment at this position, has, I would argue, the most radical implications yet considered for how we evaluate students' learning. This is the true 'paradigm shift' in our thinking about these issues; boys' and girls' forms of life in relationship and entanglement with their teachers' must be part of our evaluations of their response to assessment tasks and tests. Such a perspective will considerably change how we view their learning, how we understand how learning takes place, and what we are actually doing when we attempt to capture and *measure* boys' and girls' achievements.

References

Aczel, A (2003) *Entanglement: the greatest mystery in physics*. Chichester: Wiley.

Alperstein, JF (2005) Commentary on girls and boys, test scores and more. *Teachers College Record*, 16 May. www.tcrecord.org ID number 11874 (accessed 15 June 2005).

Baird, J (2002) Challenges of computerized assessment. Paper presented to the 27th Annual Conference of the International Association for Educational Assessment, Brazil, May 2001.

Bennett, R, Jenkins, F, Persky, H & Weiss, A (2003) Assessing complex problem-solving performances. *Assessment in Education*, 10: 347–60.

Black, P (1999) Assessment, learning theories and testing systems, in Murphy, P (ed) *Learners, learning and assessment* (pp 118–34). London: Paul Chapman.

Black, P & Wiliam, D (1998) Assessment and classroom learning. *Assessment in Education*, 5: 7–71.

Black, P & Wiliam, D (2005) Lessons from around the world: how policies, politics and cultures constrain and afford assessment practices. *Curriculum Journal*, 16: 249–61.

Black, P, Harrison, C, Lee, C, Marshall, B & Wiliam, D (2003) *Assessment for Learning: putting it into practice*. Buckingham: Open University Press.

Bloor, D (1983) *Wittgenstein: a social theory of knowledge*. New York: Columbia University Press.

Broadfoot, P (1996) *Education, assessment and society*. Milton Keynes: Open University Press.

Bruner, J (1999) Culture, mind and education, in Moon, B & Murphy, P (eds) *Curriculum in context* (pp 148–78). London: Paul Chapman.

Bruner, J & Haste, H (1987) *Making sense: the child's construction of the world*. New York: Routledge.

Centre for Educational Research and Innovation (CERI) (2005) *Formative assessment – improving learning in secondary classrooms*. Paris: OECD.

Cobb, P (1999) Where is the mind? In Murphy, P (ed) *Learners, learning and assessment* (pp 135–50). London: Paul Chapman.

Elwood, J (1995) Undermining gender stereotypes: examination and coursework performance in the UK at 16. *Assessment in Education*, 2: 283–303.

Elwood, J (1998) Gender and performance in the GCE A level: gender-equity and the 'gold standard'. PhD dissertation, University of London, Institute of Education.

Elwood, J (2001) Examination techniques: issues of validity and effects on pupils' performance, in Scott, D (ed) *Curriculum and assessment* (pp 83–104). Westport, CT: Ablex.

Elwood, J (2005) Gender and achievement – what have exams got to do with it?, *Oxford Review of Education*, 31: 373–93.

Elwood, J & Comber, C (1996) *Gender differences in examinations at 184: final report*. London: Institute of Education for the Nuffield Foundation.

Elwood, J & Murphy, P (2002) Tests, tiers and achievement: gender and performance at 16 and 14 in England. *European Journal of Education*, 37: 395–416.

Epstein, D, Elwood, J, Hey, V & Maw, J (eds) (1998) *Failing boys? Issues in gender and achievement*. Buckingham: Open University Press.

Fordor, J (2000) *The mind doesn't work that way: the scope and limits of computational psychology*. Cambridge, MA: MIT Press.

Francis, B, Robson, J, Read, B & Melling, L (2003) Lecturers' perceptions of gender and under-graduate writing style. *British Journal of Sociology of Education*, 24: 357–73.

Gipps, C (1999) Socio-cultural aspects of assessment. *Review of Research in Education*, 24: 355–92.

Gipps, C & Murphy, P (1994) *A fair test? Assessment, achievement and equity*. Buckingham: Open University Press.

Goldstein, H (1996a) Statistical and psychometric models for assessment, in Goldstein, H & Toby, L (eds) *Assessment: problems, developments and statistical issues* (pp 41–56). Chichester: Wiley.

Goldstein, H (1996b) Group differences and bias in assessment, in Goldstein, H & Lewis, T (eds) *Assessment: problems, developments and statistical issues* (pp 85–94). Chichester: Wiley.

Grayling, AC (2001) *Wittgenstein: a very short introduction*. Oxford: Oxford Paperbacks.

Hargreaves, A, Earl, L & Schmidt, M (2002) Perspectives on alternative assessment reform. *American Educational Research Journal*, 39: 69–95.

Herbert, N (1985) *Quantum reality: beyond the new physics*. New York: Anchor Press.

Ivinson, G & Murphy, P (2003) Boys don't write romance: the construction of knowledge and social gender identities in English classrooms. *Pedagogy, Culture and Society*, 11: 89–111.

Joint Council for General Qualifications (JCGQ) (2004) *National provisional GCSE full course results June 2004 (all UK candidates)*. www.jcgq.org.uk/exam-result-date/gcse-statsistics-summer.2004.pdf (accessed 13 February 2005).

Lave, J & Wenger, E (1991) *Situated learning: legitimate peripheral participation*. Cambridge: Cambridge University Press.

Leathwood, C (2005) Assessment policy and practice in higher education: purpose standards and equity. *Assessment and Evaluation in Higher Education*, 30: 307–24.

Lemann, N (2000) *The big test: the secret history of the American meritocracy*. New York: Farrar, Straus and Giroux.

Lillis, TM (2001) *Student writings: access, regulation and desire*. London: Routledge.

Martin, MO, Mullis, IVS, Gonzales, EL, Gregory, KD, Smith, TA, Chrostowski, SJ, Garden, RAV & O'Connor, KM (1999) *TIMSS 1999 International Science Report: findings from the IEA's repeat of the Third International Mathematics and Science Study at the Eighth Grade*. Boston, MA: Boston College.

McDermott, RP (1999) On becoming labelled – the story of Adam, in Murphy, P (ed) *Learners, learning and assessment* (pp 1–21). London: Paul Chapman.

McGinn, M (1997) *Wittgenstein and the philosophical investigations*. London: Routledge.

Moore, F (2001) Rethinking measurement in psychology and education: a quantum perspective. Doctor of Education dissertation, Queen's University Belfast, Northern Ireland.

Morrison, H (2005) Personal communication.

Murphy, P (1995) Sources of inequity: understanding students' responses to assessment. *Assessment in Education*, 2: 249–70.

Murphy, P (ed) (1999) *Learners, learning and assessment*. London: Paul Chapman.

Murphy, P & Elwood, J (1998) Gendered experiences, choices and achievement: exploring the links. *International Journal of Inclusive Education*, 2: 85–118.

Murphy, P & Ivinson, G (2004) Gender differences in educational achievement: a socio-cultural analysis, in Olssen, M (ed) *Culture and learning: access and opportunity in the curriculum*. Greenwich, CT: Information Age Publishing.

National Assessment of Educational Progress (NAEP) (2000) *Trends in academic progress: three decades of student performance*. Washington, DC: National Centre for Educational Statistics.

Organisation for Economic Co-operation and Development (OECD) (2000) *Knowledge and skills for life: first results from PISA 2000*. Paris: OECD.

Organisation for Economic Co-operation and Development (OECD) (2004) *Learning for tomorrow's world – first results from PISA 2003*. Paris: OECD.

Pinkerton, M (2002) Quantification, standards and the elusive search for transparency in monitoring school performance. Doctor of Education dissertation, Queen's University Belfast, Northern Ireland.

Pirie, M (2001) How exams are fixed in favour of girls. *The Spectator*, 20 January.

Read, B, Francis, B & Robson, J (2004) Re-viewing undergraduate writing: tutor's perceptions of essay qualities according to gender. *Research in Post-Compulsory Education*, 9: 217–38.

Read, B, Francis, B & Robson, J (2005) Gender, 'bias', assessment and feedback: analysing the written assessment of undergraduate history essays. *Assessment and Evaluation in Higher Education*, 30: 241–60.

Rogoff, B (2003) *The cultural nature of human development*. Oxford: Oxford University Press.

Rust, C, O'Donovan, B & Price, M (2005) A social constructivist assessment process model: how the research literature shows us this could be the best practice. *Assessment and Evaluation in Higher Education*, 30: 231–40.

Sadler, R (1998) Formative assessment: revisiting the territory. *Assessment in Education*, 5: 77–84.

Shepard, L (2000) The role of assessment in a learning culture. *Educational Researcher*, 29: 4–14.

Stobart, G, Elwood, J & Quinlan, M (1992a) Gender bias in examinations: how equal are the opportunities? *British Educational Research Journal*, 18: 261–76.

Stobart, G, White, J, Elwood, J, Hayden, M & Mason, K (1992b) *Differential performance in GCSE maths and English – final report*. London: SEAC.

Sutherland, G (1996) Assessment: some historical perspectives, in Goldstein, H & Toby, L (eds) *Assessment: problems, developments and statistical issues* (pp 9–20). Chichester: Wiley.

von Glasersfeld, E (1987) Learning as a constructive activity, in Janvier, C (ed) *Problems in the representation in the teaching and learning of mathematics* (pp 3–18). Hillsdale, NJ: Erlbaum.

von Glasersfeld, E (1989) Cognition, construction of knowledge and teaching. *Synthese*, 80: 121–40.

Vygotsky, L (1978) *Mind in society*. London: Harvard University Press.

Wertsch, J (1991) *Voices of the mind: a sociocultural approach to mediated action*. Cambridge, MA: Harvard University Press.

Wilder, GZ & Powell, K (1989) *Sex differences in test performance: a survey of the literature*. New York: College Board Publications.

Willingham, WW & Cole, NS (eds) (1997) *Gender and fair assessment*. Mahwah, NJ: Laurence Erlbaum.

7

Portfolios and Assessment in Teacher Education in Norway: A Theory-based Discussion of Different Models in Two Sites

Olga Dysthe and Knut Steinar Engelsen

[...]

Introduction and contextualization

[...]

The project reported in this article, 'Alternative assessment in teacher education', involves three Norwegian teacher institutions: the Department of Teacher Education at the University of Oslo, which runs a one-year programme for students who have finished their subject specialization, and the Departments of Teacher Education at the University Colleges of Vestfold and at Stord/Haugesund, both of which have four-year teacher programmes. The two latter institutions are included in our study. The Alternative Assessment Project is connected to an ICT project, and digital portfolios are part of a larger effort to develop technology-rich learning environments in Norwegian teacher education. A constructivist perspective on knowledge and learning is common to most portfolio use in teacher education (McLaughlin & Vogt, 1996). Our project is based on social constructivist and sociocultural perspectives and a major concern is how collaborative learning can be supported in the portfolio processes. Our focus in this chapter is on describing and discussing the portfolio models and typical learning and assessment processes in the two sites, with a particular emphasis on the learning potential and areas of improvement. Our main questions are:

- What are similarities and differences in the portfolio models that are implemented by our two sites?
- What are particular areas for further improvement?
- What are critical factors in portfolio work as regards students' learning processes?
- How is the digital aspect of portfolios utilized and what are unused potentials?

In order to answer these questions, we have developed what we call a model of analysis for portfolio processes which we use as an instrument to describe variations within each site and across sites. Our data come from three sources: project reports from each site, semi-structured

From: *Assessment and Evaluation in Higher Education*, 29 (2), 2004, pp.239–58. Reprinted by permission of the publisher (Taylor & Francis Ltd, http://www.informa world.com).

interviews with teachers, student evaluations, and reports from semi-monthly meetings in the project group during the autumn semester 2001, 2002 and the spring semester 2003.

A model of analysis for portfolio processes

Zeichner and Wray (2000) distinguished between the 'learning portfolio', often used throughout the duration of a pre-service teacher education programme, the 'credential portfolio', often used to assess prospective teachers' readiness to receive an initial teaching licence, and the 'employment portfolio', a showcase portfolio representing students' best work and used when students applied for teaching positions (pp. 615–616). The portfolio type we discuss in this chapter does not correspond to any of these categories, as it is a discipline-based 'learning and assessment portfolio'.

Before presenting our theoretical perspectives, we will outline our model of analysis. Defining the portfolio in education is no easy task. One of the most commonly used definitions is by Paulson et al. (1991):

> A portfolio is a purposeful collection of student work that exhibits the student's efforts, progress, or achievements in one or more areas. The collection must include student participation in selecting contents, the criteria for judging merit, and evidence of the student's self-reflection. (p. 60)

Our understanding of digital portfolio is embedded in the same definition. In addition, a digital portfolio is stored and organized digitally and it utilizes digital tools in the learning process and in the documentation (Otnes, 2003).

The definition by Paulson et al. is normative and excludes some of the portfolio models we present in this chapter, and we will discuss this point later. In international literature, there is a great variety of portfolio models (Black et al., 1994; Brown et al., 1997; Yancey & Weiser, 1997), but common to most of them seem to be 'collection, reflection, selection' as well as postponement of summative assessment (Hamp-Lyons & Condon, 2000; Klenowski, 2002). Portfolios were first widely used in the arts and in writing, and consensus has developed in these subject areas about the usefulness of these characteristics. The model presented in Figure 7.1 is based on a collection-reflection-selection framework, and as such it can be seen as a benchmark to determine the success of portfolios in the two sites we report from. But because of the rapid spread of portfolios to a great variety of disciplines and contexts in Norway, it is important to discuss whether this framework is equally useful everywhere. There was no unified conception of portfolios among teachers in our participating sites. It is also worth noting that none of the institutions had any previous experience of using portfolios.

By presenting this model, we want to raise awareness of advantages and disadvantages of different ways of practising portfolios. Our model is primarily a descriptive and analytic tool, and our purpose is to illustrate how the learning potential at different stages in the portfolio processes depends on what choices are made regarding some key factors in each of the 'learning phases'. We have chosen this term because we are particularly interested in how the portfolio can support student learning. In real life the portfolio learning processes are continuous and iterative, not linear. Our model of analysis is meant to help identify critical factors for improvement, especially in institutions where they have just started using portfolios. Figure 7.1 summarizes the questions we asked in order to describe portfolio processes in the two teacher institutions, and Figures 7.2–7.5 show some characteristics of portfolio use in two disciplines in each of them.

Learning phase 1

This phase comprises activities and processes resulting in a variety of objects (written, oral, visual, practical), which are collected in a working portfolio. Learning is dependent on a number of factors that vary from site to site. We have identified a number of key questions to ask in order to identify how portfolios are used in phase 1. Some questions relate to the macro level, some to the micro level:

- *Organization*. How are learning processes organized? (i.e., are they mainly lecture-based, case-based, project- or problem-based?) What combinations?
- *Individual-collective*. How is the relationship between individual and collective/collaborative work? What kinds of work dominate?
- *ICT*. Is ICT used primarily for individual writing and for organization of portfolio processes, or also for feedback, discussion and collaboration?
- *Writing and feedback practices*. What are the recommended writing strategies? Who gives feedback and how is it organized? (peer/teacher, written/oral, individual/group, digital/paper-based)
- *Meta-processes*. To what extent are reflection as well as discussion and negotiation of criteria integrated in the work with theoretical and practical aspects of the subject area?

Teacher and peer feedback are widely recognized as crucial aspects of formative assessment.

Learning phase 2

In our model of analysis, this phase is connected with students selecting documentation for their Presentation Portfolio (PP). Important questions to ask in order to determine what and how students learn in phase 2 are:

- *Self-assessment*. Are students involved in self-assessment as part of selecting what goes into the PP, and do they use criteria and reflection in doing so?
- *Criteria*. Have students been given explicit criteria for what counts as good quality work? Have these been developed in cooperation with the students or negotiated with them?
- *Reflection*. Are students asked to write reflective texts for their PP?

Several studies have documented that self-assessment of portfolio work is an important aspect of formative assessment as well as students' need for criteria (Topping, 2003).

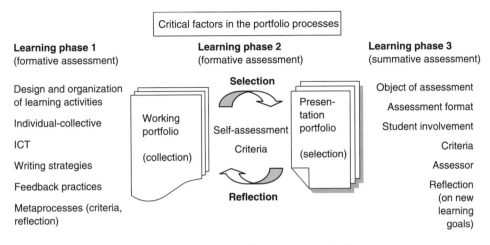

Figure 7.1   A model of analysis for portfolio processes in the project 'Alternative assessment in teacher education in Norway'

Learning phase 3

Summative assessment is centre-stage in phase 3, which covers a very short period of time compared to phase 1. By also calling this a 'learning phase', we want to emphasize the learning potential also in the summative assessment process, and we have identified some critical factors:

- *Object and format of assessment*. What is being assessed? The portfolio itself? Portfolio-based oral performance or written essays? Combination of portfolio and traditional exam?
- *Student involvement*. Is the student directly involved? What degree of control does the student have over the object of assessment?
- *Criteria*. Are the criteria implicit or explicit? Do the criteria include process or just product?
- *Assessor*. Is the traditional Norwegian pattern of external assessors + teacher still dominant? Are peer and self-assessment used for summative purpose?
- *Reflection*. Is there any space for setting new learning goals on the basis of assessment results?

Portfolios in the light of sociocultural theories of knowledge and learning

From sociocultural perspectives, knowledge and learning are viewed as situated, social, distributed and mediated, dependent on language and dependent on participation in communities of practice (Säljö, 2000; Dysthe, 2001). [...] These perspectives also govern our understanding of assessment as closely integrated in the learning processes instead of as a separate event after learning has taken place (Gipps, 1994; Greeno et al., 1996).

Portfolios as mediating artefacts

The cultural historical school of Vygotsky, Luria and Leont'ev underlined the fact that human beings develop and use physical, technical and semiotic tools. Tools are intellectual and practical resources which we have access to and which we use to understand the world around us and to act on it. Portfolios are mediating cultural tools, and the physical and cultural aspects of them are important, as well as the rules and routines and processes the portfolios are surrounded by and embedded in. If portfolios are seen solely as an assessment form, the main focus is usually on the products. We look at portfolios primarily as tools or artefacts that mediate learning. Digitalization of portfolios provides an interesting example of how learning processes change when the mediating tool changes. The first step is often to use digital portfolios just as a different medium of storage, and the next one is to ask what new learning potential digitalization offers (Otnes, 2002). [...]

Learning as situated, social and distributed

The term 'social' is used in at least two meanings when related to learning (Wertsch, 1998); one emphasizes the historical and cultural *context* which the learner is situated in, the other the relational and interactional aspect. Both are relevant to portfolio processes.

The second meaning of 'social' focuses on *interaction* processes. As shown in Figure 7.1, collaborative learning in various forms are at the centre of what we have called 'Learning phase 1'. [...]. While Bruffee (1993) focused on the goal of collaboration as enculturation into communities of practice, Roschelle and Berend (1995) described it as mutual engagement in problem solving. Salomon (1995, p. 149) emphasized 'genuine interdependence' as the main prerequisite for collaborative teamwork, and he has also pointed out some of the common pitfalls for productive group collaboration. Technology should ideally serve as support to collaborative processes (CSCL) and a long-term goal of our project is therefore to find out in what ways the digital portfolio may enhance collaborative learning processes.

When knowledge development and knowledge *production* is in focus instead of knowledge *reproduction*, the notion that knowledge is *distributed* becomes of practical importance in the learning activities. Learning is dependent on how well the group is able to draw on the different skills and insights of its members and thus extend beyond the capacities of the individual. Digital portfolios may open up new opportunities of making visible how the knowledge of different students complement each other, for instance, because they gain access to other students' portfolios and to different kinds of collective shared documents, and because they can make hypertextual connections. The mother-tongue models from Vestfold and Stord/Haugesund and their elements of collaboration across institutional borders are examples of this. An important issue is whether co-production of knowledge and distributed learning actually takes place, or whether it is only a juxtaposition of different persons' knowledge? The latter is often the case when students coordinate different learning tasks without utilizing each other's knowledge. Do the portfolios reflect not only the contributions of each member but also the 'added learning value' of dialogical interaction of different voices? (Dysthe, 1996a, b).

From a sociocultural perspective, language is not just a mediating tool for learning, but closely bound up with thinking itself (Vygotsky, 1986). Language is part and parcel of all phases of portfolio work, not only when the documentation is a written product. Collaborative learning processes are dependent on shared oral and written information and on dialogic interactions at all stages of knowledge production.

Learning as participation in communities of practice

In theories of 'situated cognition', learning is seen basically as a process of enculturation into a community of practice (Brown et al., 1989; Lave & Wenger, 1991). A community is characterized by mutual engagement, joint enterprise and shared repertoires (Wenger, 1998). Students in teacher education participate in several communities of practice during their education, most noticeably the learning community of peers and teachers at the particular teacher institution and the community of practitioners in the school(s) where they are student teachers. Within each of these communities, students may also participate in a number of others, for instance, the various disciplinary communities and various peer groups. In order to define a teacher education class or a peer group as 'a community of practice', the students must share a mutual engagement in learning, be willing to define the particular learning task as a joint enterprise and share 'repertoires', for instance, strategies for group work, for how to give response or for how to create hypertextual links. A portfolio assignment may be located within different communities of practice, and the particular context where it is situated will make a difference regarding the opportunity space it affords for the students.

'Participation' is both personal and social, and the term describes 'a complex process that suggests both action and connection. It combines doing, talking, thinking, feeling, and belonging' (Wenger, 1998, p. 56). Participation includes all kinds of relations, not just collaborative, but also conflictual and competitive. This is in keeping with Bakhtin's view of dialogue where the creative potential lies in the tension between multiple voices and conflicting perspectives (Bakhtin, 1986; Dysthe, 2001). An important question to ask is therefore whether portfolio assignments pre-suppose students' participation in and across different communities of practice or only individual engagement with the tasks.

'Reification' is a concept introduced by Wenger (1998) which etymologically means 'making into a thing'. Wenger uses reification in a more general sense about processes that give form to our experience by producing objects, processes that include, for instance, 'making, designing, representing, naming, encoding' (Wenger, 1998, p. 59), as well as the products of such processes. The concept is a difficult one, but we will nevertheless explore some implications of seeing portfolios as reification of practices.

One implication is the close connection between process and product. When a certain understanding is given a form, for instance, in a portfolio artefact, this form then becomes a focus for negotiation of meaning. Reification does not simply translate meaning into an object; such translation is never possible and 'therefore the process and product always imply each other' (Wenger, 1998, p. 60). In portfolio artefacts, the process is implicit in the product. To what extent the process itself should be documented, and thus reified, is a recurrent question of discussion in portfolio literature. Portfolio products may vary from written or multimedia texts to material objects or a video of a drama performance, and even though the latter may contain more of the process than a written text does, in principle the product always implies the process. It is therefore important to realize that portfolio artefacts 'are only the tip of an iceberg, which indicates larger contexts of significance realized in human practices. Their character as reifications is not only in their form, but also in the processes by which they are integrated into these practices' (Wenger, 1998, p. 61). We will discuss some of the implications of looking at portfolios as reification of practice in the last section of the chapter and tie this to identity formation for teacher education students.

Variations of portfolio models in two Norwegian teacher education institutions

After a brief contextualization of the use of portfolio in teacher education at Vestfold and Stord/Haugesund University College, we present figures that illustrate how portfolios are used in two disciplines in each site. Our brief comments relate to characteristic aspects of each phase and the degree and use of digitalization.

Teacher education at Vestfold University College

Contextualization and brief description

At Vestfold University College, the faculty board decided on a model very similar to our model of analysis as a framework for the use of portfolios in all subjects, but there are nevertheless considerable disciplinary variations regarding content, structure, assignments, processes and assessment of the portfolio. Our data indicate that this institution utilizes the potential of ICT in the portfolio process, also as a means of achieving a collaborative learning environment, to a higher level than Stord/Haugesund has managed so far. In Norwegian (mother tongue education), the use of hypertext for building collective structures is a significant aspect. In the Vestfold examples, the final assessment is divided in two: Assessment of the presentation portfolio (50%) and an oral exam based on the working portfolio (50%).

Commonalities of all the portfolio models at this site: (1) the portfolio is stored and organized digitally, either Net-based or in a closed Learning Management System, i.e. ClassFronter, a Norwegian LMS, and students are supposed to utilize the digital medium, for instance, multimedia texts, interactive communication and hypertext; (2) the portfolios are in principle open and accessible to a general public, with the exception of sensitive material regarding pupils or the students themselves. Transparency is an important principle at the Vestfold site and this implies that fellow students can access each others' portfolios as a necessary prerequisite for cooperative learning and collective processes;

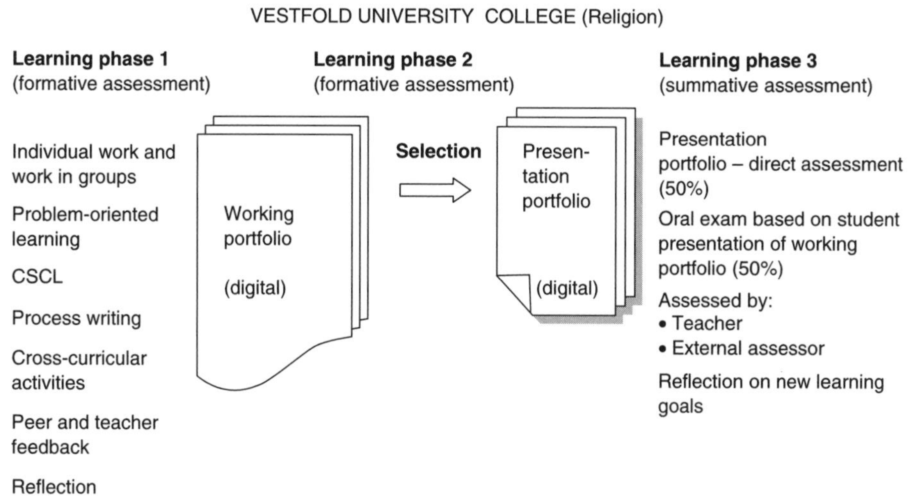

VESTFOLD UNIVERSITY COLLEGE (Religion)

Learning phase 1
(formative assessment)

Learning phase 2
(formative assessment)

Learning phase 3
(summative assessment)

Individual work and
work in groups

Problem-oriented
learning

CSCL

Process writing

Cross-curricular
activities

Peer and teacher
feedback

Reflection

Working
portfolio

(digital)

Selection

Presen-
tation
portfolio

(digital)

Presentation
portfolio – direct assessment
(50%)

Oral exam based on student
presentation of working
portfolio (50%)

Assessed by:
• Teacher
• External assessor

Reflection on new learning
goals

Figure 7.2   Portfolio model of Religion, Vestfold

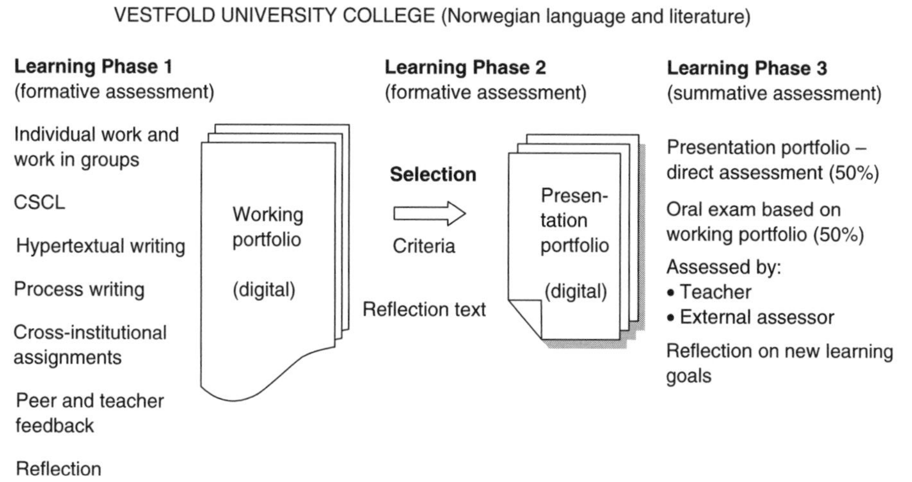

VESTFOLD UNIVERSITY COLLEGE (Norwegian language and literature)

Learning Phase 1
(formative assessment)

Learning Phase 2
(formative assessment)

Learning Phase 3
(summative assessment)

Individual work and
work in groups

CSCL

Hypertextual writing

Process writing

Cross-institutional
assignments

Peer and teacher
feedback

Reflection

Working
portfolio

(digital)

Selection

Criteria

Reflection text

Presen-
tation
portfolio

(digital)

Presentation portfolio –
direct assessment (50%)

Oral exam based on
working portfolio (50%)

Assessed by:
• Teacher
• External assessor

Reflection on new learning
goals

Figure 7.3   Portfolio model of Norwegian language and literature, Vestfold

and (3) collaborative processes are built into portfolio assignments, including reflection
and peer/teacher feedback (learning phase 1).

Religion emphasizes cooperation with other subjects, for instance, art, and students
build their own syllabus as an integrated part of the portfolio process.

The Norwegian language and literature model has a strong emphasis on building collective texts through the use of hypertext. It is also characterized by extensive use of Net-
based dialogue among the students, especially chat. It is possible to log this chat dialogue,
and in Vestfold there are examples of how the log is used as a resource in individual and

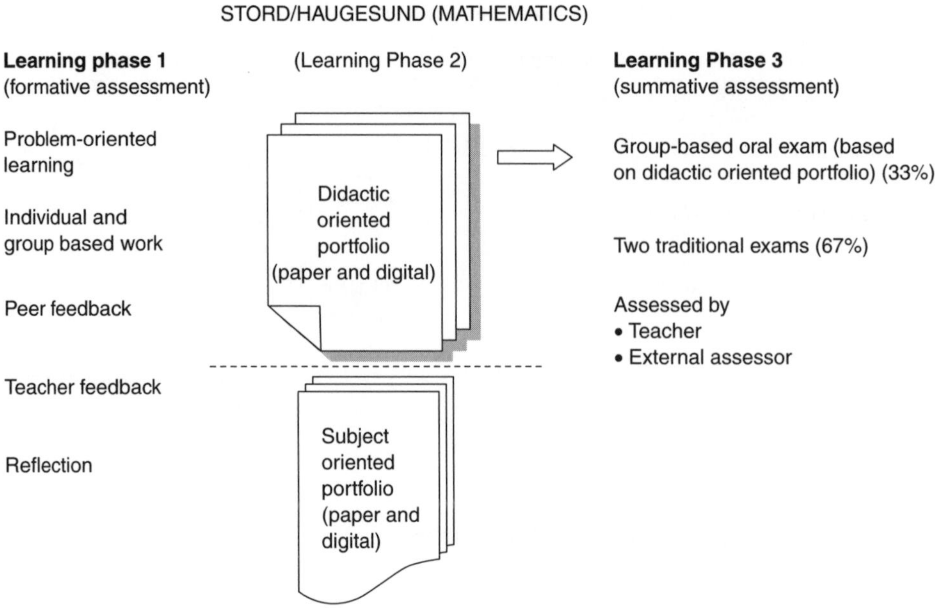

STORD/HAUGESUND (MATHEMATICS)

Learning phase 1 (formative assessment)	(Learning Phase 2)	Learning Phase 3 (summative assessment)

Learning phase 1
(formative assessment)

Problem-oriented
learning

Individual and
group based work

Peer feedback

Teacher feedback

Reflection

(Learning Phase 2)

Didactic
oriented
portfolio
(paper and digital)

Subject
oriented
portfolio
(paper and
digital)

Learning Phase 3
(summative assessment)

Group-based oral exam (based
on didactic oriented portfolio) (33%)

Two traditional exams (67%)

Assessed by
• Teacher
• External assessor

Figure 7.4   Portfolio model of Mathematics, Stord/Haugesund

collective metaprocesses. The written chat dialogue seems thus to function as a comple-ment to the oral discussion in the learning community (Otnes, 2003).

The criteria for selection are mainly defined by the teachers (learning phase 2). The selection process involves a focus on new learning goals. The oral exam is based on the student presenting selected aspects of his or her portfolio.

Teacher education at Stord/Haugesund University College

Contextualization and brief description

The two examples from Stord/Haugesund differ a great deal from our model of analysis, especially in relation to learning phase 2, where selection and criteria work is absent. A specific characteristic is that the portfolios are not being assessed directly, only indirectly through an oral exam (Mathematics) or a home-based essay exam (mother tongue), both based on portfolio content. Both subjects also use traditional syllabus-based exams in addi-tion to the portfolio system.

We have chosen to present the portfolio model in Mathematics as well as in Norwegian language and literature, in order to illustrate differences within this site. In Mathematics, one third of the grade was based on the portfolio related oral exam and two thirds on two traditional written exams. The portfolios are stored digitally and thus made accessible to

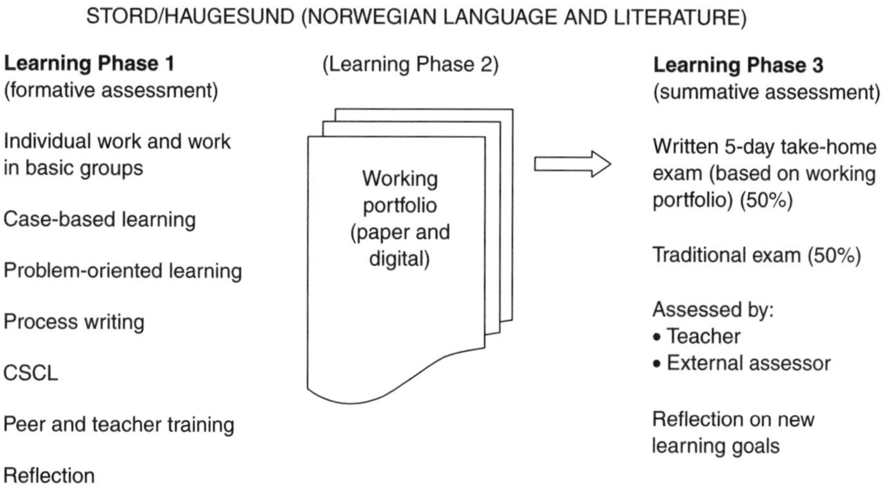

STORD/HAUGESUND (NORWEGIAN LANGUAGE AND LITERATURE)

Learning Phase 1
(formative assessment)

Individual work and work
in basic groups

Case-based learning

Problem-oriented learning

Process writing

CSCL

Peer and teacher training

Reflection

(Learning Phase 2)

Working
portfolio
(paper and
digital)

⇨

Learning Phase 3
(summative assessment)

Written 5-day take-home
exam (based on working
portfolio) (50%)

Traditional exam (50%)

Assessed by:
• Teacher
• External assessor

Reflection on new
learning goals

**Figure 7.5   Portfolio model of Norwegian language and literature
(mother tongue), Stord/Haugesund**

all students, mostly through the LMS (ClassFronter). Net-based discussion is not a significant aspect in this model.

In Mathematics, learning phase 1 combines both a working portfolio (containing regular maths assignments) and a presentation portfolio containing didactic oriented coursework set by the teacher.

A particular feature of this model was the lack of connection between the students'
working portfolio and the presentation portfolio. Students made no selection and therefore
they did not work specifically with quality criteria. Learning phase 2 was seemingly
non-existent, but students did choose which aspects of all portfolio group assignments to
present for discussion with the external assessor and the teacher. Reflection and self-
assessment were not prominent in this model.

The portfolio model in Norwegian language and literature contains just two learning
phases as there is no selection and very little self-reflection or self-assessment. The
aspects of learning phase 1 are similar to those in the model of analysis and includes both
individual and group work, problem oriented learning, process writing and CSCL. The
latter is mostly connected to 'Database-mediated dialogue', used in the early literacy
course. In this dialogue the students collect authentic pupil-texts, analyse them and pub-
lish both the text and the analysis within the database system. Afterwards, the analyses
are discussed with peers, teachers and practice teachers (Engelsen, 2002, 2003; Bjørlykke
& Økland, 2003). The discussions are also mediated through and stored within the database system.

The portfolio assignments are mainly stored digitally, some on the Web and some in
ClassFronter. A few of the portfolio assignments are collective and emphasize the use of
hypertext for building thematic structures, e.g., websites for children's literature based on
student work.

All components in the portfolio must be accepted by the teacher in order for the student to be assessed. The summative assessment consists of a 5-day take-home essay

exam. This is based on portfolio contents, but the assignment is made by the teacher. Students are expected to reflect on their work as part of the exam. External assessor and teacher grade the essay, which only counts for 50% of the grade. The remaining 50% is based on a traditional written exam. The criteria are largely implicit and not discussed with students.

Summary and discussion

Some general findings

1   Portfolios influence the pedagogical processes in both sites and have improved formative assessment.
2   There is considerable emphasis on social learning processes in both sites.
3   Unless cooperation and collaboration are built into the portfolio assignments, individual work continues to be dominant. Assignments are therefore crucial.
4   Developing an integrated portfolio and ICT pedagogy is a major change and takes time.
5   Written Net-based dialogues complement oral dialogues both among students and between students and teachers.
6   Increased workload is a problem both for teachers and students, especially in the first semester, due to the demands of developing the specific competencies in using the mediating tools (i.e., computer literacy, collaboration competence, portfolio genre knowledge).
7   None of the sites utilize fully the learning potential in all the three phases of the model of analysis. Some improvement areas are: (a) criteria work in phase 1 and 2; (b) student written reflective texts; and (c) self-assessment and selection. The lack of focus on selection and criteria work seems to be significant in both sites, and students are not likely to be involved in reflection and self-assessment unless this is built into the assignment or specifically asked for in phase 2.
8   The summative forms of assessment can be characterized as hybrid in the sense that traditional exams are mixed with portfolios in various ways. The most successful innovation in summative assessment is a portfolio-based oral exam.

How do the sites utilize the learning potential in each of the phases?

In this section, we want to discuss the questions raised in connection with the presentation of our model of analysis.

Learning phase 1: Formative assessment

[…] In our sites, the use of portfolios and ICT has resulted in changes in the way student learning is organized. There are concerted efforts to change from lecture-based teaching to project- and problem-based learning. This includes creating a more collaborative learning environment and emphasizing peer tutoring as well as teacher feedback. In teacher education, formative assessment by teachers has always existed, but portfolios afford more systematic use of peer feedback, mainly individual, but also in the form of response groups. Developing and negotiating quality criteria for student work may be a necessary next step in order to make students aware of standards and strengthen the formative element of peer assessment.

Collaborative knowledge production may be documented in individual portfolios, group portfolios or through thematic portfolios constructed across individual portfolios. Ideally both the quality of products and processes should be documented. With a few exceptions, the portfolios in this project have all been individual, though Vestfold reports that the fact that the portfolios are transparent has strengthened the collaborative activities among the students. Since students so far have more experience producing individual products and teachers likewise have more experience in assessing those, there is a need for developing expertise on collective portfolios. A major issue for further discussion is how to handle the dilemma of collective work processes and traditional individual assessment.

Another dilemma has to do with control. Teacher education in Norway has traditionally a strong focus on teacher and curriculum control. The data from our examples indicate that learning in all sites is still mainly teacher and curriculum controlled and that moving the locus of control to students is a hard and difficult process.

Both our sites utilize digital tools for building collective, thematic structures between the portfolios. Vestfold has come a long way in exploring the new learning potential in hypertextual writing and collaboration across institutional sites. Stord/Haugesund has utilized hypertext as well as database dialogue. In both sites, written Net-based dialogue (both synchronous and asynchronous) seems to establish a complementary position to oral dialogue. In the beginning, the two seemed to compete, especially at Stord/Haugesund, and our material indicates, not surprisingly, that enhanced competency leads to positive attitudes and more use. While ICT in the early phases was regarded mostly as a problem by students and teachers alike, ICT increasingly becomes a transparent aspect of the learning activities and opens new arenas for dialogue and new ways of collaboration.

Learning phase 2: Formative assessment

Phase 2 is weakly represented in our project. Some examples do not distinguish between a working and a presentation portfolio, and neither of the sites has a strong focus on selection, criteria work and self-assessment. This raises the question whether the 'collection-reflection-selection' framework of our model of analysis actually can be used as a benchmark to evaluate the success of portfolio use, or whether it is unsuitable in some contexts. What is quite clear from a wider range of portfolio experiments in higher education in Norway, is that short courses only provide time for a limited number of projects or assignments and as a result the working portfolio and the presentation portfolio are identical. The Quality Reform of higher education mentioned initially in this chapter, introduces both portfolio assessment and modularization of all courses (half a semester's workload). It is therefore a paradox that modularization reduces the possibility of producing a varied collection of artefacts for the portfolio. In teacher education and other professional studies, however, it is possible to collect work over two or more semesters. In both our sites, Norwegian language and literature exemplify this, and students have a broad collection of artefacts from which to select what to present for assessment.

There is much evidence in the international portfolio literature that the selection process promotes self-assessment and focuses students' attention on quality criteria (Seegers et al., 2003). This is why we think there is a considerable improvement potential in our two sites in the area of self-assessment, whether or not it is connected to a selection for a presentation portfolio. Collective work on quality criteria has to be strengthened and closely tied to the individual reflection essays that students have to write in some of the examples from our sites.

A particular feature of phase 2 in our examples is due to the fact that the portfolios are not assessed directly but indirectly in a portfolio-based oral or written exam. Students therefore select what to present digitally and orally or what aspects of the portfolio they want to develop further in a written essay. This definitely involves self-assessment and reflection, and we will discuss advantages and disadvantages under the next heading.

Learning phase 3: summative assessment

Our material presents very varied forms of summative assessment. There are three main models of assessment where portfolios are involved: (1) the portfolio itself is being graded; (2) the portfolio is the source from which students extract material to present digitally at an oral exam; and (3) written exams, where students more or less directly develop some aspects of portfolio contents. In addition, there may be traditional written exams used as a supplement to portfolios, for instance, in order to check student coverage of curriculum content or to test students' ability to solve math problems. Interestingly, none of the disciplines in our study base students' grades solely on the portfolio. Neither is self- or peer assessment involved in the summative assessment process, and the assessment commission, consisting of external assessor and the teacher, determines the final grade.

There are several ways of interpreting these findings. It seems to us that the traditional exam regime still has a very strong hold on both institutions, in spite of the progressive development work and efforts to create student-centred and collaborative learning processes around the portfolios. Thus hybrid assessment formats have been developed which give the portfolio a role to play, but where exams are still dominant. The control aspect is strong. There seems to be a discrepancy between the importance of the portfolio in learning phase 1 and the lack of importance given to it in the summative assessment. Student evaluations, however, show that students invest a lot of time and effort in portfolio assignments even though they are not directly assessed! Whether this is due to the Hawthorne effect and a feeling of being pioneers, we do not know, but it seems realistic to think that interest in portfolios may decline unless they count more in the summative assessment.

A positive aspect according to the students is the new oral, portfolio-based exam, where students are given 10–15 minutes for a digital presentation of selected portfolio work, followed by questions and discussion. Students are very satisfied with this assessment format, and they emphasize that it gives them more control than traditional exams (Wittek, 2002).

Both Vestfold and Stord/Haugesund are in a transition phase where they are cautiously trying out new forms of summative assessment, but they have not yet come to terms with how to use portfolios as both formative and summative assessment tools, nor do they utilize their full potential. In our view, student portfolios need to count more directly towards the grade in order to make it worthwhile to invest time and effort in them, assessment criteria should be developed and negotiated together with the students, and meta-reflective processes need to be fully integrated in all the phases.

The potential of communication and digitalization

In all the four examples, ICT is an aspect, but its importance varies. ICT is used both for peer and teacher response, but the problem is the time factor. The Stord/Haugesund math example indicates low activity in Web-based discussion, the explicitly expressed reason being that both students and teachers find face-to-face oral communication to be less time-consuming than written Net-based communication. The mother-tongue example from Stord/Haugesund also indicates that student and teacher competency training in feedback is an area for improvement. The Vestfold Norwegian literature and language example shows that synchronous dialogue (chat) enhances Net-based dialogue, and in Religion the transparency afforded by Net-based portfolios seems to have a positive impact on peer collaboration. In general, our data show that the participants are optimistic about Net-based communication and its potential to improve portfolio processes.

Is it possible to conclude that digital portfolios provide qualitatively new learning opportunities for students? Is the portfolio just a filing cabinet or also a learning arena (Otnes, 2003)? Both Vestfold and Stord/Haugesund provide examples of digital portfolio processes that bring new dimensions to the learning environment. Constructing collective, thematic Web-structures across individual portfolios provides new learning opportunities. There are also examples in our material of structures crossing institutional borders through joint projects. Here students literally built new knowledge by utilizing the distributed knowledge of their fellow students. Collective structures *across* portfolios amount to more than the sum of the individual portfolios.

The use of dialogues around the pupil-text database at Stord/Haugesund is also an example of a portfolio assignment that would have been impossible without the web. The database consists of text produced through collaborative activity, where students, college teachers and partner schoolteachers participate (Bjørlykke & Økland, 2002; Engelsen, 2002b). This is also one of the few examples in our material where portfolio assignments are designed to connect different communities of practice.

In spite of these notable examples, our material indicates that in neither of our sites is ICT fully integrated into the learning ecology. There is an unexploited potential in portfolios used both as a learning tool and as an assessment tool.

A theory-based discussion of three critical aspects of portfolio work

In this section we want to limit our discussion to three aspects of portfolio work that our empirical material has shown to be critical: negotiated portfolio assignments, reflection/self-assessment and the format of summative assessment. We will explore some implications of looking at *portfolios as reifications of practice* for each of these.

Negotiated, authentic assignments—a key to tapping the learning potential of portfolios?

If we look at portfolios as reification in the way Wenger uses the term (Wenger, 1998), portfolio assignments must provide opportunities for rich and complex learning situations, where students experience central aspects of professional practice, and are challenged to bring together both disciplinary content and didactics. Assignments should also signal the need for collaboration. The key question for teachers to ask initially is: what kind of practice do we want students to document in the portfolio? Asking students to reproduce information or to solve problems where there are right and wrong answers make uninteresting portfolio assignments in a teacher education context. Problems need to be complex even if reification of individual cognitive activity is the goal, and when reification of multifaceted and collective practices is the desirable goal, assignments need to be carefully designed.

In our view, portfolio assignments in teacher education need to have some degree of *authenticity*. According to Schaffer and Resnick (1999, p. 197), 'thick authenticity' means that it is personally meaningful, it relates to 'real life', it demands disciplinary thinking and self-reflection. We would add that such assignments need to be discussed and negotiated with students, and in cases where other partners are implicated (for instance, practice teachers), also with them (Vines, 2002). […] Because of the complexity of portfolio assignments aiming at tying together theory and practice, the groundwork for successful learning in all three phases is laid in the assignment. Both sites provide examples of authentic portfolio assignments, both involving cooperation with pupils and practice teachers and students at other university colleges.

Reflection and self-assessment as vital elements of professional identity building

We have argued that reflection and self-assessment are closely tied to the act of selecting texts or artefacts for the presentation portfolio (learning phase 2). […]

Reflection and self-assessment can be argued for from different theoretical perspectives. From a sociocultural viewpoint, these features of portfolio work are elements of students' identity building, and for future teachers, this is a particularly important aspect. Wenger (1998) underlines the close relationship between identity and practice. The way students participate in their communities of practice shape their identities as teachers, whether they are conscious of it or not. Reflection and self-assessment strengthen these identity-forming processes by making them explicit and we think it is vital that they are part of the portfolio work and also documented in the form of text. Whether or not reflective texts should be assessed, has been a controversial question. We advocate great caution here because identity issues are not well suited for grading. This does not mean, however, that criteria become irrelevant for reflective texts. Quality criteria are important for students in order to self-assess, but these criteria also need to be negotiated in order for students to make them their own. Wenger sees identity as emerging from 'negotiated experience of self (in terms of participation and reification)' (p. 150). The clue to enhancing the learning potential in reflection and self-assessment for teacher education students may rather lie in sharing them with trusted peers and teachers instead of in grading such texts.

From what we have seen in our two sites, teacher education portfolios have a potential for bringing a number of experiences and practices together for the students and thus play an important role in developing their identities as future teachers. Much of this potential is, however, still unused.

Student participation in summative assessment—an underrated learning potential?

From a theoretical understanding of portfolios as reification of practice, it does not make sense to let an assessor grade the portfolio as an isolated act. We will argue here for the students' participation in the summative assessment process, both in the form of the oral presentation, and by involving students more directly in self- and peer assessment. According to Wenger, participation and reification both require and enable each other: 'it takes our participation to produce, interpret and use reification; so there is no reification without participation. On the other hand, our participation requires interaction and thus generates shortcuts to coordinated meanings that reflect our enterprises and our takes on the world' (Wenger, 1998, p. 66). In our two sites, students have presented their portfolio for the assessment commission. [...] Students who have been interviewed about this summative assessment situation where they presented their portfolios said that they felt more in control than world be the case if they just handed in a portfolio for grading. They were also able to focus on the portfolio processes, not just the products. The dialogic interaction with the commission was yet another advantage. Students reported that the significance of such an exam did not stop with the grade, but that they used the feedback from the commission to reflect on their future as teachers (Wittek, 2002).

Involving students in self- and peer assessment as part of the formative portfolio assessment process is uncontroversial, but it is still not used systematically, nor are students trained for the task. Involving students in self- and peer assessment as part of summative assessment is controversial and not tried in Norway, but especially for prospective teachers it seems worthwhile to also participate in this way.

Concluding remarks

The core issue in the assessment discussion seems to be the relation between formative and summative assessment, and our experience is that discussion about changing the assessment system from traditional exams to a portfolio-based system is often reduced to the question of how to secure fairness and justice according to psychometric ways of thinking. Our model of analysis emphasizes collaborative and meta-reflective aspects, criteria development and self- and peer assessment. A stronger focus on these aspects involves a shift of focus from summative to formative assessment which seems fundamental for increasing the learning potential of portfolios, a perspective that we have aimed to legitimize through our theoretical perspective. In addition to this, we have also shown the learning potential in new summative assessment formats. Altogether, this implicates the hard process of shifting the locus of control and giving legitimate roles to the learners as equal members of the communities of practice (Wenger, 1998).

Changing the assessment system has more to do with learning in general than with assessment as an isolated phenomenon. Our analysis shows that the meta-reflective aspects are still underdeveloped and our two sites are themselves aware that further development in these areas is necessary in order to enhance student learning.

In Norway, we are now in a transition phase where cultures of learning and cultures of assessment are changing and live side by side in all educational institutions. It is therefore necessary to analyse what characterizes the cultural contexts in higher education, particularly what view of knowledge and learning the teachers adhere to. Traditional sit-down exams where student collaboration is banned, was the result of a view of knowledge as objective and transferable and individually based. It is therefore logical that reproduction of knowledge and not the production was foregrounded in this assessment culture. If portfolio assessment is introduced into a culture dominated by a traditional view of knowledge and learning, the outcome may either be an instrumentalization of portfolios or a change in the culture itself. Portfolios are a strong change agent, but there is always a danger that it will be used only to document knowledge reproduction. We will argue that this is the case if teaching goes on as before and the only difference is that students on an individual basis produce artefacts that are collected in a portfolio. In a traditional assessment culture, where the control aspect of evaluation is highlighted, there will be considerable resistance against making portfolios alone the basis of assessment. The compromise is often a combination with a traditional exam, where the latter accounts for most of the grade.

Teacher education must provide students with basic disciplinary knowledge and teaching skills that enable them to function well in their first job as teachers. It is impossible, however, to provide them with everything they need, and therefore one of the most important tasks of teacher education is to educate teachers with the ability to self-assess their own work, to discern for themselves what they need to learn and adopt adequate strategies of learning. In school contexts, this means among other things to be able to learn from their colleagues (peers) and be critical to established cultures at the same time. Maybe this is the ultimate goal of collaborative portfolio models? In that case, teacher education needs to be much more audacious in transferring responsibility and control to the students.

References

Bakhtin, M. M. (1986) *Speech genres and other late essays* (Austin, TX, University of Texas Press).

Bjørlykke, B. & Økland, N. (2002) Database som læringsrom, in: S. Ludvigsen & T. L. Hoel (eds) *Et utdanningssystem I endring* [Database as learning space] (Oslo, Cappelen Akademisk Forlag).

Bjørlykke, B. & Økland, N. (2003) *Database som læringsrom* 2 [Database as learning space 2] (Stord/Haugesund University College).

Black, I. et al. (eds) (1994) *New directions in portfolio assessment. Reflective practice, critical theory and large-scale scoring* (Portsmouth, NH, Boynton/Cook, Heinemann).

Brown, G., Bull, J. & Pendlebury, M. (1997) *Assessing student learning in higher education* (London, Routledge).

Brown, J. S. Collins, A. & Duguid, P. (1989) Situated cognition and the culture of learning, *Educational Researcher*, 18(1), 32–42.

Bruffee, K. (1993) *Collaborative learning: higher education, interdependence, and the authority of knowledge* (Baltimore, MD, John Hopkins University Press).

Dysthe, O. (1996a) The multivoiced classroom, *Written Communication*, 13, 385–425.

Dysthe, O. (ed.) (1996b) *Ulike perspektiv på læring og læringsforskning* [Different perspectives on learning and research on learning] (Oslo, Cappelen Akademisk Forlag).

Dysthe, O. (ed.) (2001) *Dialog, samspel og læring* [Dialogue, interaction and learning] (Oslo, Abstrakt Forlag).

Engelsen, K. S. (2002) Reflection and collective knowledge building structured through a database dialogue, paper presented at *NERA-congress*, Tallinn 7–9 March.

Engelsen, K. S. (2003) Mapper og IKT, in: O. Dysthe & K. S. Engelsen (eds) *Mapper som pedagogisk redskap Perspektiver og erfaringer* [Portfolios and ICT] (Oslo, Abstrakt Forlag).

Gipps, C. (1994) *Beyond testing. Towards a theory of educational assessment* (London, Falmer Press).

Greeno, J., Collins, A. & Resnick, L. (1996) Cognition and learning, in: D. Berliner & R. Calfee (eds) *Handbook of Educational Psychology* (New York, Macmillan), 15–46.

Hamp-Lyons, L. & Condon, W. (2000) *Assessing the portfolio: principles for practice, theory, research* (Cresskill, NJ, Hampton Press).

Klenowski, V. (2002) *Developing portfolios for learning and assessment. Processes and principles* (London, RoutledgeFalmer).

Lave, J. & Wenger, E. (1991) *Situated learning. Legitimate peripheral participation* (New York, Cambridge University Press).

McLaughlin, M. & Vogt, M. E. (1996) *Portfolios in teacher education* (Newark, DE, International Reading Association).

Otnes, H. (2002) Collective digital text development in teacher education. Hypertext and dialogism in digital portfolios, paper presented at *NERA-congress*, Tallinn 7–9 March.

Otnes, H. (2003) Arkivskuff eller læringsarena? Lærings og dokumentasjonssjangrer I digitale mapper [Archive or learning arena? Learning and documentary genres in digital portfolios], in: O. Dysthe & K. S. Engelsen (Eds) *Mapper som pedagogisk redskap Perspektiver og erfaringer* (Oslo, Abstrakt Forlag).

Paulson, F. L., Paulson, P. R. & Meyer, C. (1991) What makes a portfolio a portfolio? *Educational Leadership*, 48(5), 60–63.

Roschelle, J. & Berend, S. (1995) The construction of shared knowledge in collaborative problem solving, in: C. O'Malley (ed.) *Computer-supported collaborative learning* (Berlin, Springer Forlag), 69–97.

Salomon, G. (1995) What does the design of effective CSCL require and how do we study its effects? In: J. L. Schnase & E. L. Cunnius (eds) *CSCL 95. Computer support for collaborative learning* (Mahwah, NJ, Lawrence Erlbaum), 147–156.

Seegers, M., Dochy, F. & Cascallar, E. (2003) *Optimising new modes of assessment: in search of qualities and standards* (Dordrecht/Boston/London, Kluwer Academic Press).

Schaffer, D. W. & Resnick, M. (1999) 'Thick' authenticity: new media and authentic learning, *Journal of Interactive Learning Research*, 10(2), 195–215.

Säljö, R. (2000) *Lärande i praktiken. Et sociokulturelt perspektiv* [Learning in practice. A sociocultural perspective] (Stockholm, Prisma).

Topping, K. (2003) Self and peer assessment in school and university, in: M. Seegers, F. Dochy & E. Cascallar (eds) *Optimising new modes of assessment: in search of qualities and standards* (Dordrecht/Boston/London, Kluwer Academic Press).

Vines, A. (2002) *Mellom forstäingsbrot og visjon. Eit eksempel frå arbeidet med ei felles nettsta-doppgåve i lærarutdanninga* [Between communication breakdown and vision. An example from teacher education] (Bergen, Bergen University).

Vygotsky, L. S. (1986) *Thought and language* (Cambridge, MA, MIT Press).

Wenger, E. (1998) *Communities of practice. Learning, meaning, and identity* (Cambridge, Cambridge University Press).

Wertsch, J. V. (1998) *Mind as action* (Cambridge, MA, Harvard University Press).

Wittek, L. (2002) *Mapper som redskap for undervisning og læring. Delrapport ILS. En intervjuundersokelse fra våren 2002 (PLUTO 3)* [Portfolios as tools for teaching and learning. Report from ILS] (Oslo, Universitetet i Oslo).

Yancey, K. B. & Weiser, I. (Eds) (1997) *Situating portfolios: four perspectives* (Logan, UT, Utah State University Press).

Zeichner, K. & Wray, S. (2000) The teaching portfolio as a vehicle for student teacher development: what we know and what we need to know, paper presented at the annual meeting of the *American Educational Research Association*, New Orleans, LA, April.

8

Participationist Discourse on Mathematics Learning

Anna Sfard

[...]

These days, being explicit about what one means while claiming "the social nature of learning" seems a necessity. In spite of the omnipresence of the word "social" in the current literature – or perhaps just because of it! – there is much confusion about how this term should be understood when applied in conjunction with learning. To avoid undesirable connotations, I use a different terminology. Due to the metaphor for learning underlying the particular family of sociocultural discourses to be presented on the following pages, I call these discourses participationist. To bring the special features of the participationism in fuller relief, I present it against the contrasting background of the more traditional acquisitionist approach. The origins of participationism can, indeed, be traced to acquisitionists' unsuccessful attempts to deal with certain long-standing dilemmas about human thinking. After surveying some of these resilient puzzles and presenting basic participationist tenets, I show how the claim that participationism, if followed in a disciplined way, leads to the claim that human thinking originates in interpersonal communication. I finish with a few remarks on the consequences of participationism for theory and practice of mathematics education and demonstrate how it helps in dealing with some of the questions that acquisitionism left unanswered.

1. Acquisitionism and its dilemmas

The roots of acquisitionist discourse on learning, which is usually seen as originating in the work of Piaget, go in fact much deeper. The underlying metaphor of learning as an act of increasing individual possession – as an acquisition of entities such as concepts, knowledge, skills, mental schemas – comes to this scholarly discourse directly from everyday expressions, such as acquiring knowledge, forming concepts or constructing meaning. To get a sense of the impact of the metaphor of acquisition on one's interpretation of human mathematical activities, let me take a look at the following episode, featuring young children talking with grownups about numbers. The brief scene is the beginning of a series of conversations about numbers between my colleague Irit Lavi and two young girls: 4 year old Roni, Irit's daughter, and 4 year 7 months old Eynat, Roni's friend. The event took place in Roni's house.

From: Maasz, J. and Schloeglmann, W. (eds.) *New Mathematics Research and Practice* (Rotterdam, Netherlands: Sense Publishers, 2006). Reproduced by kind permission of the publisher.

Episode: Comparing boxes with marbles

Speaker	What is said	What is done
1. Mother	*I brought you two boxes.* Do you know what is there in the boxes?	*Puts two identical closed opaque boxes, A and B, on the carpet, next to the girls.*
2. Roni	Yes, marbles.	
3a. Mother	Right, there are marbles in the boxes.	
3b. Mother	I want you to tell me in which box there are more marbles.	*While saying this, points to the box A close to Eynat, then to box B.*
3c. Eynat		Points to box A, which is closer to her.
3d. Roni		*Points to box A*
4. Mother	In this one? How do you know?	*Points to box A*
5. Roni	Because this is the biggest than this one. It is the most.	*While saying "than this one" points to box B, which is close to her*
6. Mother	Eynat, how do you know?	
7. Eynat	Because... cause it is more huge than that.	*Repeats Roni's pointing movement to box B when saying "than that"*
8. Mother	Yes? This is more huge than that? Roni, what do you say?	Repeats Roni's pointing movement to box B when saying "than that"
9. Roni	That this is also more huge than this.	*Repeats Roni's pointing movement to box B when saying "than that"*
... ...	... ...	... ...
10a. Mother	*Do you want to open and discover? Let's open and see what there is inside. Take a look now.*	
10b. Roni		*Abruptly grabs box A, which is nearer to Eynat and which was previously chosen as the one with more marbles.*
11. Roni	*1.. 1.. 1.. 2, 3, 4, 5, 6, 7, 8.*	*Opens box A and counts properly.*
12. Eynat	1, 2, 3, 4, 5, 6.	*Opens box B and counts properly.*

13. Mother	So, what do you say?	
14. Roni	6.	
15. Mother	Six what? You say 6 what? What does it mean "six"? Explain.	
16. Roni	That this is too many.	
17. Mother	That this is too much? Eynat, what do you say?	
18. Eynat	That this too is a little.	
19. Mother	That it seems to you a little? Where do you think there are more marbles?	
20. Roni	I think here.	*Points on the box, which is now close to her (and in which she found 8 marbles)*
21. Mother	You think here? And what do you think, Eynat?	
22. Eynat	Also here.	

The episode is likely to leave the acquisitionist researcher unimpressed. The girls' mastery of counting would only confirm what she knows only too well from previous studies: 4 and 5 year old children are usually advanced enough in their "acquisition of the concept of number" to be able to count properly (for a summary of the relevant research, see e.g. Nunes & Bryant, 1996, Dehaene, 1997). Nor will the acquisitionist researcher be struck by the fact that in spite of their well developed counting skills, the girls did not bother to count the marbles or even to open the boxes when asked to compare these boxes' invisible contents. Extensive acquisitionist research on early numerical thinking, in which young children have been observed implementing different versions of Piagetian conservation tasks, has shown that at this age, this behaviour is quite normal: "Children who know how to count may not use counting to compare sets with respect to number" (Nunes & Bryant, 1996, p. 35).

And yet, knowing what children usually do not do is not enough to account for what they actually do. An unprejudiced observer, whose analysis is not biased by the sole interest in the girls' ability to "operate with number", is likely to ask questions to which the acquisitionist researcher may have no answers. Thus, the young interviewees' apparently arbitrary response to the question "Which box has more marbles?" cannot be accounted for simply by the reference to 'underdeveloped number schemes'. Similarly, the fact that the girls agreed in their surprising decisions does not seem to have much to do with insufficiency of their "conception of number". Finally, one should rather not count on acquisitionist explanation while wondering what made the children "justify" their choice in a seemingly adequate way in spite of the fact that they had no grounds for the comparative claims, such as "this is the biggest than this one", "It is the most" ([5]) and "it is more huge than that" ([7]). If there is little in the past research to help us account for this kind of phenomena, it is probably because the acquisitionists, while watching their interviewee, attended to nothing except for those actions which they classified in advance as relevant to their study. For them, the conversation that preceded opening the boxes would be dismissed as a mere 'noise'. The analysis of the remaining half of the event might even lead them to the claim that the girls had a satisfactory command over numerical comparisons, although this is not the vision that emerges when the second part of the episode is analyzed in the context of the first.

Probably the main reason for the shortcomings of acquisitionists' accounts is these researchers' belief in the invariability of learning processes across different contexts. In their research, they are tuned to cross-situational commonalities rather than differences. For them, individual minds are the principal source of their own development, whereas the task of the researcher is to discover the universal blueprint of the process. In result, acquisitionist discourse is ill equipped to deal not just with inter-personal and cross-situational differences, but also with those changes in human processes that transcend a single life span. Indeed, as long as human learning is seen as originating in the individual, and as long as this process is thought of as practically impermeable to other influences, notably those coming from interactions with other individuals, one has no means to account for the fact that human ways of doing, unlike those of other species, evolve over history. Within the confines of acquisitionist discourse, there is no cogent explanation for the fact that the outcomes of the ongoing transformations accumulate from generation to generation, constantly redefining the nature and extent of the individual growth.

2. Participationism and its solutions to acquisitionist dilemmas

Although usually traced back to the work Vygotsky and other founders of Activity Theory, participationism has, in fact, a more extensive genealogy. As a confluence of ideas coming from areas as diverse as philosophy, sociology, psychology, anthropology, linguistics, and more, this relatively new school of thought is a mélange of approaches rather than a single research discourse. Some of these approaches depart from acquisitionism only marginally, in that they merely add social considerations to the traditional individualist account. Lave (1993) speaks about 'cognition plus' whenever referring to the talk about the 'social' mounted on the top of an acquisitionist discourse. The basic claim that motivates the more radical form of participationism is that *patterned, collective forms of distinctly human forms of doing are developmentally prior to the activities of the individual.* Whereas acquisitionists view the individual development as proceeding from personal acquisitions to the participation in collective activities, strong particpationists reverse the picture and claim that people go from the participation in collectively implemented activities to similar forms of doing, but which they are now able to perform single-handedly. According to this vision, learning to speak, to solve a mathematical problem or to cook means a gradual transition from being able to take a part in collective implementation of a given type of task to becoming capable of implementing such tasks in their entirety and on one's own accord. Eventually, a person can perform on her own and in her unique way entire sequences of steps which, so far, she would only execute with others. The tendency for individualization – for turning patterned collective doings into activities for an individual – seems to be one of the hallmarks of humanness, and it is made possible by our capacity for overtaking the roles of others.

The difference between the acquistionist and the participationist versions of human development [...] manifests itself in how we understand the origins and the nature of human uniqueness. For acquisitionists, this uniqueness lies in the biological makeup of the individual. While participationism does not deny the need for special biological pre-requisites – such as, for example, the special voice cords and the ability to discern certain sounds, both of which are the basis for effective human communication – this approach views all the uniquely human capacities as resulting from the fundamental fact that humans are social beings, engaged in collective activities from the day they are born and throughout their lives. In other words, although human biological givens are what makes this collective form of life possible, it is the collective life that brings about all the other uniquely human characteristics, with the capacity for individualizing the collective – for individual reenactments of collective activities – being one of the most important. Human society emerges from the participationist account as a huge fractal-like entity, every part of which is a society in itself, indistinguishable in its inner structure from the whole.

Another notable change that happens in the transition from acquisitionist to participationist discourse is in the unit of analysis. It is this new unit which I had in mind while speaking, somewhat ambiguously, about "patterned collective doings". Other eligible candidates for the participationist unit of analysis are *form of life*, suggested by Wittgenstein (1953), and *activity*, the pivotal idea of the Activity Theory. The nowadays popular term *practice* is yet another viable option (see e.g. Wenger, 1998; Cobb, 2002). Although all these terms are used in the current literature in numerous ways, with the differences between one use and another not always easy to tell, each of them is good enough for my present purpose. Indeed, all I want, for now, is to describe participationist innovation according to those central characteristics which remain basically the same across different renderings. Whatever name and definition is given to the participationist unit of analysis and whatever claims about humans are formulated with its help, the strength of this unit is in the fact that it has both collective and individual 'editions'.

Armed with this flexible analytic focus, participationists have a chance to address the question of change that exceeds the boundaries of individual life. While speaking about human development, participationists do not mean a transformation in people, but rather in forms of human doing. This non-trivial discursive shift is highly consequential, as it removes the sharp acquisitionist distinction between development of an individual and the development of collective. The developmental transformations are the result of two complementary processes, that of *individualization of the collective* and that of *collectivization of the individual*. These two processes are dialectically interrelated and, as a consequence, both individual and collective forms of doing are in a constant flux, resulting from inevitable modifications that happen in these bi-directional transitions. [...]

3. Consequences of participationism for the discourse on mathematics thinking and learning

3.1 What is thinking?

[...] More than any other human activity, thinking appears biologically determined and growing 'from inside' the person. Still, participationist tenets speak forcefully against this deeply rooted conviction. The next thesis to explore is that interpersonal communication is the collective activity that morphs into thinking through the process of individualization.

A powerful, even if indirect, argument comes to mind immediately when one tries to substantiate this conjecture. The ability to think in the complex way people do is absent in other species – and so is the human highly developed ability to communicate. At a closer look, communication, like thinking, may be one of the most human of human activities. This is not to say that the ability to communicate is restricted to people. At least some animals do seem to engage in activities that one may wish to describe as communication. And yet, human communication is special, and not just because of its being mainly linguistic – the feature that, in animals, seems to be extremely rare, if not lacking altogether. It is the role communication plays in human life that seems unique. The ability to coordinate our activities by means of interpersonal communication is the basis for our being social creatures. Our very survival, not to speak about our distinctive forms of living, depends on our being always a part of a group. And since communication is the glue that holds human collectives together, even our ability to stay alive is a function of our communicational capacity. We communicate in order to ascertain the kind of mutuality and collective doing that provides us with what we need and cannot attain single-handedly. The list of human needs that would remain unsatisfied without interpersonal communication is long and multifarious, and it includes not just the most advanced and complex cultural needs, but also the most primitive biological ones, of the kind that most animals are able to take care of by themselves, with only marginal collaboration of other individuals. In the view of all this, it is not surprising that Leont'ev (1930), one of the founding fathers of participationism, declared the capacity for communication as the hallmark of humanness: "[W]e do not meet in the animal world any special forms of action having as their sole and special end the mastery of the behavior of other individuals by attracting their attention" (p. 59).

All this, as important as it may sound, is not yet enough to substantiate the claim that thinking could be defined as a form of communicating. In fact, the current discourses go directly against this vision when they present these two basic human activities as separate, even if tightly connected. This, indeed, is how thinking and communicating are pictured in colloquial forms of talk, through expressions such as 'communicating one's thoughts' or 'putting thoughts in words'. Our speaking about thoughts as being conveyed (or expressed) in the act of communication implies two distinct processes, that of thinking and that of communicating, with the former slightly preceding the latter and constantly feeding into it. According to this vision, the outcomes of thinking, pictured as entities in their own right, are supposed to preserve their identity while being "put in other words" or "expressed somehow differently".

Whereas acquistionists have been working with this dualist vision of human cognition for centuries, participationists are likely to view the idea of "thought-conveyed-in-communication" as but a direct result of an unhelpful objectification. With Wittgenstein (1953), they believe that "Thought is not an incorporeal process which lends life and sense to speaking, and which it would be possible to detach from speaking" (p. 108). Having accepted this claim, one can also see that it remains in force when the somewhat limiting word speaking is replaced with the more general term communicating. Consequently, thinking stops being a self-sustained process separate from and, in a sense, primary to any act of communication, and becomes an act of communication in itself, although not necessarily interpersonal. All this justifies the claim that thinking may be usefully defined as the individualized form of the activity of communicating, that is, one's communication with oneself. Of course, this self-communication does not have to be in any way audible or visible, and does not have to be in words. In the proposed discourse on thinking, cognitive processes and processes of interpersonal communicating are thus but different manifestations of basically the same phenomenon. To stress this fact, I propose to combine the terms cognitive and communicational into the new adjective commognitive. The etymology of this last word will always remind us that whatever is said with its help refers to these phenomena which are traditionally included in the term cognition, as well as to those usually associated with interpersonal exchanges.

To complete the task of defining thinking as an individualized form of communication, I need yet to explain how this latter term should be understood in the present context. Since the patterned nature of communication is due to the fact that different people act in similar ways, communication needs to be considered as a collective activity, and should thus be described in terms of its global patterns. Restricting the field of vision to a single node, or to single pair of 'sender' and 'recipient', as is done in the majority of known definitions, would be as unproductive as trying to understand the rules of chess from the individual moves of one checker. The following formulation seems to fulfill this requirement: Communication is a collectively-performed, rules-driven activity that mediates and coordinates other activities of the collective. More specifically, individuals who participate in the activity of communicating perform actions that are customarily followed by a certain type of re-action of other individuals. The re-actions may be either practical actions or other communicational moves. By practical actions, I mean actions resulting in a change in the physical environment. Opening a window or adding a brick to a wall while building a house are good examples of practical actions. Communicational actions are those that affect members of the community and have no direct impact on the environment, although some of them may, in the end, lead to another person's practical (re)action. In human activities, communicational and practical actions are usually simultaneously present and inextricably interwoven. Clearly, communication is what enables the inter-person coordination needed for the collective implementation of complex practically-oriented activities, from preparing foods and garments to building houses, publishing newspapers, producing films, transporting goods, etc. This said, let me add that it is also typical of humans to have long chains of purely communicational interactions, in which every re-action is, in itself, a communicational action bound to entail yet another communicational re-action. In this process, the participants alternate between the roles of actors and re-actors, often playing both these parts in one communicational move.

Let me finish this introduction to the participationist discourse on thinking with a number of remarks. First, the definition of communication speaks about rules that regulate communication (and thus the commognition in general). It is important to stress that these rules are to be understood as observer's constructs, and not as guiding principles, followed by individual actors in a conscious, deliberate way. Another fact to remember is that the rules of commognition, are not in any sense "natural" or necessary, as nothing "in the world" can possibly necessitate the given types of associations between actions and re-action. The source of the patterns is in historically established customs. This contingent nature of communicational patterns is probably the reason why Wittgenstein (1953) decided to speak about communication as a kind of game. Second, because of its being rules-driven, commongnition has dynamics of its own, and it would not be possible without the natural human tendency for alignment. This said, it is equally important to note that in commognition, like in any other historically established activity, human players do have agency. Communicative action almost never determines a re-action. More often than not, both action and re-action are a matter of construction, to be performed according to rules that constrain but do not dictate. Third, whereas practical actions are direct actions on objects, commognitive actions are about objects, that is, they focus interlocutors' attention on an object. Fourth, commognitional actions are performed with the help of mediators, which can have auditory, visual or even tactile effects on individuals. In humans, language, which has both vocal and visual editions (as in the case of written exchanges) is the principal, although not the only, form of commognitive mediator.

Finally, just as there is a multitude of games, played with diverse tools and according to diverse rules, so there are many types of commognition, differing one from another in their patterns, objects, and the types of mediators used. Like in the case of games, individuals may be able to participate in certain types of communicational activity and be unable to take part in some others. The different types of communication that bring some people together while excluding some others will be called discourses. Given this definition, any human society may be divided into partially overlapping communities of discourses. To be members of the same discourse community, individuals do not have to face one another and do not need to actually communicate. The membership in the wider community of discourse is won through participation in communicational activities of any collective that practices this discourse, be this collective as small as it may.

3.2 What is mathematics?

Given the participationist vision of thinking as a form of communication, mathematics can be seen as a special type of discourse, made distinct, among others, by its objects, mediators and rules. Let me be more specific.

A discourse counts as mathematical if it features mathematical words, such as those related to quantities and shapes. The conversation between Roni, Eynat and Roni's mother, presented in the beginning of this chapter, is replete with such mathematical terms as number-words and comparison-words (e.g. more, bigger), and can thus count as a case of mathematical discourse. This, however, is just one out of several possible types of mathematical communication. While many number-related words may appear in non-specialized, colloquial discourses, mathematical discourses as practiced in schools or in academia dictate their own, more disciplined uses of these words. As will be argued below, neither Roni nor Eynat is using any of the mathematical words the way they are used by mathematically versed interlocutors (and I do not mean just the grammatical imperfections of the girls' talk).

Visual mediators used in mathematical discourses tend to be quite unlike those used in many other types of discourses. While colloquial discourses are usually mediated by images of material things, that is, by concrete objects that are identified or pointed to with nouns or pronouns and that may be either actually seen or just imagined, mathematical discourses often involve symbolic artifacts, created specially for the sake of this particular form of communication. Such symbolic mediation, however, is still absent from the incipient numerical talk of our young interviewees. Quite understandably, the only form of visual mediation that can be found in our data is concrete rather than symbolic: The mathematical task performed by the girls is described in terms of sets of marbles provided by Roni's mother, and is visually (and tangibly) mediated by these sets.

Endorsed narratives are sets of propositions that are accepted and labeled as true by the given community. Mathematical narratives, to be endorsed, have to be constructed and substantiated according to a set of well-defined rules, specific to this discourse. In the case of scholarly mathematical discourse, these endorsed narratives are known as mathematical theories, and this includes such discursive constructs as definitions, proofs, and theorems. In addition to the generally endorsed "abstract" narratives such as those listed above, one can speak about more specific narratives that pertain to concrete objects and may be endorsed in a given situation. The aim of Roni and Eynat's activity, at least in the eyes of the grownups, is to create such locally endorsable narratives: The girls are supposed to explore the boxes with marbles and to come up with endorsable statements that answer the mother's question "Which of the boxes has more marbles"?

Routines are well-defined repetitive patterns characteristic of a given discourse. Specifically mathematical regularities can be noticed whether one is watching the use of mathematical words and mediators or follows the process of creating and substantiating narratives about number. In fact, such repetitive patterns can be seen in almost any aspect of mathematical discourses: in mathematical forms of categorizing, in mathematical modes of attending to the environment, in the ways of viewing situations as "the same" or different, which is crucial for the interlocutors' ability to apply mathematical discourse whenever appropriate; and in production of narratives and their further substantiation. Routines may be algorithmic, and thus deterministic, or just constraining. The canonic routine of numerical comparison, which, in our example, the mother expects her daughter to perform, is an example of algorithmic routine.

3.3 What is mathematics learning?

Learning mathematics may now be defined as individualizing mathematical discourse, that is, as the process of becoming able to have mathematical communication not only with others, but also with oneself. Through the process of individualization, the personal creativity of the learner comes in.

Let me now go back to the comparing sets of marbles episode and see whether this definition helps to make a better sense of children's actions. It is now natural to assume that the observed phenomena are related to the fact that the children have not yet individualized the numerical discourse – they did not yet turn this form of talk into a discourse for themselves. Indeed, there are many signs showing that the girls are probably at the very beginning of the process. The first evidence can be found in the fact that the girls do not use the compare-by-counting procedure on their own accord: The question "[I]n which of the boxes [are there] more marbles?" ([3b]) is clearly not enough to get them started, and nothing less than a clear hint by the mother ("Do you want to open and discover?", [10a]) would help. Further, the children need mother's scaffolding in order to perform the procedure in its entirety (note, for example, that they stop after having counted the marbles and they need to be prompted in order to draw the conclusion; see the mother's question [15]). It is thus clear that if the girls participate in the numerical discourse, it is on other people's accord and according to other people's rules. This can be summarized in the following way: What for the grownups is the routine of exploration, geared toward enhancement of one's arsenal of "factual knowledge" (endorsed narratives), for the children is a ritual – a game played with others for the sake of the togetherness that game playing affords. Note that touching the marbles one by one while also pronouncing subsequent number words is not unlike incantation of meaningless rhymes which is often a part of children's play. What is now but a ritual, will turn into exploration in the course of individualization.

The fact that the girls' participation in the numerical discourse is ritualized and undertaken for the sake of connecting with others becomes even more evident when children's actions in the second part of the episode are compared with what they do in the first. When the conversation begins, the girls spontaneously respond to the mother's query with pointing to one of the identical boxes. Evidently, the question "[I]n which of the boxes [are there] more marbles?" when first asked, is not received as a prompt for a conversation on numbers but rather as an invitation to what the children usually do on their own accord and willingly: to choosing one of the boxes for themselves. Making choices, unlike numerical comparisons, is the kind of activity which the girls have already individualized. It will yet take time until the two types of routines – those of choosing and those of comparing – combine one with the other into an individual activity of the child.

It is reasonable to assume that a certain proficiency in a discourse is a prerequisite for its individualization. Roni and Eynat do not yet exhibit sufficient fluency in numerical talk. For example, they have yet to change their use of number words. Right now, these words are for them but a part and parcel of counting. In the future, the words will be used in many different types of sentences and in multiple roles, as adjectives and as nouns, among others. Above all, the use of these words will become objectified: more often than not, expressions such as one, two or two hundred will be used as if they referred to self-sustained, extra-discursive entities. Similarly, the children's use of connectives such as because will change dramatically. Right now, this use is clearly ritualized: if the girls answer mother's why questions in a seemingly rational way (see Roni's utterance [5] and Eynat's utterance [7], which both begin with the word because), it is obviously due not to their awareness of the relations between boxes but to their familiarity with the form of talk which is expected by the grownups in response to this kind of question. At this point, the girls are already aware of how to talk when answering a request for explanation, but are not yet fully aware of when – under which circumstances – it is appropriate to apply them. At this point, the mere appearance of the word why in the interlocutor's question may be enough to prompt an utterance that begins with because and then simply repeats, in a somewhat modified form, what the question was asking about. It seems reasonable to conjecture that in the process of individualization, the awareness of how discursive routine should be performed usually precedes the ability to tell when such performance would be appropriate. One may even hypothesize that it is the ability to make independent decisions about when to apply a given discursive procedure which is the ultimate sign of its individualization.

The manner in which all these changes in the girls' numerical discourse are supposed to happen is implicated in the very claim that learning mathematics is the process of individualization of mathematical discourse: discursive change can only originate in communicating with experienced interlocutors. This vision is quite different from the one professed by the acquisitionist who assumes, if often only tacitly, that learning results from the learner's attempts to adjust her understanding to the externally given, mind independent reality. Contradicting the participationist belief in the primacy of the collective, this latter version implies that learning, at least in theory, could take place without participation of other people.

Not every mathematical conversation is an opportunity for learning. For a discursive change to occur, there must be some discrepancy – a communicational conflict – between interlocutors. Such conflict arises whenever different participants seem to be acting according to differing discursive rules. The difference may express itself in a disparity in the interlocutor's uses of words, in the manner they look at visual mediators or in the ways they match discursive procedures with problems and situations. More often than not, these differences find their explicit, most salient expression in the fact that the different participants endorse differing, possibly contradicting, narratives. The dissimilarities between Roni and Eynat's numerical discourse and the numerical discourse of the grownups express themselves in different uses of words and disparate routines, and thus constitute a good example of communicational conflict, likely to result in considerable learning.

In order to fully individualize numerical discourse Roni and Eynat will have to overcome this conflict. This is not going to be easy. If the child is to ever use the numerical discourse in solving her own problems, she must be aware of the advantages of the relevant discursive procedures. For example, she needs to realize that she may benefit from choosing according to number. And yet, in order to become aware of these advantages, she has to already use the numerical discourse. The process is thus inherently circular. The next question to ask is what can possibly motivate the child to engage in the demanding task of overcoming the circularity.

3.4 Why do we learn mathematics?

The circularity implies that learning mathematics requires readiness to engage in the new discourse even before one can see its problem-solving potential and inner logic. In other words, the child needs to be prepared to participate in the numerical discourse in a ritualized way before she is able to practice the discourse while engaging in self-initiated explorations. The child's motivation for such ritualized action is its immediate social reward: Roni and Eynat perform the ritual as an act of solidarity with the grownups and in the attempt to win their approval. Giving the answer that is expected by the interlocutor may be read as an act of pledging allegiance.

More generally, when the child first engages in mathematics learning, it is because of her overpowering need for communication, which grows out of the even more fundamental need for social acceptance. This social concern can clearly be seen all along the conversations with the girls. The way Roni monitors her mother's face, talks to her and follows her lead clearly indicates that getting the parent's attention and approval is the girl's main concern. This wish competes, and is successfully combined, with an equally strong need to belong with the peer. While making their choices, Roni and Eynat are careful to stress that their decisions are shared (in the further parts of our transcripts, this need for solidarity with the friend is further evidenced by Roni's repetitive use of the word we, through which she asserts the joint ownership of solutions.)

To sum up, the children have different goals than those envisioned by the grownups. While counting and comparing, the girls are in fact preoccupied with the delicate social fabric of their little group, and the conversation on boxes with marbles is, for them, as good an occasion for inter-personal engineering as any other. While grownups count in order to get closer to the truth about the world, the children count to get closer to the grownups. The "exploratory" activities of the young participants are therefore a form of community-building ritual.

4. Consequences of participationism for the practice of mathematics teaching and learning

Our ability to make sense of what we see depends on our uses of words. As illustrated above, the interpretation of the notion "social" that gave rise to the commognitive framework made a significant difference in our vision of learning and in this vision's theoretical entailments. In particular, it allowed to account for phenomena that escaped acquisitionists' explanations and it offered alternative explanations for some others. Thus, for example, what acquisitionists interpreted as showing children's unawareness of the "conservation of number" became, in our interpretation, the result of the simple fact that in the situation of choice, young learners had no reason to privilege the ritual of counting over other routines that they had already at their disposal.

Perhaps the most dramatic difference between the acquisitionists' and participationists' visions of mathematical thinking is in their respective messages about the origins of mathematical learning. Whereas acquisitionists view learning as resulting from the learners' direct efforts to arrive at a coherent vision of the world, participationists see learning as arising mainly from one's attempt to make sense of other people's vision of this world. The former perspective implies that learning, at least in theory, could take place without participation of other people. In contrast, the idea of mathematics as a form of discourse entails that individual learning originates in communication with others and is driven by the need to adjust one's discursive ways to those of other people.

Participationism also provokes second thoughts about some common pedagogical beliefs. For instance, it casts doubt on the current call for "learning with understanding," at least insofar as this call is interpreted as the exhortation to never let the student practice routines which she cannot properly substantiate. According to the present analysis, students' persistent participation in mathematical talk when this kind of communication is for them but a discourse-for-others seems to be an inevitable stage in learning mathematics. If learning is to succeed, all the interlocutors must agree to live with the fact that the new discourse will initially be seen by the newcomers as a game to be played with others, and that it will be practiced only because of its being a discourse that others use and appreciate. It is thus now time to rehabilitate the learning that is based on ritualized action and on thoughtful imitation of the grownups' ways with words. Trying to figure out and then to meet the expert participants' expectations is sometimes the only way to initiate the long process of individualization of discourses. Making sense of another person's thinking is not any less demanding (or respectable!) than the direct attempts to understand reality. Indeed, entering "foreign" forms of talk (and thus of thought) requires a genuine interest and a measure of creativity. To turn the discourse-for-others into a discourse-for-oneself, the student must explore other people's reasons for engaging in this discourse.

[…]

References

Cobb, P. (2002). Reasoning with tools and inscriptions. *Journal of the Learning Sciences, 11*, 187–216.

Dehaene, S. (1997). *The number sense: How the mind creates mathematics*. Oxford, UK: Oxford University Press.

Lave, J. (1993). Situating learning in communities of practice. In L. B. Resnick, J. M. Levine, & S. D. Teasley (eds.), *Perspectives on socially shared cognition*. Washington, DC: American Psychological Association, 17–36.

Leont'ev, A. N. (1930). Studies in the cultural development of the child. II. The development of voluntary attention in the child. *Journal of Genetic Psychology, 37*, 52–81.

Nunes, T. and Bryant, P. (1996) *Children doing mathematics (understanding children's worlds)*. Oxford: Blackwell.

Wenger, E. (1998). *Communities of practice*. New York: Cambridge University Press.
Wittgenstein, L. (1953). *Philosophical investigations*. Oxford: Blackwell.

Bibliography

Bakhtin, M. (1981). *The dialogic imagination*. Austin, TX: University of Texas Press.

Bauersfeld, H. (1995). "Language games" in mathematics classroom: Their function and their effects. In P. Cobb & H. Bauersfeld (eds.), *The emergence of mathematical meaning: Interaction in classroom cultures*. Hillsdale, NJ: Lawrence Erlbaum Associates, 271–292.

Blumer, H. (1969). *Symbolic interactionism: Perspective and method*. Englewood Cliffs, NJ: Prentice-Hall.

Cobb, P. & Bauersfeld, H. (eds.) (1995). *Emergence of mathematical meaning: Interaction in class-room cultures*. Hillsdale, NJ: Lawrence Erlbaum Associates, 25–129.

Cobb, P., Wood, T. & Yackel, E. (1993). Discourse, mathematical thinking, and classroom practice. In E. Forman, N. Minick, & A. Stone (eds.), *Contexts for learning: Sociocultural dynamics in children's development*. New York: Oxford University Press, 91–119.

Edwards, D. (1997). *Discourse and cognition*. London: Sage.

Engeström, Y. (1987). *Learning by expanding: An activity-theoretical approach to developmental research*. Helsinki: Orienta-Konsultit.

Ernest, P. (1993). Conversation as a metaphor for mathematics and learning. *Proceedings of the Day Conference*. Manchester, UK: Manchester Metropolitan University, 58–63.

Ernest, P. (1994). The dialogical nature of mathematics. In P. Ernest (eds.), *Mathematics, education and philosophy: An international perspective*. London: The Falmer Press, 33–48.

Garfinkel, H. (1967). *Studies in ethnomethodology*. Englewood Cliffs, NJ: Prentice-Hall.

Goffman, E. (1958). *The presentation of self in everyday life*. Edinburgh: University of Edinburgh, Social Sciences Research Centre.

Greeno, J. G. (1997). On claims that answer the wrong question. *Educational Researcher, 26* (1), 5–17.

Harré, R. & Gillett, G. (1995). *The discursive mind*. Thousand Oaks, CA: Sage.

Holquist, M. (1990). *Dialogism. Bakhtin and his world*. London: Routledge.

Krummheuer, G. (1995). The ethnography of argumentation. In Cobb, P. & Bauersfeld, H. (eds.), *The emergence of mathematical meaning. Interactions in classroom culture*. Hillsdale, New Jersey: Erlbaum, 229–269.

Lave, J. (1988). *Cognition in practice*. Cambridge: Cambridge University Press.

Lave, J. & Wenger, E. (1991). *Situated learning: Legitimate peripheral participation*. Cambridge: Cambridge University Press.

Leont'ev, A. N. (1947/1981). *Problems of the development of mind*. Moscow: Progress Press.

Marková, I. (2003). *Dialogicality and social representations: The dynamics of mind*. Cambridge, UK: Cambridge University Press.

Nardi, B. C ed., (1996). *Context and consciousness: Activity theory and human-computer interaction*. Cambridge, MA: MIT Press.

Schutz, A. (1967). *Collected papers: The problem of social reality*. Hague, Netherlands: Martinus Nijhoff.

Sfard, A. & Lavie, I. (2005). Why cannot children see as the same what grownups cannot see as different? – early numerical thinking revisited. *Cognition and Instruction, 23* (2), 237–309.

Voigt, J. (1985). Patterns and routines in classroom interaction. *Recherches en Didaclique des Mathematiques, 6* (1), 69–118.

Vygotsky, L. S. (1987). Thought and speech. In Rieber, R. W. & Carton, A. S., *The collected works of L. S. Vygotsky*, Vol. 1. New York: Plenum Press.

Section 3

Identities, Agency and Learning

9

Literacies and Masculinities in the Life of a Young Working-Class Boy

Deborah Hicks

[…]

This narrative history of the life of one young reader draws on my three-year research study of two children growing up in blue-collar, or working-class families and attending a local public primary school. Between kindergarten and the beginning months of third grade, I observed and documented the home and school learning experiences of Laurie and Jake, recording their work and play in classrooms and spending time with them in the context of their family lives. That work drew on my own childhood experiences growing up in a white, working-class family, though in a very different time and place. My research purposes were to document children's negotiation of cultural and textual spaces between home and school as they participated in two different cultural settings. My interpretive lens is focused in this chapter on Jake, in particular on the complex ways in which he negotiated gendered identities and textual practices as he moved through primary school. As I compose Jake's history as a young reader, I reflect on how the social practices and relationships he experienced at home were brought to bear on the task of becoming a reader in school. My history of Jake's classroom learning moves between home and school as I construct a narrative that details the complex particulars of his values, feelings, and practices in a social context. My home visits with Jake as well as regular classroom observations of him in grades K–2 are threaded into Jake's story.

[…]

Kindergarten apprenticeships

An image from Jake's kindergarten year: he is working at the puzzles center, putting together an overlay of "Fireman Dan" (i.e., putting the fireman clothes and paraphernalia on Fireman Dan). While he is working, Jake begins to tell a fantasy story involving Fireman Dan, and he includes me in the story. I ask him if he wants to draw a picture of the story. He shakes his head as if saying, "Of course not." About two months later, I am again observing Jake at the puzzles center. This time he is putting together a puzzle, something he has often chosen during center times. Some of the other children working at the table have been drawing pictures. I ask Jake if he would like to draw something. He responds, "There's nothing to draw for me."

In many respects, kindergarten was a resounding success for Jake in terms of his response to formal schooling. Because of the open-ended nature of many kindergarten social and academic practices, Jake was able to construct his own points of connection with school. He engaged with classroom practices during kindergarten in ways that mirrored his modes of learning at home. Jake moved freely and independently between centers, "roaming" as his teacher, Ms. Thompson, described it in our summary review of his kindergarten year. He very often chose tasks involving three-dimensional objects, seemingly preferring practices that involved building things or putting together puzzles and, less frequently, choosing tasks involving drawing, painting, or writing. In general, Jake created forms of textuality that involved manipulative *doing*. He worked for long periods of time at centers that involved building vehicles or working with objects. For much of his kindergarten year, Jake resisted activities that involved two-dimensional texts: reading or pretend reading; writing, drawing, and dictating stories; performing symbolic tasks that involved numeracy. His early response to textual practices like book reading, drawing, or writing seemed to be one of disinterest or "tuning out." During whole-class, shared readings, for instance, Jake often sat in the back of the rug area, not participating verbally in the choral book reading. Defining himself as an independent agent within the social spaces of the classroom, Jake could become passionately engaged in activities that were of interest to *him*. Instructional efforts to nudge him toward school-like practices were, however, often met with the firm "no way" kind of response that I encountered at the puzzles center. As Ms. Thompson commented about Jake's engagement in academic practices, "He's always on task; it just might not be your task."

Part of my objective in writing Jake's history in kindergarten is to uncover the threads of love and identification that he experienced as a young boy that shaped how he responded to classroom literacies. Jake's response to textual practices in his earliest weeks and months in school was a reflection of his home relationships and values. […]

Love and independence

Some images from early home visits with Jake and his family evoke the loving acceptance and expectations for independence that shaped Jake's early learning experiences. On a chilly winter day, Jake had gone out back to show me how he could hit plastic softballs (he could hit them all the way into neighbors' yards). Lea Ann, his younger sister, was playing on the wooden swingset that happened to be within range of Jake's flying softballs. I voiced concern about her getting hit, but Jake's father, standing nearby, assured me, "Don't worry, she's really tough." On a later visit in the fall of Jake's first-grade school year, Jake was learning how to play umpire in a batting session with his father and some neighborhood children. He insisted on standing right behind a girl batting, in part because he wanted to bat himself. Warning Jake in a no-nonsense tone that he had to stand back, Jake's father added gruffly, "He's gonna find out himself."

Relationships and activities within Jake's close and extended family are fluid and shifting; social spaces in this home are therefore typically buzzing with ongoing talk and activity. One of Jake's two grandmothers or a visiting cousin might be sitting in the family living room watching TV or chatting with his mother as Jake and his sister (and later a baby brother) move freely from one self-chosen activity to the next. Amid these fluid social relationships, the task of caring for Jake during his early years in school was distributed among family members. Jake spent the night at his grandparents' home during kindergarten, so he could sleep a little later in the morning (he attended the afternoon kindergarten program). Jake and Lea Ann (often called Lea) were the recipients of frequent attention from their mother, maternal grandmother, and other family members who shared their home. These close family relationships provided strong support for Jake's learning experiences at home. However, neither Jake nor Lea Ann were necessarily treated as young "students" in need of explicit direction and constant protection. Jake's mother voiced her family's philosophy of teaching and learning this way: children need to learn from their mistakes, to learn for themselves. Minor bumps and mishaps along the way were an accepted part of how Jake and his younger sister learned through participation and *doing* within their family.

The ways in which Jake and Lea participated as members of this extended family reflected their differences in age (Lea being about three years younger than Jake) and gender. Both Jake and Lea were treated as independents who could figure out things for themselves, given a reasonable degree of support within the family. Each received open expressions of love and affection from extended family members. However, their identities as learners and family members reflected the ways in which gendered relations were lived in their home. Lea's bedroom was painted in pink pastel colors and outfitted with a toy stove, replica kitchenware and china, and baby dolls. For Halloween, during Jake's second-grade school year, Lea dressed up as a fairy. Modeling her new Trick-or-Treating outfit for a video camera (I sometimes filmed the children during home visits), Lea was reminded by her "mom-mom" (her maternal grandmother) of how beautiful she was. That same Halloween, Jake had dressed up as a NASCAR driver, wearing the yellow and red "Kellogg's" racing colors worn by his personal favorite racing celebrity, Terry Labonte.

Growing up as a boy amid this close and extended family, Jake was drawn to the values and passions lived by his father, a no-nonsense or "direct" (as Jake's mother teasingly noted) man. Jake's father was a self-taught man—a ninth-grade dropout who had subsequently taught himself (through reading and apprenticeships) the professions of carpentry and mechanical contracting. He was a gifted carpenter whose craftsmanship astonished me during early home visits. His backyard workshed seemed the workspace of an artisan. Its walls were intricately lined with tools and wood materials, and a large powersaw was placed in the middle. Jake also had a powersaw, and he sometimes worked alongside his father, cutting small pieces of wood or painting objects his father had made. Jake demonstrated the use of his powersaw to me during my first "tour" of this amazing carpentry workshed. I watched (at first horror-struck) as he struck his finger in the vibrating needle that would cut wood but not small fingers. His own workspace in the shed was set up so that he could work alongside his father. However, in no sense was this required of him. Jake chose this activity as one of many forms of participation he embraced, and was one of many expressions of identification with his father's values and interests.

Jake also joined his father in a family (but especially male) passion for car racing and collecting small replica racing cars. In his parents' room was his father's extraordinary collection of miniature racing cars, each displayed with a picture of the car's driver. Hung in Jake's bedroom was an emerging collection of race car miniatures. As early as his kindergarten year, Jake could identify each NASCAR vehicle and its driver, "reading" details such as racing colors and insignia, car configurations, and print. He was, as a young boy, strongly immersed in the stories and practices that were lived by his father and seen by the women in his family as being aspects of identities Jake shared with his father.

At home, Jake "roamed" (to use Ms. Thompson's phrasing) between activities that met his particular interests and goals. Jake was nearly constantly in motion, sitting down only to perform a task (like cutting a piece of wood on his child-safe powersaw), then moving right on to the next activity. Jake was more than capable of sustaining a passionate interest in a particular project or activity. His love for NASCAR racing and his emerging interest in joining his father in constructive jobs are things that could sustain him for long stretches of time, engaging his imagination and intellect. Jake's energy and his movement between activities did not preclude his doing more reflective activities like reading (Jake often listened to books read by his mom-mom), painting wooden objects made by his father in the workshed, or figuring out the particulars of how something worked (Jake sometimes joined his father on certain tasks around the house and even on some mechanical contracting jobs outside the home). Sustained interest in an activity, however, required that the task make sense to Jake. A task had to be something that needed to be done. Otherwise, as Jake would later say about some academic tasks, it was just plain "stupid."

A scene from a first-grade home visit: Jake's mother and his mom-mom are sitting with me in the family living room, having a chat about Jake and his responses to school. Jake's maternal grandmother tells the story of how Jake's dad educated himself, after dropping out of high school, through reading manuals and then practicing his crafts. He could have gone into any number of professions, she noted; he was gifted in a number of arenas. Jake too was a gifted learner, she added as our conversation went on. After I asked what she thought Jake would do later in life, she commented that Jake would be his own person. Jake would probably end up doing not one thing, but different things. She noted how quickly Jake picked up knowledge and expertise at home—things like helping put together the family swimming pool. These words about Jake echoed themes from his father's life story: independence, giftedness as a learner, reluctance to box himself into one single profession or passion. These family stories of father and son were threads of the male identities and values he was later to bring to first- and second-grade literacy practices.

Embodied fictions versus school textualities

All during his kindergarten year, Jake had not one but two imaginary dogs: Max 1 and Max 2. He was very able to distinguish the Maxes from one another when asked which was present at a particular time. Out on the playground, Jake would throw one of his dogs a ball, follow the trajectory of the ball with his eyes, and then run at full speed if Max tried to run away with the ball himself. It turns out, as Jakes's mother explained to me one day, that Max 1 was a fictional representation of the real "Max," a beagle who belonged to Jake's teenage cousin. The real Max would sometimes come along when Jake's cousin visited, and all the children present would pursue Max as he outran them easily. Max 2 was completely fictional—this seemed to be Jake's own dog, something for which he longed. In second grade, Jake composed in his Writer's Notebook a story that reflected his desires to have his own Max:

> Today i myt [might] get a Dog. a Begt [Beagle]
> i am name [naming] hem max
> because my
> cosint [cousin] haves a Dog so i want a
> Dog i am going to the Farmrs
> makit [market] to get my Dog today
> and wan [when] i came

home i will thaek [take]
ham [him] for a wak [walk]
(Jake's Writer's Notebook entry, second grade)

During kindergarten, Jake's "Max" fantasies were enacted or performed on the playground and at home. His entire body expressed the narrative as he demonstrated, sometimes at the request of an adult, how Max (1 or 2) could perform tricks for his owner.

As a boy growing up, Jake's fictional worlds seemed largely constructed around physically enacted texts, texts that involved a high degree of movement and that often involved media forms. A special passion of his was Sega video games. He had acquired a Sega video player in kindergarten (for Christmas), and Sega action games like the Lion King, car racing games, Sonic the Hedgehog, and football games were clearly textual forms that Jake valued highly. During my home visits, he demonstrated his command of various Sega games, his whole body becoming engaged in the physical action as he manipulated the Sega controls and tried to avert the disasters that loomed for characters like Sonic the Hedgehog. My field-note descriptions from one such set of observations in the fall of Jake's first-grade year evoke the forms of textual enactment that Jake practiced at home with his Sega games:

> As soon as we entered Jake's room, he insisted on showing me a sample of his current collection of Sega video games. The first video game he inserted into the Sega player was a football game. Jake was able to choose which teams to set against one another, and he clicked on the 49ers versus the Dolphins. I was not able to follow all the rapid movements of his choices on the controls; he used the controls to decide tackles and other movements. During the Sega football game, Jake was extremely physically active. His verbalizations ("I tagged him," "I pushed him down") were uttered in the voice of one actually engaged in the game itself. Jake seemed to be on the field with the football players, his whole body moving with each hit. After Jake had played through a few football tackles, he switched to a race car video. In this Sega video game, the action occurred from the point of view of someone inside a car. The video game was constructed as if the player were inside the car, looking out the very rapidly passing landscape. At various key points in the "race," there would be an obstacle to avoid in order not to crash. Rather than what I would picture as a race track, the course was set in a landscape area—with hills, trees, etc. Jake was once again completely physically engaged in his enactment or performance of the video game. He used body movements and loud sound effects to perform the movement of the race car. He was the driver of the car, maneuvering it through the dangers of the race course. At one point, a slightly older visiting cousin, Cheryl, commented that Jake was always loud. A very physically engaged and vocal player was certainly on view during these Sega games.

Gilbert and Gilbert (1998) argue that such electronic and video game cultures are typically linked to discourses of masculinity. Video games like the ones played by Jake are marketed for young boys to play, and boys find the games exciting and fun. Boys get to experience "playing the body" (Gilbert & Gilbert, 1998, p. 78) as a means of practicing the masculinities that they will perform outside of video game contexts. Gilbert and Gilbert (1998) read such practices through a critical lens, pointing out how the video games can position boys in hegemonic discourses of masculinity, ones that align masculinity with "power and aggression, with victory and winning, [and] with superiority and strength" (p. 72). They argue that:

> Although some girls do play and enjoy electronic games, electronic gaming is constructed predominately as a male activity and a male field of pleasure. Just as the "Barbie" culture constructs a highly gendered representational field targeted at girls, the "Game Boy" world of video games offers much the same to boys and young men. Through participation in the multimedia practices associated with electronic gaming, boys and young men enter into a discursive field in which constructions of hegemonic masculinity dominate, and within which they can practice and play at masculinity, and at what it comes to represent. (Gilbert & Gilbert, 1998, p. 73)

As played out in the particularity of Jake's life, video games were indeed a discursive field in which he practiced the masculinities that were so integral to his gendered identities. In order to understand the passion that Jake felt for Sega games, however, it is important to see the embeddedness of the video games in his relationships at home. The ways in which Jake was able to enact fantasies of male power and control through Sega games stood between wider discourses of masculinity and the particular relationships and identities that Jake constructed at home. As part of that personal history, the Sega games were harmonious with the values and discourses Jake was coming to live in relation to others. The game were forms of textuality rooted in Jake's family life and in the feelings and practices that enveloped him relationally as a young boy.

Ideally, schooling in the primary grades should be an opportunity for children to experience new identities and new ways of engaging with social and textual worlds. Dyson (1991, 1993, 1995) describes how children from diverse communities can engage in textual practices that draw upon and also extend or "pluralize" the means by which they mediate the boundaries of self and other, written text and embodied action. Children from poor and working-class communities, communities whose cultural discourses may differ from those of educational institutions, should be able to construct *hybrid discourses* that ultimately enrich their possibilities for living and knowing. Rather than giving up the cherished social practices they have come to live at home, students like Jake should be able to place those social practices and identities in dialogue with new ones. A richer consciousness, argues Bakhtin (1981), is one that is more dialogically engaged or hybridized. The instructional movement toward such cultural pluralism or hybridity, however, requires first that the learner's primary values, passions, and identifications—ones that emerge in the particular relationships constitutive of family and community life—be an integral part of the cultural climate of the classroom. Without the acceptance within the classroom walls of what James Paul Gee (1996) refers to as *primary discourses*, poor and working-class students are faced both with the challenge of appropriating language practices and values that may seem unfamiliar, even unwanted and with the risk of losing integral threads of what they most love and value. For Jake to engage with the kinds of literacy practices valued by school, he would first have to see a cultural space for the things he most valued.

As my history turns to Jake's engagement with first- and second-grade literacies, it will become clear that just the opposite occurred as academic practices became more formal and bounded. In kindergarten, there was space for Jake to interface with school literacy practices on his own terms, as an independent. In first and second grade, Jake's self-reliance and his reluctance to engage with formal literacy practices began to be seen as forms of resistance. The young boy who was so gifted a learner at home increasingly distanced himself from classroom values and social practices.

[...]

Coming to know and be in two discourse communities

School reading practices are often conveyed in educational research literatures as a set of competencies or cognitive skills, as indeed they are measured by the standardized tests so valued among educational institutions. Such portrayals readily miss the embeddedness of reading in the particularity of cultured and gendered (embodied) lives. It becomes all too easy to lose sight of the fact that reading involves a set of cultural *practices*, as integrally embedded within the webs of relationships as any other social act of living and knowing (see Lankshear & O'Connor, 1999, for discussion). If we ignore the cultured and gendered specificity of reading practices we risk missing how conflictual school reading can be for students like Jake, students whose identities so readily fall outside the box of institutional practices. How Jake came to negotiate the cultural boundaries of home and school reading practices is an integral part of his story in first and second grade. The fine detail of that history has to take into account how both men and women engaged in reading with Jake at home, and then later how Jake approached school reading practices, which was shaped, in his case, by women teachers.

My history of Jake's experiences in first and second grade turns now to how he moved between the social worlds of home and school, learning how to participate in two very different discourse communities. Jake did become a reader in first and second grade, but with some degree of struggle amid the social boundaries of classroom reading and writing practices. While learning through family apprenticeships at home, including those involving reading, Jake became, over the course of first and second grade, a struggling student; he was in danger of retention by the end of second grade. Jake's strong preferences for the forms of being and knowing that he practiced at home interfaced with first and second grade expectations. Jake's history as a reader and writer in first and second grade begins with scenes from his life as a reader at home.

Reading practices at home and school

On a late-fall visit to Jake's home during his second-grade school year, Jake's father told the story of how he had become a local expert on JFK assassination theories. He shared that he read voraciously, mostly books about the Kennedy assassination. He went on to recount an incident in a bookstore in which a store clerk had referred a customer to *him* for information on books about JFK. He told this story with a twinkle in his eye, teasingly noting how he (a working man) was considered an expert in this literary domain. He added that he owned many books on the subject of JFK's assassination.

Connected images emerge for me from my time observing as Jake engaged in reading practices at home. On an earlier home visit, in April of his first-grade year, I am sitting in the living room and talking with Jake's mother and his mom-mom about reading. I suggest that Jake needs to do a lot of reading over the summer, to help him get ready for second grade. Jake's mother shares with me how much Jake loves to read. His mom-mom adds that Jake holds back in school, and notes his giftedness as a learner. Jake's mother pulls out an informational book about U.S. presidents and begins quizzing Jake (who is sitting in the living room with the adult women) about various presidents and other political figures. She asks questions like, "Who was the second president?" and "What did George Washington chop down?" At one point, Jake turns to an appendix that lists presidents and facts about them, making use of graphophonic cues and his memory to read or pretend-read presidential facts. He seems to make use of some graphophonic cues to read or pretend-read some of these historical facts. Other facts seem come to him from memory. For instance, when his mother asks him a question about the black man who was shot, Jake responds from memory that it was Martin Luther King. All the while, Jake holds the large informational book in his lap, occasionally consulting it to support his responses.

A second image from observing Jake at home in first grade: on a sunny, fall day, I am introduced to the first Charlotte, a very large spider sitting in its web spun along the side of the swimming pool. Jake's mother asks him to recite the spider's name, and then asks for the names of other characters in the children's book, *Charlotte's Web*. Later on that same afternoon, I meet the second Charlotte, who would narrowly escape demise from a softball hit by Jake. This second Charlotte has spun a web under the eaves of the front porch.

Literary references threaded into ongoing experience, and talk about a love of reading were an important part of Jake's home life during his primary school years. His childhood was richly informed by the literary interests of his mother and maternal grandmother, and by his father's passion for historical and informational books. In his bedroom was a bookshelf full of children's books—mostly books like the Dr. Seuss books (e.g., *Green Eggs and Ham*) and beginning children's readers that his mother ordered from a mail-order service. Some of these mail-order books came with "sight word" flashcards using words from the text. Frequently, adult family members noted how much Jake loved to read himself. His identity as a reader seemed to be embedded in a general family valuing of reading for enjoyment and information.

These rich and varied reading practices at home, however, did not seem to connect easily for Jake with first-grade reading practices. The boundaries between school reading practices and the cultural practices that shaped his life as a young reader at home were difficult for Jake to negotiate. Reading practices in school included whole-class readings of anthology selections (with children following along with their pointing fingers); independent reading during DEAR (Drop Everything And Read); and a variety of Morning Paper and skills activities (e.g., graphophonics, word analysis), often designed to go along with the children's anthology selections. For Jake, bringing with him as he did a history that placed *reading* amid the social practices in his family, many of these activities were constraining and pointless. Reading practices at home were more typically immersed in the ebb and flow of work, recreation, and intimate family relationships. Jake listened to stories when spending nights with his grandmother. Literary connections were made in relation to actual spiders who had spun webs around Jake's home. Race car magazines and information books were typical of the books that Jake read in ways that mirrored the interests and values of his father. When Jake encountered reading practices that emphasized the analysis of parts of texts, or when he read children's stories that were not of any particular use or interest to him, he could become disengaged, perplexed, or frustrated. For instance, in May of his first-grade year, when asked to fill in a story map worksheet with plot information from the story "Strange Bumps" (a selection in Jake's anthology reprinted from an Arnold Lobel book, *Owl at Home*), Jake seemed disengaged and perplexed. "I'm not sure what it is," he commented in frustration. "What *what* is?" I asked, trying to figure out how he was responding to the story map activity. "This *paper*," he said.

Reading and writing masculinities

In second grade, Jake encountered reading practices that hearkened back in some ways to his kindergartern year. Jake's second-grade teacher, Ms. Williams, tended to ascribe to the philosophies and methods embraced by whole language advocates (e.g., Edelsky, Atlwerger, & Flores, 1991; Goodman, 1986). She had attended special workshops given by prominent language arts educators like Lucy Calkins. Jake's teacher based her reading and writing instruction largely around the *workshop* as a pedagogical space and metaphor (see Atwell, 1987). Children read daily in Reader's Workshop, and they composed narratives and other genre pieces in Writer's Workshop. At the same time, she wove a considerable amount of "traditional" instruction in graphophonic relations, word analysis, and genre characteristics into her language arts teaching. Like many contemporary language arts teachers, Ms. Williams strove for teaching methods that balanced out children's need for a focus on whole texts and their structural parts.

Given Jake's history of independence and apprenticeship-style learning at home, and his preference for certain kinds of texts, the Reading and Writing Workshops seemed well suited to Jake's hope of finding a cultural and discursive space for himself amid school reading practices. Although Reader's Workshop was still a space where interaction was not boundless (children had to do certain kinds of reading that excluded three-dimensional textualities), there was a considerable degree of latitude. Children could move about during Reader's Workshop—stretching out on the rug, sitting in a rocking chair, or huddling in a corner off to themselves. Moreover, as long as he was reading, Jake could choose books of interest to him. During Reader's Workshop, Jake often sequestered himself in a corner, defining himself as an "independent" in ways evocative of his kindergarten year. He alternated between choosing narrative texts, often beginning level narrative books like *Popcorn*, *Caps for Sale*, and *Frog and Toad*, as well as informational books. […]

Jake also enjoyed writing in Writer's Workshop. The practices that constituted writing in this workshop afforded a pedagogical space for the kinds of textual enactments that Jake valued. On the pages of his Writer's Notebook, he could negotiate textual boundaries that drew on those practices that he lived at home. Though Jake could not *perform* his fantasies and experiences, as in the Sega and "Max" stories he enacted at home and in kindergarten, he could begin to negotiate the sometimes difficult crossing of textual and cultural worlds. On the pages of his Writer's Notebook, Jake composed entries that reflected his embracement of the gendered practices and identities that shaped his life as a young boy at home. In the two Writer's Notebook entries below, Jake composes scenes of boyhood: accompanying his Dad to the car racing store, and hitting some balls in the front yard with his baby brother, Brad.

> yesterday i want [went]
> to [store name]
> it is a racing stor
> me and bab [dad] we go

to the stor to go
to get nascar sthav [stuff]
and pay for it thend
we go home to pat [put]
it in oro [our] rooms
wana [when] war [we're] don
we eat Banta [dinner] then
we go to bud [bed]

(Jake's Writer's Notebook entry, 12/9)

me and Brad play baesball
out fraint [front] in the grss
and Brad hits home runs
and i hit home runs to
I hit the ball ovar
a van the ball allmost
hit the van. Brad hit
the samft [soft] ball it hit the wndooe
of the van. But it didn't
bast [bust] the wndooe on the van
at my house in the drivway
the red mieni [mini] van wndooe
it hit the van tier [tire]
[not?] the wandooe I feal cool and
I faet [felt] like the big boys.

(Jake's Writer's Notebook entry, 5/15)

These narrative fictions, or shaping of events (Davis, 1987), seemed situated somewhere between home and school cultural practices. Jake could write the culturally specific masculinities he lived at home, while appropriating the rhetorical forms that helped align him with those discourse practices valued in second grade.

Although Jake ended the school year on the very positive note of having made enormous gains in school literacy practices, he was about six months behind his more successful (i.e., on target vis-a-vis grade-level expectations) peers. Midway through his second-grade year, Jake had just begun to interface with textually focused story and chapter books, like Arnold Lobel's *Frog and Toad*. Toward the end of the school year, when more successful readers in his classroom were reading short novels, Jake was still working with short informational books and beginning chapter books. His accomplishments as a reader and writer in second grade, though impressive, did not match up with the expected sequence of achievements for children at the end of primary school. Jake was to enter third grade as a fragile reader amid the values and expectations that constituted reading in a formal or institutional sense. And yet, the complexities of Jake's story do not begin or end with reading fluencies, as important as these might be within an institutional setting.

In September, I observed as Jake participated in a thematic unit on communities, including the buildings that made up different communities. Ms. Williams was reading the book, *Up Goes the Skyscraper*, a book that chronicles the sequential building of a skyscraper. Pictures and text depict the process of constructing a skyscraper, and Ms. Williams' discussion and reading drew on terminology and concepts from construction and engineering. I noticed that Jake, typically distant and disengaged during such whole-class read-alouds, was extremely alert and engaged. Some of the text and pictures depicted the construction of heating and air conditioning systems in the new building. At one point, Jake raised his hand and commented that his father worked as a heating and air conditioning repairman.

Two additional images come from my classroom observations in Jake's second grade. In early December, he puts his head down on his desk and pretends to fall asleep during a math activity in which children were doing "take away" problems. As I walk by him to see what he is doing (and to try to figure out why he's doing it), he whispers softly to me and tells me this story: The night before, his father had awakened him in the middle of the night to take him along for a heating repair emergency. Jake's words are, "I had to" [i.e., I had to be up all night]. He is aware that he is losing focus on the math activity, and so he creates a fantasy that reflects a reasoned (i.e., consonant with family life) explanation for why things would be so difficult right now.

A second image comes from an observation I made in March. Jake had been having a lot of trouble in school that week. For days, he had written nothing in his Writer's Notebook. Ms. Williams had expressed her concerns that week that Jake was still reading on a first-grade level though he was now in second grade. After a whole-class read-aloud of a chapter from the children's novel *How to Eat Worms*, I try to gain a better understanding of the meaning that Jake is making of late second-grade reading practices. During the read-aloud, he had put his head on his desk, seemingly disengaged, though I wasn't sure. After the read-aloud, as children are getting ready for lunch, I ask Jake if he was listening, and what he was thinking about when he put his head down on his desk. He was listening, Jake assures me. He tells me how he was thinking of the time when he went fishing and threw out a line with live bait. He demonstrates physically, enacting the motion of throwing out the fishing line.

I think that Jake struggled to align school reading practices with the particularity of his life as a reader at home, including the gendered relationships and identities that shaped reading amid the intimacy of family life. His history as a reader at home, as this was embedded in the ways of knowing and being that he embraced as a young boy, certainly did not preclude becoming a reader in school. However, the cultural spaces, practices, and values that defined classroom reading also made it sometimes difficult and risky for Jake to read successfully in school. Jake did on occasion find hybrid cultural spaces—a cultural and discursive borderland in which the values and practices he lived at home came together with classroom values and practices. The whole-class reading and discussion of *Up Goes the Skyscraper* was one such moment for him. More typically, however, Jake struggled to find meaning in many classroom reading practices. Reading, like other practices in his community life, had to make good sense before they became something of value to Jake. Adult men, at least in his family world, did not bother with cultural practices that were not linked to constructive *doing* or informational learning. Jake searched to find a place for himself as a school reader, and he was only partly successful in doing this.

Things were not dramatically different for Jake in second grade than they had been in kindergarten—in terms of the ways in which he drew connections between the stories and identities he lived within his family and the particular textualities and identities valued in school. What was different was that, by second grade, the stakes were getting higher. In kindergarten, there was more room for Jake to express his gentle resistance and independence.

He could walk away from a center and simply choose one more to his liking. Rarely did he tune out amid kindergarten social spaces and practices; he was constantly in physical motion, much like at home. By second grade, social spaces and practices were much more bounded and constrained. Within those more bounded practices, Jake's options were more limited. He continued to express an open and trusting warmth toward adults; he still typically had a huge smile on his face upon entering the classroom each morning. Alongside that trust in adults more generally, however, was an increasing dislike of academic practices, and on occasion the teachers who insisted upon them. By second grade, Jake had begun telling family members that he didn't like school, and he had begun resisting things like homework.

At the same time that Jake was struggling with academic practices and identities in school, he was thriving as a young apprentice in family projects and hobbies and in his father's business. In kindergarten and first grade, Jake had helped with home projects like putting together a large Christmas train set and building a backyard swimming pool. In second grade, be had begun to accompany his Dad on those repair jobs where it seemed appropriate to bring him along. By this time, his family had started a mechanical contracting business, and Jake had been named vice president (his mother was the office manager and secretary; all in the family were co-owners and business partners). Sitting at the kitchen table after the more difficult chore of getting through homework, Jake's mother shared thoughts about the future. Following my comment that Jake needed to read over the summer to get ready for third grade, she noted that Jake needed to learn to read well to go on to college. Jake replied quickly and firmly that he would not go to college. Passing through the kitchen, Jake's father added his two cents worth: that Jake would take over the family business. As if in enactment of this prediction about him, Jake picked up the phone nearby and began demonstrating how he answered calls for the family business.

The stories voiced about us, by those whom we most love and value, shape our identities and values in ways that are sometimes more powerful than even the most authoritative institutional systems of cultural power and social regulation can muster. Caught between the discourses of home and school, deeply committed to the practices and relationships lived within his family, Jake struggled to negotiate a space for himself as a young reader and writer in the classroom. He practiced school literacies—sometimes giving himself up to the task of writing about car racing or family events, or reading books reflective of his interests. His embrace of those storylines voiced about him within his family, however, often seemed to exert a stronger pull for him, a more powerful shaping of his identities as a young boy. Presented with the substantial risks he faced if he challenged school textual practices, ones that would require him to think and be in new and unfamiliar ways, Jake chose what must have seemed a safer route: tune out, fantasize, resist; then go home to live the practices and identities that so warmly embraced him. That there was sometimes room in primary school for Jake to enact the identities he lived at home as a young apprentice is testimony to the skill and compassion of his teachers.

Toward hybrid discourses of instruction

Literacy education for poor and working-class children is sometimes viewed as a process of helping children move *from* the familiar language and cultural practices of home and community, *to* the more unfamiliar textual practices of the classroom. Children from ethnic minority and poor and working-class communities, it is argued, bring divergent *primary* discourses to their primary grade classrooms (e.g., Gee, 1996; Michaels, 1981). The process of becoming literate in school, then, entails the appropriation of cultural, textual forms and practices that are more typical of institutional life—what literacy theorist James Paul Gee (1996) calls *secondary* discourses. […] Literacy educators working toward more socially just relationships have argued, on the whole, that something must be done to equalize children's opportunities in classrooms and later in the workforce.

While such metaphors of literacy learning and instruction certainly provide a well-grounded depiction of cultural conflict in the classroom, and, in this case, of Jake's lived classroom experiences, they do not fully capture the moral particularity of lived experience. Nor do they reflect the rich potential of cultural hybridity in the classroom. To suggest that the movement from home and community discourses is a unidimensional process of cultural appropriation (i.e., a movement *from* one thing to something else) is to miss the particularity of readers' histories in relationship to schooling. In writing the history of one young reader, a boy growing up in a blue-collar family and community setting, I have tried to reveal the complex ways in which he came to know and be in multiple ways, even as he struggled with the personal conflict that this process sometimes entailed for him. Jake's history as a reader and writer in school suggests the intricate and hybrid ways in which one young boy moved from the particular loves and identifications he experienced at home, to create points of intersection with school social practices and values. He managed to construct hybrid pedagogical spaces for himself, and he did this on his own terms. In kindergarten, Jake could know and be in familiar ways, while trying on some new textual practices and identities. Once he bumped up against the more constrained textual practices of first and second grade, things became more challenging and conflictual for him. However, Jake's occasionally rich engagements with school reading and writing practices speak to his willingness to risk change and explore new ways of being and knowing.

There are many things that mitigate against such cultural hybridity and change, including the educational mandates and "accountability" measures that are now *de rigeur* in public school systems. Jake's teachers struggled with the extreme pressures they faced in teaching responsively to children's needs while satisfying the administrative bureaucracies that seemed to limit their options as teaching professionals. Larger even than the individuals working within the system, however, and the wider cultural practices that shape schooling in relation to gender, social class, and ethnicity. The politics of schooling leave little room for the kind of hybridity that I think would been enriching for Jake. […] Rather, he lived his life in school in a kind of cultural borderland, one that entailed increasing resistance on his part.

Hybrid discourses of instruction for boys like Jake need to make space for the particular identities and textual practices that are valued and practiced by men and boys in culturally specific settings. Though highly capable of multiplicity and change, Jake also needed space to "roam," to *do*, and to live his passions throughout primary school. Rich school apprenticeships for Jake would entail space for movement as well as reflective activity, for independence as well as social relationship, and for reading and writing in ways that reflect boys' textual interests and performances. Hybrid pedagogical spaces require the radical move of opening up the curriculum to practices and forms of textuality valued by boys like Jake, and creating an instructional dialogue that both embraces and extends.

[…]

References

Atwell, N. (1987). *In the middle: Writing, reading, and learning with adolescents*. Portsmouth, NH: Heinemann.

Bakhtin, M. M. (1981). Discourse in the novel. In M. Holquist (ed.), C. Emerson & M. Holquist (Trans.), *The dialogic imagintion: Four essays by M.M. Bakhtin* (pp. 259–422). Austin, TX: University of Texas Press.

Davis, N. Z. (1987). *Fiction in the archives: Pardon tales and their tellers in sixteenth-century France*. Palo Alto, CA: Stanford University Press.

Dyson, A. H. (1991). The word and the world: Reconceptualizing written language development, Or do rainbows mean a lot to little girls? *Research in the Teaching of English*, 25(1), 97–123.

Dyson, A. H. (1993). *Social worlds of children learning to write in an urban primary school*. New York: Teachers College Press.

Dyson, A. H. (1995). Writing children: Reinventing the development of childhood literacy. *Written Communication*, 12(1), 4–46.

Edelsky, C., Altwerger, B., & Flores, B. (1991). *Whole language: What's the difference?* Portsmouth, NH: Heinemann.

Gee, J. P. (1996). *Social linguistics and literacies: Ideology in discourses* (2nd ed.). Bristol, PA: The Falmer Press.

Gilbert, R., & Gilbert, P. (1998). *Masculinity goes to school*. New York: Routledge.

Goodman, K. (1986). *What's whole in whole language?* Portsmouth, NH: Heinemann.

Lankshear, C., & O'Connor, P. (1999). Response to 'Adult literacy: The next generation.' *Educational Researcher*, 28(1), 30–36.

Michaels, S. (1981). 'Sharing time': Children's narrative styles and differential access to literacy. *Language in Society*, 10, 423–442.

10

Positional Identities

Dorothy Holland, William Lachicotte Jr, Debra Skinner and Carole Cain

[…]

Another facet of lived worlds, that of power, status, relative privilege, and their negotiation, and another facet of lived identities, that of one's self as entitled or as disqualified and inappropriate, must also receive theoretical attention. In order to highlight these facets, we make an analytic distinction between aspects of identities that have to do with figured worlds—storylines, narrativity, generic characters, and desire—and aspects that have to do with one's position relative to socially identified others, one's sense of social place, and entitlement. These figurative and positional aspects of identity interrelate in myriad ways. Sometimes they are completely coincident; sometimes one dominates over the other. Two incidents from our fieldwork in Nepal give a sense of the positional aspect of identity formation.

One day when [Debra] Skinner [author] was recording songs from three of the girls of Naudada, Tila Kumari, who owned the house Debra was renting, came storming onto Debra's porch and began to yell at the girls. She accused them of eating fruit and cutting fodder from her property:

> You stupid girls … Why do you cut grass from our fields? Are you not ashamed? … Everyone has seen the guavas here, but only you have eyes for them … Go to your husband's or father's field to eat. You have no fear to cut the grass in another's field. After telling your parents, I will weed your hair … I will complain like the daughter of Hari [a local adolescent notorious for her bad temper].

All three girls were upset about this scolding. Muna, one of the three, said:

> We hadn't done anything. I can't figure out why they made such a scandal out of it … I felt like crying. I couldn't retaliate. I do not do such things. I thought, who was she to tell someone like my mother such things? We did not get angry because we had not done anything wrong. That's why I felt bad and wanted to cry.

On another day, Shanta, Tila Kumari's six-year-old daughter, was berated because she ventured into an activity to which she had no right. Shanta was in the field where her older brother was plowing. As he steered the oxen past her, she reached out playfully and touched the plow. Immediately her brother began to hit and rebuke her. Her father and other brothers ran from the house to join in the scolding and beating, and her father told her it was a sin for a girl to touch a plow and threatened to beat her severely if she ever touched it again. Shanta cried and trembled for hours. When asked about the incident several weeks later, she remembered it well, repeating her father's words and promising never again to touch the plow. Although Shanta did not understand the wider moral universe in which her act was defined as a sin, she did learn in a dramatic way that, because she was a girl, she was restricted from acts that her brothers could freely perform.

Positional identities in figured worlds

Shanta and the three girls had become embroiled in incidents in which their activity was constrained; they had encountered rebuffs to their freedom of movement and freedom of action, limitations of what we will call their social position. Others treated their actions as claims to social positions, positions that, on account of gender in Shanta's case and perhaps of relative caste position in the girls' case, they were denied. In Tila Kumari's eyes Muna and the other girls were appropriate targets for demeaning. By the acts she suspected they had committed—entering her yard and taking her fruit—they had claimed positions to which they were not entitled. The same fault could be found in Shanta's innocent intrusion into the male domain of the plow.

Sociolinguistics has long made much of the socially constitutive import of language choice (see Gumperz and Hymes 1972). One's choices of dialect, register, pronouns, and genre are not socially neutral. Such decisions partake of powerful systems that index claims to the social relationships between speaker and hearer and to the speaker's general social position. Linguistic choice is but one of these indexical systems. There are other systems of artifacts [...] that carry with them a "theory of the person" who uses them. There could well be fields of sociosartorial studies, sociocognitive studies, even sociomotive studies, since styles of dress (Turner 1969), displays of knowledge (Gearing et al., 1979; McDermott 1974; Lutz 1995), and expressions of emotion (Lutz 1988, 1990) all index social categories of persons. Spaces, too, imbue and are imbued by the kinds of persons who frequent them; conventional forms of activity likewise become impersonated. The dialect we speak, the degree of formality we adopt in our speech, the deeds we do, the places we go, the emotions we express, and the clothes we wear are treated as indicators of claims to and identification with social categories and positions of privilege relative to those with whom we are interacting.

This is the stuff of positional or relational identities, and much research in anthropology and other fields shows that this aspect of identities is important. Relational identities have to do with behavior as indexical of claims to social relationships with others. They have to do with how one identifies one's position relative to others, mediated through the ways one feels comfortable or constrained, for example, to speak to another, to command another, to enter into the space of another, to touch the possessions of another, to dress for another.

[...]

Hindu religious tenets posit a world of the sacred. In that extensively elaborated world, different castes are more or less intrinsically pure, and one's caste affects how polluting one can be to others. Perhaps Tila Kumari's reactions to the girls in her yard had to do with concerns about pollution. But her treatment of Muna and the other girls was not cast in these religious terms but rather in terms of forbidden territory and forbidden goods. It was more about what we will call positional identity than about what we have called figurative identity. Positional identities have to do with the day-to-day and on-the-ground relations of power, deference and entitlement, social affiliation and distance—with the social-interactional, social-relational structures of the lived world. Narrativized or figurative identities, in contrast, have to do with the stories, acts, and characters that make the world a cultural world. Positional identity, as we use the term, is a person's apprehension of her social position in a lived world: that is, depending on the others present, of her greater or lesser access to spaces, activities, genres, and, through those genres, authoritative voices, or any voice at all.

[…]

Positions and markers that cut across figured worlds

Relational identities and the cultural artifacts through which they are claimed may be specific to a figured world. […] Other positional identities and markers may, however, be less specific and cut across such worlds.

In the testimony of witnesses in court cases, O'Barr and Atkins (1980) identified several patterns of speech—such as the use of "hedges," locutions like "there may be" or "perhaps"—that experimental studies later showed to undermine the credibility of the testimony of any witness who exhibited them. There was a correlation between the use of these nonassertive patterns of speech and being female and/or of low "social power." O'Barr and Atkins see these speech behaviors as responses Americans use in formal situations that include people who are more powerful than the speaker. These speech behaviors are not peculiar to the figured world of law courts; instead, hedges, "intensifiers," and "hesitation forms," among others, communicate relative position in other figured worlds as well. They are indices of relational identities that are not particular to any figured world.

In Naudada, too, there were cultural artifacts or resources for positioning self and other that crossed a number of figured worlds, those of domestic/household relations, school, and *parma* (reciprocal work groups). One important set concerned food. Taking certain kinds of food directly handled by another allows a kind of intimate contact that can be considered polluting if the handler is of lower status. To refuse food handled by another, then, is to claim greater moral worth and a higher social position. Conversely, accepting food indicates either one's affiliation and equality of status with its handler or one's deference to a higher-caste donor.

Besides artifacts, social categories also can have meaning across many figured worlds. These categories are by and large associated with the major social divisions—gender, class, race, ethnicity—that separate those who are routinely privileged from those who are not. Cross-cutting markers tend to become stereotypically associated with these social categories, if not actually demanded of their members in practice. Studies in the United States have found that women use hedges, "tag questions," and other deferential forms more often than men (Lakoff 1975; O'Barr and Atkins 1980; Cameron et al. 1988). In Naudada, Bahuns were popularly stereotyped as greedy and maliciously clever, always looking to take advantage of others. These stereotypic associations between marker and category are the (practical) part and (cultural) parcel of the reproduction of social division, and of the categories that are its elements.

A controversy has raged in anthropological linguistics over women's styles of speaking in the United States and whether they should be viewed in the enduring, almost essentialist terms of "subculture" or in the relational terms of situated practice. Tannen (1990) and others take the former position, which we have called culturalist. Women grow up learning a set of values and ways of being in the world, which they translate into ways of speaking. McConnell-Ginet (1988, 1989; Eckert and McConnell-Ginet 1992), among others, takes a more constructivist position, arguing that women (and men) grow up learning how positions of relative power are communicated. Since women are often forced into positions of lesser power, they end up using deferential speech strategies more often than men.

Our approach does not automatically give us the answer to the controversy, but it does suggest that the situation is too complex to be settled by adopting either the culturalist or the constructivist position. It seems to us a double mistake to think of these cross-cutting relational identities as somehow cleanly separable from figured worlds. First, it is erroneous to believe that figured worlds all partake of these differentia in like manner. Rather, conventions of privileged access associated with gender, caste, or some other major social division may or may not have been taken up, elaborated, and made hegemonic in a particular figured world or field of power. In the schools of Naudada, the language of hierarchy communicated through the rules of exchanging food and water was being used to subvert the system of caste privilege; in the tea stalls, the same language was being used to maintain it.

A second mistake, the reverse of the first, is to think that styles of indicating relative social position can be cleanly separated from a figured world of moral meanings—that they are arbitrary indicators which evoke no figured world of their own. In the world of academia, being verbally aggressive may be a sign of high status and position; but for a person who has formed an identity in a figured world where maintaining egalitarian relations is important, verbal aggressiveness has connotations of a moral failing.

Signithia Fordham (1993), drawing from a long-term study of Capital High School in Washington, D.C., provides an example of both of these points. She reveals the nuanced ways in which major social divisions may be elaborated and made crucial in a localized figured world. She describes some of the excruciating consequences of participating in social formations where the styles of one social category are taken as indices of quality and achievement for all people. She writes especially about African-American women and their disposition to silence themselves in the academic activities of the high school. Although Capital High's student body had, at the time of her study, an African-American majority, the space of its activities ideologically privileged styles that were white and male. The school was oriented toward a particular style and way of being a student. Its model of the good student was one who behaved as did white men. The African-American women students, as a result, were in a place where the styles meaningful at home were considered signs of being a poor student.

That these styles of speaking and acting could not simply be put on or taken off at will is evident from Fordham's analysis as well. There were especially bleak results for the African-American women who tried to suppress their own styles and move toward the valued styles—who tried to "pass." By passing, Fordham means a more subtle and figurative kind of performance than the literal passing for white: "Passing implies impersonation, acting as if one is someone or something one is not. Hence, gender passing [for African-American women] suggests masquerading or presenting a persona or some personae that contradict the literal image of the marginalized or doubly refracted 'Other'" (1993: 3). Too much passing, she argues, drawing upon Said, can result in a potentially subversive self where the person can no longer speak or even think in his or her "native voice." Such persons lose their creativity: because they are compelled to assume the identity of the "Other"—in exchange for academic success—they cannot represent themselves; they are forced to masquerade as the authentic, idealized "Other" (26).

Taking up social positions

What Fordham shows us in vivid detail are the results of a long process. Many of the women she studied had developed what we call a positional identity, a sense of their relative social position, which, among other things, led them to silence themselves within the figured world of school. Fordham also describes other young women who had developed an oppositional stance, rejecting the strategy of effacing themselves in order to conform to the model of a good student. How had the young women at Capital High arrived at these positional identities? What interests us is the processes of development over the long term. The long term, however, happens through day-to-day encounters and is built, again and again, by means of artifacts, or indices of positioning, that newcomers gradually learn to identify and then possibly to identify themselves with—either positively or negatively, through either acceptance or rejection.

In the groups that we studied, as in any group engaged in jointly creating and participating in a figured world, day-to-day practices always positioned the participants situationally, relative to one another. That is, participants in collaborative activities—be they staff members producing a treatment plan in a mental health clinic, old hands welcoming a newcomer to an AA meeting, or a romantically involved couple going out to see a film—engaged in conversation and interaction that invariably constructed their own social position and their social relations with one another.

As social constructivists emphasize, these "discourses" and the other forms of cultural artifacts used in everyday practices construct subjects and subject positions. The positions are, at least provisionally, imposed upon parties to the practice. The sociologist R. W. Connell provides an example of this idea when he sums up the argument that gender is more appropriately treated as a process or a practice than as a static attribute or an enduring characteristic. He suggests that "gender" would be more transparent if it were a verb rather than a noun: that its significant qualities would be clearer if we said, "I 'gender' you, you 'gender' me, she 'genders' him"; or, better yet, "I try to 'gender' you, you try to 'gender' me," and so on (Connell 1987: 140).

Entitled people speak, stand, dress, emote, hold the floor—they carry out privileged activities—in ways appropriate to both the situation of the activity and their position within it. Those who speak, stand, dress, hold the floor, emote, and carry out activities in these proper ways are seen to be making claims to being entitled. Speaking certain dialects, giving particular opinions, and holding the floor are indices of claims to privilege.

[…]

In Naudada, husbands usually addressed their wives with the less respectful pronominal form used to address children and animals. The respect and deference owed to superiors were communicated through other pronouns. Thus each time he used this form of address a husband afforded his wife a position inferior to his own. In reply, the usual, respectful forms of address that wives employed for husbands would accord him the greater deference. Their social relationship—his superordination, her subordination—was constantly reconstituted by the very media of this discursive practice.

Another example of the affording of a position comes from a practice in Naudada that depends upon the food etiquette of castes. The tea stall owners of Naudada served members of the Damai and other "untouchable" castes, but required them to wash their own cups and glasses. Because people of higher castes avoided food or utensils that had been touched by people of castes considered to be so impure as to pollute, tea stall owners, by enforcing this rule about washing, implicitly claimed to be, or positioned themselves as, pure, superior, and keepers of purity for others. They claimed the qualities of the higher castes, elaborated in relation to the figured world of caste relations, at the same time inviting customers of lower castes to enact a subject position of inferiority. For similar reasons, and with similar implications for the parties' relative positions, husbands refused to eat leftover food from their wives' plates, but it was not expected that wives would refuse their husbands' leftover food.

Viewed over the long term, these day-to-day practices are social work, acts of inclusion/exclusion, of allowing/compelling only certain people to evince the sign, that maintains positions and the value of artifacts as indices of position. [...]

Much of the inclusionary/exclusionary work of sign restriction is done simply by the inclusion or exclusion of certain types of people from sites where the signing knowledge is interacted as a matter of course (see Rogoff 1990). Trosset (1986) describes the difficulties of a foreigner learning to speak Welsh in Wales. For various reasons, Welsh speakers invariably switch to English in the presence of a non-Welsh speaker, thus effectively limiting the signal means to their identity as Welsh, the ability to speak the everyday tongue.

Gearing and colleagues (1979) describe how processes of inclusion/exclusion work in the absence of clear control—that is, even when dialects can be overheard, or more privileged ways of acting can be directly observed and therefore imitated. They analyze the means by which children in school are kept from learning skills that are taken as indices of social position. They emphasize that knowledge (reading, knowledge of chemistry, skills in repairing machinery) is proprietary; that it is generally associated with, or belongs to, a recognized category of people; and that, by virtue of this relation, the use of knowledge signals identity. Hence, even in situations where all students are admitted to the arena of learning, learning is likely to become unevenly distributed in its specifics. Teachers will take some students' groping claims to knowledge seriously on the basis of certain signs of identity. These students they will encourage and give informative feedback. Others, whom they regard as unlikely or even improper students of a particular subject (girls and shop skills, working-class students and philosophical essays), are less likely to receive their serious response.

[...]

Late learners are impeded not only by their sense of inferior propriety or right to act, which their late access signals, but also by the withholding of aid and the acts of disapproval (such as sarcasm, practical jokes, and straight misinformation) through which knowledgeable associates enforce their superior claim. Many never overcome that awkwardness, which inevitably affects the acceptance of their claims and reproduces the situation of inferiority. They are always lesser than. And they may always feel self-conscious, linking durably in their persons the structures of privilege to the dispositions of silencing and acceptance that such structures demand. These are the dimensions of difference to which Lykes (1985) alludes when she argues that individuals have different senses of self because, senses of self being grounded in experiences of power, individuals have differential access to the positions of power that afford the experience. People develop different relational identities in different figured worlds because they are afforded different positions in those worlds.

[...]

How social position becomes disposition

[...]

The development of social position into a positional identity—into dispositions to voice opinions or to silence oneself, to enter into activities or to refrain and self-censor, depending on the social situation—comes over the long term, in the course of social interaction. Relational identities are publicly performed through perceptible signs. People "tell" each other who they claim to be in society in myriad ways. In Naudada, Skinner found, children learned early that a woman's marital status was expressed by diverse signs: by the *tilhari* (a type of necklace) that married women wear, for example, or the vermilion powder worn in the part of their hair. They learned that tea stall owners would not wash the glasses of a lower-caste person, nor would high-caste persons allow lower-caste persons to enter their homes. But much of this learning may happen in a nonreflective way.

Embodiment versus mediated positional identities

In the ordinary developmental sequence proposed by the sociohistorical approach, the child first *interacts* the sign in concert with others. The interaction of the sign, for the child, is part of a behavioral sequence that may have no meaning in and of itself. It is likely that relational identities are borne in a similar way, in what phenomenologists used to call the natural attitude, the uninterrupted flow of everyday life, Bergson's *durée*. The meaning of actions remains transparent or taken for granted in the natural attitude, and response follows as a matter of course. The formation of identity in this posture is a byproduct of doing, of imitation and correction, and is profoundly embodied. Positional identities inhabit the landscape of Bourdieu's habitus.

Adults too can be drawn into a figured world and develop a relational identity without much reflection upon the social claims carried in the forms of their action. Kondo (1990) provides a telling illustration of the effects of such embodied processes. Kondo, a Japanese American who grew up in the United States, relates something that happened to her after a period of fieldwork in Japan, a time in which she had immersed herself in the daily lives of people in her neighborhood. She went shopping one day:

> Promptly at four P.M., the hour when most Japanese housewives do their shopping for the evening meal, I lifted the baby into her stroller and pushed her along ahead of me as I inspected the fish, selected the freshest looking vegetables, and mentally planned the meal for the evening. As I glanced into the shiny metal surface of the butcher's display case, I noticed someone who looked terribly familiar: a typical young house-wife, clad in slip-on sandals and the loose, cotton shift called "home wear," a woman walking with a characteristically Japanese bend to the knees and a sliding of the feet. Suddenly, I clutched the handle of the stroller to steady myself as a wave of dizziness washed over me, for I realized I had caught a glimpse of nothing less than my own reflection. (16–17)

Kondo had acquired the dress, posture, and habits of a young Japanese housewife (or so she identified them) simply by immersing herself in social activity from the position that her gender and her associates assigned her. Her acquisition of the dispositions that marked a particular, gendered identity had occurred without her awareness, and the moment of recognition was disorienting. The image of herself in the butcher's display case and the image of herself in her mind's eye did not match, and that disparity led Kondo to distance herself from her fieldwork. Immersion gave way to a reticence in which she gauged her activity according to the recalled standards of her self-image.

No doubt many aspects of positional identities develop out of one's awareness, as Kondo's had before she caught a glimpse of herself. No doubt many behaviors develop out of awareness, unmediated by one's reflection upon them as claims to social position. One simply participates in the typical arrangements of people in houses, say, where one is more likely to find, in the United States, women in the kitchen and men in the work-shop or yard; or in Naudada, women at the hearth, men at the tea shop. Or one simply takes part in everyday activities and finds young Japanese -American) women walking about with sliding steps and slightly bent knees, pushing babies in strollers as they shop in the afternoon.

Occasionally, a child may be admonished in a way that includes mention of social posi-tion. A mother may tell her daughter that girls don't do x. Shanta was certainly warned away from the plow in a dramatic and upsetting way, but perhaps the usual path to rela-tional identity is through simple associations that pass unnoticed in any conscious way. It may not be until later that the associations between social positions and entitlements become a matter of reflection. The child at first, and perhaps for a very long time, may not associate the access that she gains or does not gain to spaces and activities with the lan-guage of social claims. She may not consciously realize that her developing dispositions are caste-specific. Especially at first, she undoubtedly does not say to herself, "Tila Kumari is a Bahun. To go into her yard is to claim to be of higher caste than I am. If I go there, she is likely to mistreat me."

Other indices of positional identities, however, become conscious and available as tools that can be used to affect self and other. Muna interpreted Tila Kumari as accusing her and her friends of being morally bad. She defended herself, to herself and to Debra, as not deserving such an evaluation. In the lived world of Naudadan domestic and community relations, a woman's social worth was figured according to the life path of the good woman

[…]. Girls of Muna's age had long been used to hearing and using terms such as *radi* (widow) to insult others. These were derogatory terms for women who had strayed from the life path of the good Hindu woman. They had even come to understand why radi was a negative term—a widow was a woman who had fallen from the life path by outliving her husband. Further, the girls cared about their own moral standing in the community and often constructed for Skinner representations of themselves as good daughters and sisters […]. Muna's emotional response to Tila Kumari's scolding indicated her attachment to the understanding of herself as a good person.

In other words, some positional identities and their associated markers are clearly figured. In Naudada, good works and good behavior, when contrasted to the misbehavior that constitutes *pap* (sin), are noted and related to the script of the life path of a good person. In the world of romance of college students in the American South, attractiveness as a form of symbolic capital, a measure of one's social worth, was figured extensively, not only as a key element in the development of romantic relationships, but also as a motive for numerous projects, practices, and artifacts of beautification. Perhaps these figured aspects of relational identities become relatively conscious for anyone successfully recruited into the figured world where such qualities are deemed important. The everyday aspects of lived identities, in contrast, may be relatively unremarked, unfigured, out of awareness, and so unavailable as a tool for affecting one's own behavior.

We do not mean to imply that identities subsist in two exclusive forms, one type a pure product of imagination and the other of unreflected action. Rather, consider two orientations or attitudes to the production of social activity. Figured identities arise and are reproduced in the special attitude of play or, more precisely, imaginative framing. […], Vygotsky describes play as a special social form of activity, one in which the conditions and modes of action are not those of the "actual," that is, everyday setting, but of an imagined template cast over the everyday. He uses the simple example of a child's playing at riding a horse, when what the child rides is "merely" a broom. What counts in play, and what counts in the identities of figured worlds, is the cultural relations, the "rules," that govern the movements of a game. The meanings of play, like the meanings of *langue*, are only attached or assigned to the material tokens that instantiate them. Their source lies in the imaginative system.

Mundane activities, in contrast, have become a matter of habit. By differentiating between mundane activities and the more dramatic, remarked activities singled out in figured worlds, we create not a dichotomy but a continuum.

[…]

Vygotsky called the process in which the historical sources and the distinctiveness of behavior are erased by its automation "fossilization." In a sense, some imaginative frames become "fossilized" in mundane daily life. But fossilization is not irreversible. Ruptures of the taken-for-granted can remove these aspects of positional identities from automatic performance and recognition to commentary and re-cognition. (Kondo's experience is an excellent example.) This hermeneutic moment leads persons to specify the figured world that prefigures everyday activity.

This disruption happens on the collective level as well. Some signs of relational identity become objectified, and thus available to reflection and comment, in relation to the social category. Alternative figurings may be available for interpreting the everyday, and alternative ways of figuring systems of privilege may be developed in contestations over social arrangements. We heard in Naudada figurings of caste that differed from those given in Brahmanical texts. Schoolboys told Skinner that the blood of the lower castes was red, like that of the higher castes—members of different castes were at root the same, and not "naturally" different.

At some point, the lower-caste child may begin to grasp consciously the emotional, evaluative nature of the signs that are used to position him as inferior, as a source of potential pollution for all those whose caste is higher than his own. By drinking from the glass at a tea stall, the Damai, the Sarki, the Kami pollutes it. At some point, the child may begin to use the sign in relation to social category and in turn as a symbolization of how others experience him. Typically, a child will reproduce the comments of adults in his own ego-centric speech, that is, in the speech stream that frames, comments upon, and comes to manage action. Through continually objectifying or symbolizing himself enacting the sign, he becomes able to experience a version of himself as an object in a social world given meaning by these signs. Eventually, this means of objectification, which is a form of self-management, becomes what Vygotsky and Bakhtin called inner speech [...], and what we consider an element of the imagination. One particular lower-caste boy so resented the position assigned him because of his caste that he dreamed of returning to Naudada as a doctor, a figure of such importance that higher-caste people would have to accept food and water that he had touched (Skinner and Holland 1996).

The women in Holland's study of romance often talked about such objectifications of themselves and ruminated upon them. Often these representations took the form of voices, of Bakhtin's (1981) vocal images, while others were visual images. Similar processes of objectification were evident for the children that Skinner followed in Nepal. These visions often seemed to motivate (plans for) action, sometimes even life-changing action. Kondo suggests that for her, too, the image reflected in the display case became a mediating device; it allowed her to think about what she had become, and to attempt to change it.

Children in their development and neophytes entering into a figured world, then, acquire positional dispositions and identities. At some level of apprehension, they come to know these signs as claims to categorical and relational positions, to status. More important, they learn a feel for the game, as Bourdieu calls it, for how such claims on their part will be received. They come to have relational identities in their most rudimentary form: a set of dispositions toward themselves in relation to where they can enter, what they can say, what emotions they can have, and what they can do in a given situation.

[...]

References

Bakhtin, Mikhail M. 1981. *The Dialogic Imagination: Four Essays by M. M. Bakhtin.* ed. M. E. Holquist, trans. Caryl Emerson and Michael Holquist. Austin: University of Texas Press.

Cameron, D., F. McAlindon, and K. O'Leary. 1988. "Lakoff in Context: The Social and Linguistic Function of Tag Questions." *In Women in Their Speech Communities: New Perspectives on Language and Sex*, ed. J. Coates and D. Cameron, 74–93. New York: Longman.

Connell, R. W. 1987. *Gender and Power: Society, the Person and Sexual Politics.* Palo Alto: Stanford University Press.

Eckert, P., and S. McConnell-Ginet. 1992. "Think Practically and Look Locally: Language and Gender as Community-based Practice." *Annual Review of Anthropology* 21: 461–490.

Fordham, Signithia. 1993. "Those Loud Black Girls': (Black) Women, Silence, and Gender 'Passing' in the Academy." *Anthropology and Education Quarterly* 24(1): 3–32.

Gearing, F., T. Carroll, L. Richter, P. Grogan-Hurlick, A. Smith, W. Hughes, B. Tindall, W. Precourt, and S. Topfer. 1979. "Working Paper 6." In *Toward a Cultural Theory of Education and Schooling*, ed. F. Gearing and L. Sangree, 9–38. The Hague: Mouton.

Kondo, D. K. 1990. *Crafting Selves: Power, Gender, and Discourses of Identity in a Japanese Workplace*. Chicago: University of Chicago Press.

Lakoff, Robin. 1975. *Language and Woman's Place*. New York: Harper and Row.

Lutz, Catherine. 1988. *Unnatural Emotions: Everyday Sentiments on a Micronesian Atoll and Their Challenge to Western Theory*. Chicago: University of Chicago Press.

———— 1990. "Engendered Emotion: Gender, Power, and the Rhetoric of Emotional Control in American Discourse." In *Language and the Politics of Emotion,* Lutz and Abu-Lughod, eds., 69–92.

———— 1995. "The Gender of Theory." *In Women Writing Culture*, ed. R. Behar and Deborah A. Gordon, 249–266. Berkeley: University of California Press.

Lykes. M. B. 1985. "Gender and Individualistic vs. Collectivist Bases for Notions about the Self." *Journal of Personality* 53(2): 357–383.

McConnell-Ginet, Sally. 1988. "Language and Gender." In *Linguistics: The Cambridge Survey*, ed. F. J. Newmeyer, 75–99. Cambridge: Cambridge University Press.

———— 1989. "The Sexual (Re)production of Meaning: A Discourse-based Theory." In *Language, Gender and Professional Writing*, ed. F. W. Frank and P. A. Treichler, 35–50. New York: Modern Language Association.

McDermott, R. P. 1974. "Achieving School Failure: An Anthropological Approach to Illiteracy and Social Stratification." In *Education and Cultural Process: Toward an Anthropology of Education*, ed. G. D. Spindler, 82–118. New York: Holt, Rinehart and Winston.

O'Barr, William, and Bowman Atkins. 1980. "'Women's Language' or 'Powerless Language'?" In *Women and Language in Literature and Society*, ed. Sally McConnell-Ginet, Ruth Borker, and Nelly Furman, 93–110. New York: Praeger.

Rogoff, Barbara. 1990. *Apprenticeship in Thinking: Cognitive Development in Social Context*. New York: Oxford University Press.

Skinner, Debra, and Dorothy Holland. 1996. "Schools and the Cultural Production of the Educated Person in a Nepalese Hill Community." In *The Cultural Production of the Educated Person*, ed. B. A. Levinson, D. E. Foley, and D. C. Holland, 273–299. Albany: SUNY Press.

Tannen, Deborah. 1990. *You Just Don't Understand: Women and Men in Conversation*. New York: Morrow.

Trosset, Carol S. 1986. "The Social Identity of Welsh Learners." *Language in Society* 15(2): 165–192.

Turner, Terrence. 1969. "Tchikrin: A Central Brazilian Tribe and Its Symbolic Language of Bodily Adornment." *Natural History* 78: 50–59.

Bibliography

Bourbieu, Pierre. 1993. *The Field of Cultural Production: Essays on Art and Literature*. New York: Columbia University Press.

Brenneis, Donald. 1990. "Shared and Solitary Sentiments: The Discourse of Friendship, Play, and Anger in Bhatgaon." In Lutz and Abu-Lughod, eds., 1990, 113–125.

Brown, Penelope. 1980. "How and Why Are Women More Polite: Some Evidence from a Mayan Community." In *Women and Language in Literature and Society*, ed. Sally McConnell-Ginet, Ruth Borker, and Nelly Furman, 111–136. New York: Praeger.

Crapanzano, Vincent. 1980. *Tuhami: Portrait of a Moroccan*. Chicago: University of Chicago Press.

Davies, B., and Harré, R. 1990. "Positioning: The Discursive Production of Selves." *Journal for the Theory of Social Behavior* 20: 43–63.

Gumperz, John, and Dell Hymes, eds. 1972. *Directions in Sociolinguistics: The Ethnography of Communication*. New York: Holt, Rinehart and Winston.

Harré, R., and L. Van Langenhove. 1991. "Varieties of Positioning." *Journal for the Theory of Social Behavior* 21: 391–407.

Kulick, Don. 1993. "Speaking as a Woman: Structure and Gender in Domestic Arguments in a New Guinea Village." *Cultural Anthropology* 8(4): 411–429.

Lave, Jean, and Etienne Wenger. 1991. *Situated Learning: Legitimate Peripheral Participation*. Cambridge: Cambridge University Press.

Lederman, Rena. 1984. "Who Speaks Here? Formality and the Politics of Gender in Mendi, Highland Papua New Guinea." *In Dangerous Words: Language and Politics in the Pacific,* ed. D. L. Brenneis and F. R. Myers, 85–107. New York: New York University Press.

Van der Veer, René and Valsiner, Jaan. 1991. *Understanding Vygotsky: A Quest for Synthesis*. Oxford: Blackwell.

Willis, Paul. 1981. *Learning to Labor: How Working Class Kids Get Working Class Jobs*. New York: Columbia University Press.

11

Gender and Subject Cultures in Practice

Patricia Murphy

Introduction

In England in the 1990s, the use of league tables as a mechanism for accountability made public national test and examination results by individual and by school. This allowed simple comparisons of boys' and girls' overall achievements, which revealed that girls as a group were consistently achieving more and higher qualifications than boys at the end of compulsory schooling. The form of reporting masked the evidence that progression year on year was occurring for both groups and that the female advantage did not occur consistently across all subjects or aspects of subjects (Murphy and Whitelegg, 2006) or across subgroups and schools (Gorard, 2000; Connell, 2005). Nevertheless, because of the convergence of a number of socio-historical and political factors (Mahoney, 1998), this evidence achieved heightened significance, gender moved on to the educational agenda and pedagogy became the focus for ameliorating strategies.

Pedagogy was identified as the 'problem' and teachers were required to solve it through changes in their practice that addressed the presumed differential needs of boys and of girls. However, policy recommendations about effective pedagogy that foregrounded single-sex teaching were not informed by accounts of *how* gender emerges between people as teachers orchestrate settings in a range of subject contexts. Researchers evaluating strategies to enhance girls' participation in science, for example, acknowledged the potential of single-sex organisation but only when combined with other practices co-ordinated by teachers with an understanding of how gender mediates learning (Parker and Rennie, 2002). Without this understanding, the adoption of generalized practices reduces gender to a matter of biology as sex groups are treated as homogenous and within group diversity is ignored.

It is a significant challenge for teachers to first understand gender and how it shapes practice and then to apply this understanding to enact practice that enables the participation of diverse learners. What is more, at the level of classroom interaction there is only limited research available about the gender mediation of individual knowledge construction. The chapter offers insights to inform the development of gender aware practices drawing on extracts of data from an ethnographic study in a co-educational school of single-sex settings involving students aged 13–14 years old (see Ivinson and Murphy, 2007 for a full account). The extracts are from two subject settings, science and technology, although the research involved a wider range. They reveal how teachers' understanding of gender influenced by subject cultures, emerged in practice and differentially positioned students and impacted on their learning. A sociocultural perspective is adopted in conceptualizing the issues and in the data collection and analysis. In a sociocultural view gender operates at a number of levels: as part of the symbolic mode, it is a historically produced discursive construct (Kotthoff and Baron, 2001) shared by members of a community; and in the lived world an aspect of social situations, a 'moment in action' (Penuel and Wertsch, 1995), as people negotiate and commit to meanings and positions in social activities. As an analytical perspective, a sociocultural approach allows consideration at both levels as it 'reformulates relations between the level of analysis of social practice in the everyday world and that of the constitutive order in relations with which experience in the lived world is dialectically formed' (Lave, 1988: 171).

Institutions like schools are situated and exposed to practices beyond their boundaries (Bruner, 1996). Activities within schools and the practices associated with them are part of broader cultural systems of relations, social structures, within which they have meaning. Aspects of culture, of which gender is part, exert their influence not just through structural entailments such as educational policies but also through the cultural myths that circulate and fashion 'intentional activity in the lived-world' (Lave, 1988: 178). These cultural beliefs are embodied in our thinking and inscribed in our routines and behaviours. They are the 'taken for granted' ways of a culture, or 'cultural illusions' (McDermott, 1996). The data extracts reveal how when confronted with a problem of gender without support or insights into its operation, teachers draw on cultural legacies about gender in relation to their subject. Consequently, rather than working to open up spaces and extend or 'pluralise' the means by which students mediate the boundaries of self (Dyson, 1995), teachers unwittingly constrain them. The data extracts reveal in some small ways instances where cultural spaces were made available or closed down or sometimes a borderland, a legitimate peripheral position (Lave and Wenger, 1991) was found by students themselves.

Agency and identities in learning

In the chapter, learning is understood as a movement into and through social existence (Lave, 1988). From this participationist viewpoint, 'patterned collective forms of distinctly human forms of doing are developmentally prior to the activities of the individual' (Sfard, 2006: 157). Learning and knowing are therefore perceived as relations among people in activity and have to be understood with respect to practice as a whole, within a community of learners in a subject setting, and within the world at large (Lave and Wenger, 1991: 114). Wenger (1998) argues that identity is the pivot between the individual and the collective. Taking this view focuses attention in settings on practice and the affordances made available to enable students to negotiate of ways of being a person in a context, i.e. within the possibilities made available by the systems of relations. Thus individual agency is a situated, negotiated experience and identities emerge in the interaction between students' experiences and their social interpretations, over time. In the discussion in the chapter, the notion of learning as a process of 'becoming' and 'belonging' encapsulates the key perspectives within a sociocultural account of learning as a movement deeper into practice and as a transformation of identity where identity is understood as evolving forms of competence or trajectories (Wenger, 1998: 153). Learning is not just about appropriating ways of knowing and acting valued in subject practices but essentially about the formation of an identity, becoming a competent schooled person within that subject. Wenger (1998) conceptualises identities as trajectories to incorporate the past and the future in the process of negotiating the present. An identity conceived as a trajectory is not a fixed path, rather continuous motion. A sense of a trajectory, he argues, gives individuals ways of determining what matters, what is salient and what is not.

Subject cultures and the positioning of students

Perceptions of gender set up expectations of what it is to be identifiably masculine or feminine that are more or less stable factors of a culture. Davies (2003: 9–10) talks of children's need to 'get it right': 'Getting it right means practising the culture in an identifiably individual way and to do this students have to know the ways in which cultural practices can be varied'. Cultural scripts about how people are or how they figure in the world are often played out in oppositional terms – these terms or markers of masculinity and femininity are culturally specific and draw on deep historical legacies that align with subjects.

For example, in relation to science and technology from early times the metaphors of dominion and of nurture were embedded in our religions, and language. Prior to the scientific and technical revolution, the metaphor of the female, living, nurturing world was dominant and shaped human relations with the world (Merchant, 1983). With the advancement of technological development through the 16th and 17th centuries, the dominion metaphor came into ascendancy to enable correspondence between new cultural activities and culturally sanctioned behaviour. Scientific inquiry was no longer forbidden. Francis Bacon argued in his writing about the scientific method that by digging into the mine of natural knowledge, mankind could recover the lost dominion. In his depictions of nature, Bacon maintained the association of nature with femininity and characterised its problematic essence by drawing on images of nature 'in error' and 'recalcitrant' nature, and describing matter as the 'common harlot'. As matter, the known – the feminine, was separated from the knower and by implication the knower was associated with man. At the same time as the scientific method was being articulated, Descartes, through his new philosophical method of radical doubt, distinguished the internal world of the mind from the external world of natural phenomena reinforcing the symbolic separation of mind and body and mind and matter (Lloyd, 1989). Reason came to epitomise scientific practice and femininity became associated with the world outside of the reason and logic of science.

By the end of the 17th century, the modern worldview was born that unified knowledge with material power through the scientific method and mechanical technology both of which were culturally associated with masculinity. Historically, this construction of science and not science ensured that girls were excluded from many aspects of science education, particularly physics. In technology, the association of the practices with masculinity was further reinforced by the historical exclusion of women from skilled work, which was appropriated by men restricting 'women's work' to unskilled and routinised forms of employment. As Schwartz Cowan (1997) noted when industrial society was developing ideas about gender and ideas about technology were associated, 'They [society] all agreed that there was some natural and necessary connection between working with your hands, being skilled, being independent, and being a good man' (p 218). Consequently, 'technical competence' came to be understood as an integral part of masculinities and positioned women in opposition to this as the 'outsiders' or the technically incompetent (Wajcman, 1991).

Gender legacies embedded in cultural scripts such as these serve as symbolic resources that can be differentially appropriated and deployed by any individual, teacher or student. How these symbolic resources are taken up and used is not arbitrary and has social consequences as they influence how individuals, both teachers and students, position themselves and are positioned. Two data extracts exemplify this.

Science

The following extract comes from two settings from an 'all boys' class and an 'all girls' class of students in Year 9 aged 13–14 years old. The content covered in the lessons was the same in both settings, however, the teacher, Mr White, in his practice treated girls differently to boys.

Girls as 'outsiders'?

When confronted with single-sex classes, which were imposed by senior management (see Ivinson and Murphy, 2007 for details), Mr White spoke about his surprise at finding the girls to be 'confident', willing to 'join in', take risks and sometimes even 'give wrong answers'. The girls did not 'fit any of the stereotypes' he held. His surprise suggested that he had assumed girls' incompetence in science and this was evidenced in how he policed the girls' movement and access. Mr White repeatedly told the girls to 'move quietly and safely around the lab' and frequently drew attention to the potential harm they might do to themselves. Although he reminded the boys of the safety precautions, he did not constantly repeat them. The following instructions about how to set up apparatus for a distillation experiment indicate something of the way that he associated boys and disassociated girls with the practices of the subject. Instructing the girls:

> You must clamp your tube carefully right at the top but not actually on the stopper. Make sure that's right at the top but not actually on the stopper and so tip it up a bit. ... So the flame heats up the oil, without heating all the rubber bits and things at the top. This will catch fire if it gets hot. Now if you have an accident and if it does catch fire, which will happen I am sure for one or two of you, then the key thing is you don't panic, you move the burner well out the way ... and I will come and sort you out.

In response, a girl giggled 'Don't panic', as Mr White continued with his final point about safety: '...things are going to get very hot, don't touch anything that even might be possibly hot'.

He offered no such instructions to the boys about the equipment. His safety instructions also assumed competence on the boys' behalf in dealing with hot objects:

> ...you will need to pick up a cloth ... this will be hot, be very careful as you transfer into the second test tube ...When it reaches 150° again with a cloth to protect your hand, carefully move onto the third test tube.'

In introducing the risk of fire to the boys, he attributed this to the components as opposed to any 'accidents' caused by the students as he did with the girls.

I have suggested heating the oil with the flame over at this end, and moving the flame away when you transfer from one to the other then you will not have an accident. Nevertheless there will be problems and it might well be that your apparatus catches fire ... don't panic, you are to move the burner away, draw my attention to the problem please and I will come and help you. It will not be a serious problem. ...

In these exchanges, girls were positioned as people to be protected from themselves who lacked skills and competency with scientific equipment. Science was depicted as problematic for girls. The teacher through his instructions and protection wanted to engage the girls in the practices of the domain, but seemed unaware of how he positioned the girls and reinforced their outsider status. He told both groups not to panic but the discourse within which this injunction was situated conjures images of out of control girls and calm authoritative boys. The differences in the phrases he used, such as 'sorting out' the girls compared with his intention to 'help' the boys, defined the different relationships between the students and teacher and where the balance of autonomy lay. The identity he extended to girls was resisted as the giggling girl mocked his injunction not to panic. Furthermore, observations revealed that girls were more than competent in organising and using the equipment.

Interviews with departmental staff revealed that these beliefs about girls' and boys' competency and motivation to learn science were shared. For example, both male and female teachers judged that girls were passive and failed to engage with equipment unless it was 'plonked on their desk'. This was felt to be particularly the case with low ability girls. As one female teacher commented about the source of girls' timidity: '[its] in case they hurt themselves, they get burnt or whatever'. This was explained because 'they didn't know and they didn't understand what to do'. Boys on the other hand were 'very confident in their own ability'. Low ability boys' confidence was considered misplaced but explained in terms of their being excited by science. Wenger (1998) refers to mutual engagement as a prerequisite for participation and that this relies on being part of a whole. The positioning of girls as 'outside' of science to be brought in by the teacher constrains their potential to engage in the process of negotiation of meaning. This coupled with the identity of incompetency extended to them limits their potential to experience 'belonging' in the subject, which further constrains the opportunities for them to develop expertise.

Resistant materials

The next extract is from a Resistant Materials workshop. Resistant Materials evolved from Craft, Design and Technology education (CDT) which was taught to boys, and drew on the workshop skills associated with male working-class occupations and crafts. James (1999), citing Gleeson's work, described the culture of crafts and trades teachers as an 'exclusive masculinity club'. Identification depends on the images we can build of the world and ourselves in relation to it. It involves making connections across time and the social landscape that enable our identities to take on new dimensions. Identification with a subject can be expanded beyond immediate engagement through imagination both by 'association and opposition ... by connecting us and by distancing us' (Wenger, 1998: 194). Imagination can also involve stereotypes that 'project on to the world the assumptions of specific practices' (p 178). In this next extract, Mr Hunt when faced with single-sex groups of 13–14 year olds, drew on stereotypes overtly with the intention of enhancing the engagement of both boys and girls in the subject. Mr Hunt had extensive experience as a CDT teacher and was observed teaching a lesson on joins.

Opening up cultural spaces?

Although the topic of the lessons was the same, the content in the lesson for boys and the lesson for girls varied significantly. Mr Hunt in the lesson for boys situated each join type in history: 'The idea of joining material together goes way back'. He started with Stone Age *man*, progressing to *man* the voyager: 'In the high seas you might want your raft to be springy and flexible so that it does not come to harm ... that kind of join goes back possibly 3000 years'. He explained that early man learned the technique of splitting logs to make wedges to form joins. As he spoke he continually sketched three-dimensional representations of joins which the boys copied. The engagement of the boys was clear through their interactions:

Sam   The Tudors and Victorians would have not used wedges?
Mr Hunt   Yes, the Tudors probably would have because most of the roofs were made of thatch but by the time we get to the Victorians most of the roofs were not. They used nails – I will draw a nail for you.

Men were depicted, and by association the boys, as leaders of technological developments. Mr Hunt's narrative assumed mutual engagement and a joint enterprise and he made this explicit by connecting them to a history of participation. Mr Hunt associated the boys directly with the community of practice through reference to practices and tools of the builder and the DIY expert, for example, he said, 'If *you* were to take sandpaper', and 'That is the one *you* get now from B&Q'. He offered the boys 'images' that they could relate to providing them with connections across time to their current lives to enable them to perceive salience in the activity. In these ways he enabled the process of identification with the subject. Identification and salience Holland *et al.* (1998) argue are interconnected. The more salience activities have the greater the potential for identification and for students' agency to be extended and expertise developed. The boys were recognised as competent, for example, he presumed that boys could handle 3D sketching and he extended their agency by providing them with new resources to negotiate meaning in the subject.

Closing down cultural spaces?

The narrative Mr Hunt generated for the boys included heroic feats, community practices and male inventors. He had no recourse to such a history to create a narrative for the girls. To enable girls' identification with the subject, Mr Hunt fell back on cultural scripts which positioned girls as users rather than producers of technology. Like Mr White, he saw his role as bringing the girls into the subject and as a consequence he slowed the pace of the lesson and in the process of simplifying denied girls access to the tools and reifications of the subject. For example, he substituted everyday terms for technical terms and when a technical term was used he spelt it out, something he did not do for the boys. He addressed the boys as agents, while in the girls' class he invoked future husbands and fathers in DIY activities. He talked of the girls doing something only if they 'couldn't persuade your husband to fix it'. He reinforced their outsider status by addressing the girls as if they were observing items of furniture rather than making them. For example, he said, 'Just imagine having a drawer of cutlery or jewellery'. He did not refer to girls directly as engaged in the practices of the community. By treating girls as users, he limited what he made available to them referring to artefacts – home furnishings as opposed to practices to do with creating joins that transcend artefacts.

He made explicit his assumptions of girls' technical incompetence in his expectations that they would find the subject difficult. Consider Mr Hunt's first reference to the girls about joins: 'The *trouble* is you have to hold that together with something. [Pointing to a join on the drawing of a table].' He also anticipated the girls would not have skills for 3D drawing. He made this clear in comments such as: 'If you think you can handle the drawing…'; 'I would like to think you could draw…'. Another time, he said, 'For those of you who feel they can handle the three dimensional drawing, I would like you to try…' He suggested that the girls drew 'lightly' in case they made mistakes and in this way encouraged the girls to be hesitant. The teacher's representation of girls as 'outsiders' reinforced the distance between them and the subject, which limited the possibilities for identification with the community of practice and to feel a sense of belonging.

Challenging subject cultures, enabling legitimate peripheral participation?

The next data extracts are from a Resistant Materials workshop in the same school but involving a different teacher. Mr Green had a different background to Mr Hunt and this was reflected in his personal construction of the educational purposes of the subject.

> My background is electrical engineering control systems etc. although I've worked in engineering environments… People like myself, people who've been in architectural product design etc. and who hadn't been anywhere near a machine or a tool in their life, we're the second breed [of teachers]. …

He spoke of preparing students for their future life by providing them with generic 'problem-solving' skills, including boys and girls equally in this vision. The images he portrayed of the current and future practices that students would engage in were typically in the domestic realm:

> decorating your house, doing little jobs around the house themselves, the ability to cut a bit of wood, the ability to join a bit of wood, help my mum, put a shelf up, hang wallpaper, arrange tiles, carpet fitting, buying a microwave, get the dimensions [for the space of the microwave].

He gave value to the domestic while allowing for both 'masculine' and 'feminine' behaviours within it, thus reducing the distance between students' out-of-school experiences and ways of knowing and those of the subject.

Experiencing the setting – moving deeper into practice

The data are from lessons where the brief was to design and make a vehicle with four wheels that could carry a 1kg weight and travel 5 metres. The activity was enacted in single-sex settings involving Y9 boys and girls. The emphasis in the task was on meeting the brief and essentially creating a robust moving vehicle; design was secondary to the function. For the teacher, the skills acquired through the design and making a moving vehicle had an obvious relevance to life. He linked the measurement needed to locate where to drill the holes for the wheel axles to the context of putting up a shelf. Creating joins was another feature of the activity and for the teacher this knowledge would enable students to 'do those little jobs around the house'. However, for the students, their actions and their learning were associated with the task, as they understood it and its purpose. Mr Green used the same task in both groups but unintentionally orchestrated settings in which different versions of the task and the subject were made available.

All the boys interviewed identified meeting the design brief as the main aim of the activity, i.e. the task represented by the teacher. The boys worked first on the structure to ensure that it met the design criteria of stability, strength and movement. Only one boy mentioned appearance and talked of making his car 'eye catching' but in elaborating this he talked of detailed structural features such as the bonnet etc. Two boys were explicit that appearance was a secondary consideration. As one put it, 'it's the capability [not the appearance] of the designs that's key'. Mr Green in his discourse in the boys' group emphasised the functional aspects of the design and concepts such as forces and gravity in relation to this. He discouraged attention to style alluding disparagingly to the boys' interest in aesthetics by referring to 'Ferarri testosteroso', 'go-faster stripes' and 'fluffy dice' which he made clear were not legitimate within the brief. In this way, he separated the aesthetic aspects of the vehicle from the objective, technical features and aligned the boys with practices associated with the traditional 'masculine' construction of the subject.

Unlike Mr Hunt, Mr Green had experience of competent women in industry and of girls mastering tools and techniques in single-sex settings in ways not achieved in the mixed classes he had taught previously. He understood that to open up practice to girls, he needed to extend their agency and to do this, he considered that they needed to become familiar with the tools of the culture, in particular, the machinery. While he postioned the girls as in 'need' of support, he identified this need in terms of lack of experience rather than innate deficiencies. Over the research period, the girls were observed using the sanding, sawing and drilling machines and other tools, trying out their skills and in the process learning through trial and error. Girls took up the space made available to them, which was curtailed in the science laboratory. The teacher gave priority to the girls' participation enabling them to learn the purposes and meanings associated with the reifications of the community – the instruments and equipment. The identity extended to them of legitimate peripheral participants (Lave and Wenger, 1991) was recognised by the girls. Girls talked of 'knowing how to work it [the machine]' and that 'it is nice to be trusted to use the machine'. One girl commented about the purpose of the activity that it was about learning how things work 'even if you don't get it right.'

Views from the periphery

Both Mr Hunt and Mr Green assumed that boys as a group identified with the subject, shared a repertoire of skills and had equal access to the tools of the culture. An identity of belonging was extended to all boys. However, how this was experienced depended on the students. Identification was problematic for some boys who felt uncomfortable in the subject, as they did not experience, through their participation, the competency that was assumed on their behalf. To expose their needs would also threaten their gender identity, as in this setting it was associated with technical competence. One boy described himself as not very good at the subject and policed what he took home as he anticipated negative feedback. There was a tension for boys between the value the subject practices placed on the realised product and the role of the product in making visible their inadequacies. Two of the boys disliked the subject and considered themselves insufficiently skilled to participate in it successfully. One related his lack of confidence and dislike of the subject to his fear of the machines: 'I'm just afraid of hurting myself'. For these boys, the only way to resolve the identity conflicts they experienced was to leave the subject. Mr Green along with Mr Hunt, unintentionally, drew on cultural scripts that associated technical competency with boys and incompetence with girls and as a consequence made assumptions about girls' and boys' experiences. They were both unaware how students' agency and learning was constrained by the identities extended to them in the subject setting.

In giving the girls opportunities to experience a sense of belonging and becoming in the subject, Mr Green was anxious to remove constraints. In contrast, he challenged and guided the boys to think about designs in relation to needs of the brief, hence through discussions of forces and gravity he linked design to function. He did not do this with the girls. This had both a positive and a negative effect on the girls, learning. The open nature of the task space allowed girls to see a cultural space for the things they valued the most – design. Julie described resistant materials as her favourite subject. She decided to make the vehicle in the shape of a sheep. 'I made the base and I made the wheels and then I'm just making like the sort of sheep cut-outs to put on the sides'. Together with other girls, she spoke about the importance of creating a product that would be interesting and appealing to look at. However, she recognised that the vehicle might be too heavy to travel the 5 metres required. She hoped that the design of the vehicle would be good enough to get her marks even if the vehicle did not meet the other criteria. Assessment was not the most important outcome for Julia. Her competency in the subject, essential to her participation, was derived as much from her membership in her family as in the school community of the subject, if not more. Her parents' perceptions of what constituted a good product was her source of validation and their criteria were the ones she gave value to. The difference in the task reformulated by Julie and other girls was invisible to the teacher. In assessing her product, he would consider that she was unable to meet the demands in relation to the functional aspect of the product and misinterpret her potential and her future needs. To successfully negotiate the social landscape, students need to be aware of what is required to succeed in a subject in order to exercise their agency, even to challenge that of the teachers. They have to be able to calculate risks and benefits in order to act.

Kylie's interpretation of the teacher's approach was that he gave value to effort and believed learning through mistakes was as beneficial as learning through success. As she commented, the aim of the activity was to learn how things work 'even if you don't get it right'. Her sense of being part of what mattered was evident in that she felt 'a bit older by using them [the machinery]' and in both of these respects she felt her participation was legitimised. Kylie was aware of the gendered nature of the subject's practices describing them as things 'girls don't normally do'. She went on to explain her view of feminity in relation to technology and how she rejected this for herself:

> When normally you grow up they're [girls] just beauticians or working on computers and all things like that and when something goes wrong, like, my Mum, she can never do [fix] it. My Dad's got to get someone out… When I get older I just want to be able to do it all myself instead of relying on everyone else.

Like Julia, her home experiences were fundamental in how she felt positioned and positioned herself in the subject.

> My Dad's a builder and he's got them sort of things [tools] at home. I always go out to the garage and play with them and build things… Little aeroplanes and things but I'm making a doll's house at the moment. When I was little I used to watch him [Dad] making things and when he did things around the house I used to always do that and want to help and stuff and make it with him.

Kylie entered the workshop with an identity of belonging that her Dad had legitimated. Through her play in the 'garage', she moved more deeply into the practice of the community, creating her own artefacts and developed expertise and competence in using the tools of the subject. Mr Green in extending the workshop space to the girls and opening up practice further for them through participation with the machinery enabled Kylie to place cherished social practices and identities lived at home in dialogue with new ones (Hicks, 2001: 221). Both Mr Green and her father had given Kylie access to spaces, tools and know-how that allowed her to develop a sense of her own competence, expanding her vision of the future and the identities available to her. The strong sense of identification gave Kylie power to risk negotiating the task but this was not done overtly with the teacher. She talked of wanting her artefact 'to be different' and how she liked 'doing it my own way'. The teacher had stressed in his interview that he valued individuality and Kylie saw this as legitimising her reformulation of the teacher's task. Having the power to exercise agency depends on a sense of belonging as well as being able to exercise control over what we belong to (Wenger, 1998).

Taking practice forward

In the chapter, reference has been to subjects historically associated with masculinity. In subjects like Textiles, English and modern languages, for example, other gender alignments obtain (Ivinson and Murphy, 2007). The point to be made is that gender cultural scripts and subject cultural scripts intertwine and serve as symbolic resources that have recognisable gender markings that are taken up in different ways by teachers and students. They emerge in practice in subject settings and signal particular identities. As Holland et al. (1998) argue, and as the extracts revealed, this alters how some students are positioned and how teachers interact with them.

> Teachers will take some students' groping claims to knowledge seriously on the basis of signs of identity. These students they will encourage and give informative feedback. Others, whom they regard as unlikely or even improper students of a particular subject … are less likely to receive their serious response. (p 135)

This was evident in the way Mr Green and Mr Hunt responded to and guided boys but in turn there were negative consequences for students of both genders. Awareness of the relationship between cultural scripts about how people figure in the world and subject cultures will help teachers to consider which students may come into settings needing support to identify with the subject and experience a sense of belonging. This same awareness shared with students could also become resources for them to challenge identities extended to them and to take on alternative ways of being. Mr Green's practice in the all-girls setting revealed ways in which this might be achieved but also pointed to the complexity of the problem for practice.

As students move between different communities – family and school or different subject communities – they experience conflicting forms of competence and identities. The work of reconciliation they undertake is not insubstantial nor is it necessarily subconscious. Several of the girls through their interactions made it clear in both science and technology that the identities extended to them conflicted with other versions of themselves. They resisted these differences either by complying or by disengaging. Disengagement was also the resolution that the boys committed to, who were uncomfortable with the gap between their presumed expertise and associated 'masculine' identity and their sense of themselves in the technology workshop. The boy who policed what he took home recognised conflicts in the identities he wanted to maintain and that exposed by his product. Julie knew that she was taking risks with the form of competence valued in the workshop in her decision to commit to her design. Neither the process nor the efforts expended in this reconciliation work or its outcomes were visible to the teachers. Mr Green, similarly, was unaware that part of Kylie's identification and evolving competence in the subject was due to her experiencing the workshop as a space where the values and practices of home and school corresponded. This was significant as for Kylie her home practices were her hobbies and this was exactly the term she used to describe the subject and her involvement in it as a 'school hobby', not a serious subject that would retain her long-term interest.

The instructional movement towards cultural pluralism that allows spaces for students to bring together forms of competence across subject and home-school boundaries requires teachers to pay attention to, and integrate, the histories of participation and identifications that students bring into settings (Hicks, 2001). This challenge is daunting but, as with the research discussed, the best resources for teachers are their students. If the work of reconciliation is recognised and students are engaged in relationships with teachers and students where mutuality is experienced and maintained, then the possibilities for them to make visible the dilemmas and conflicts they face can become an integral part of practice.

In both respects, the changes suggested would mean that in time potential dilemmas could be anticipated and the efforts of teachers and of students redirected towards their learning.

References

Bruner, J. (1996) *The Culture of Education,* London: Harvard University Press.

Connell, P. (2005) *A Critical Review of Recent Developments in Quantitative Research on Gender and Achievement.* Paper presented at the 5th International Conference, Cardiff University, March.

Davies, B. (2003) *Shards of Glass: Children Reading and Writing beyond Gendered Identities,* Cresskill, NJ: Hampton Press Inc.

Dyson, A. H. (1995) Writing children: Reinventing the development of childhood literacy. *Written Communication,* 12 (1), 4–46.

Gorard, S. (2000) *Education and Social Justice: The Changing Composition of Schools and its Implications,* Cardiff: University of Wales Press.

Holland, D., Lachicotte Jr, W., Skinner, D. and Cain, C. (1998) *Identity and Agency in Cultural Worlds,* Cambridge, MA: Harvard University Press.

Hicks, D. (2001) Literacies and masculinities in the life of a young working-class boy, *Language Arts,* 78 (3), 217–26.

Ivinson, G. and Murphy, P. (2007) *Rethinking Single-sex Teaching: Gender, School Subjects and Learning,* Buckingham: Open University Press.

James, P. (1999) Masculinities under reconstruction: classroom pedagogy and cultural change. *Gender and Education,* 11 (4), 395–412.

Kotthoff, H. & Baron, B. (2001) Preface in B. Barron and H. Kotthoff (eds) *Gender in Interaction, Perspectives on Femininity and Masculinity in Ethnography and Discourse,* Amsterdam: John Benjamins Publishing Company.

Lave, J. (1988) *Cognition in Practice,* Cambridge: Cambridge University Press.

Lave, J. and Wenger, E. (1991) *Situated Learning: Legitimate Peripheral Participation,* Cambridge: Cambridge University Press.

Lloyd, G. (1989) 'Man of Reason', in A. Garry and M. Pearsall (eds) *Women, Knowledge and Reality: Explorations in Feminist Philosophy,* Boston: Unwin Hyman.

Mahoney, P. (1998) 'Girls will be girls and boys will be first' in Debbie Epstein, Janette Elwood, Valerie Hey and Janet Maw (eds) *Failing Boys? Issues in Gender and Achievement.* Buckingham: OU Press.

McDermott, R. P. (1996) The acquisition of a child by a learning disability, in S. Chaiklin and J. Lave (eds) *Understanding Practice – Perspectives on Activity and Context,* Cambridge: Cambridge University Press.

Merchant, C. (1983) Mining the Earth's womb, in J. Rothschild, *Machina Ex Dea,* New York: Pergamon Press.

Murphy, P. & Whitelegg, E. (2006) *Girls in the Physics Classroom: A Review of the Research into the Participation of Girls in Physics,* London: Institute of Physics Publishing.

Parker, L. H. and Rennie, L. J. (2002) Teachers' implementation of gender-inclusive instructional strategies in single-sex and mixed-sex science classrooms, *International Journal of Science Education,* 24 (9), 881–897.

Penuel, W. R. and Wertsch, J. V. (1995) Vygotsky and identity formation: a sociocultural approach, *Education Psychologist,* 30 (2), 83–92.

Schwartz Cowan, R. (1997) *A Social History of American Technology,* Oxford: Oxford University Press.

Sfard, A. (2006) Participanist discourse on mathematics learning, in J. Maasz and W. Schloeglmann (eds) *New Mathematics Education Research and Practice,* Rotterdam, The Netherlands: Sense Publishers.

Wajcman, J. (1991) *Feminism Confronts Technology,* Pennsylvania: The Pennsylvania State University Press.

Wenger, E. (1998) *Communities of Practice Learning, Meaning, and Identity,* Cambridge: Cambridge University Press.

12

Science Education as/for Participation in the Community

Wolff-Michael Roth and Stuart Lee

[...]

Background

We frame our rethinking of science education in terms of the debate about scientific literacy. Scientific literacy is, in our approach, a social practice. In a practice approach, the focus is on levels of participation, division of labor, and knowledgeability rather than on decontextualized procedural and declarative knowledge (Lave & Wenger, 1991). In the same way, we think of science and scientific knowledge in terms of social practice rather than as something that exists in human minds as concepts, skills, representations, and so on (e.g., Roth & McGinn, 1998a). Cultural–historical activity theory is most appropriate for theorizing human activities because it is centrally concerned with the primacy of lived praxis (the structures of which are theorized as "practices"). In the following, we briefly review scientific literacy and activity theory, and then articulate the former in terms of the latter.

Scientific literacy

There is no doubt that since its introduction, the notion of scientific literacy has played an important role in defining the science education reform agendas. Reform projects and conceptual change research in science education "consistently define scientific knowledge in terms of 'concepts, principles, theories, and models that are important for all students to know, understand, and use in the fields or disciplines of science'" (Lee, 1999, p. 189). The need for a general scientific and technological literacy is often based on the argument that an effective workforce participation in the twenty-first century requires a certain amount of scientific knowledge (Hazen & Trefil, 1991; Lee & Fradd, 1996). As a result, the reform agendas focused on a general (for *all*!) scientific literacy as an important goal to be achieved (e.g., AAAS, 1989). Despite the rhetoric of scientific literacy for *all* students, school science remains virtually unchanged; students are confronted with basic facts and

[This is an edited version of an extensive illustrated article].

From: *Science Education* (88), pp.263–91. © 2004 Wiley Periodicals, Inc. Reprinted with permission of John Wiley & Sons, Inc.

theories (Eisenhart et al., 1996). The standards of warrants for science knowledge claims often differ dramatically from the standards characteristic of First Nations people, residing in the authority of the cultural–historical developments of oral teachings (Fusco & Barton, 2001), or of women, who may approach science with "a feeling for the organism" (e.g., Keller, 1983). That is, the poor, people of color, and women (as well as others) may fail in school science exactly because of the nature of science and forms of knowing that are stressed in teaching (Rodriguez, 1998); many students (especially women) who leave science are discouraged by the organizational structure of science including its competitive and individualistic nature and its claims to objectivity, value-free inquiry, and being an isolated enterprise (AAUW, 1992). Unsurprisingly, minorities (e.g., African Americans, First Nations) and women often feel discouraged from studying science because its ways of knowing and everyday practices privilege White middle-class and male standpoints and interactional patterns (Eisenhart, et al., 1996; Tobin et al., 1999). The pursuit of scientific literacy promoted by recent national agendas does little to address the diverse audiences, many of whom have been squeezed out of science in traditional approaches.

Not everyone agrees that science could or should be for all. Some scientists are blatantly opposed to the possibility of a general scientific literacy, pointing out that science is an elitist calling and that "raw intelligence and special skills that far exceed what is to be expected of the average person are required to attain it" (Levitt, 1999, p. 4). It may also be that making scientific literacy available to *all* poses a threat to the hegemony of scientific expertise in everyday affairs. Science for all is a threat because it is based on the "potentially counterhegemonic principle of equality" (Eisenhart et al., 1996, p. 271). The scientific community, facing the potential to be continuously questioned in the public debate (e.g., anti-GMO demonstrations, AIDS activists), might therefore not be interested in a general scientific literacy. In this chapter, we not only subscribe to the ideal that science is for all and practiced by collectives, but we also propose that "science," "scientific literacy," and their roles in society have to be redefined.

Although the debate over scientific literacy has been long and ongoing, there remains at least one fundamental assumption that has never been questioned: scientific literacy is a property of individuals and can therefore be measured by means of traditional forms of individual assessment. While most science educators will accept that not every student needs to know how to build a house, how to repair a car, lawnmower, or washer, or how to grow one's own food in a small garden, they will insist that *all* students need to appropriate (via information transfer or construction, depending on the theory of learning) knowledge of the atomic model, Newton's laws, and other "basic facts" and, "basic principles." Thus, the debate over scientific literacy focuses on knowledge, facts, and theories that individuals are expected to possess and exhibit.

[…]

Eisenhart et al. (1996) decentered the debate by taking up three metaphors for literacy previously proposed by Scribner (1986): literacy as adaptation (proficiencies necessary for effective performance), literacy as power (enabling people to claim places in the world), and literacy as a state of grace (self-enhancing potential of literacy). Although these metaphors expand the traditionally rather narrow view on the topic, we suggest that they do not go far enough.

Studies in public understanding of science construct an image of the interaction between scientists and nonscientists that is much more complex, dynamic, and interactive than the traditional opposition between "scientific expertise" and ignorance and rejection of scientific knowledge may lead us to believe (e.g., Irwin & Wynne, 1996). In the everyday world of a community, science emerges not as a coherent, objective, and unproblematic body of knowledge and practices (Roth & Lee, 2002b). Rather, science often turns out to be uncertain and contentious, and unable to answer important questions pertaining to the specific (local) issues at hand (Jenkins, 1999). In everyday situations, citizen thinking may offer a more comprehensive and effective basis for action than scientific thinking; the former is adapted to the complexities of everyday life in the community, whereas the latter only works under the highly constrained conditions of a laboratory isolated from much of the world (Latour, 1988).

It therefore makes sense to conceive scientific literacy in terms of "citizen science," which is "a form of science that relates in reflexive ways to the concerns, interests and activities of citizens as they go about their everyday business" (Jenkins, 1999, p. 704). In our own research, citizen science is related to a variety of contexts, ranging from personal matters (e.g., accessibility to safe drinking water), livelihood (e.g., best farming practices), leisure (e.g., gardening in sustainable, organic ways) to activism or organized protest (Roth & Lee, 2002b). In the community, however, citizen knowledge is collective and distributed: our lives in society are fundamentally based on the division of labor. If we need advice for a backache, most of us go to the doctor or chiropractor; if our cars or bicycles do not work, most of us go to the car or bicycle shop. In the same way, we can think of science in the community as distributed, making the social organization rather than the individual the seat of knowing and learning (Hutchins, 1995). Thus, although many Brazilian child street vendors do not read numbers (e.g., on the currency bills) or do not perform well on school mathematics tasks, they make profits from buying and selling candy (Saxe, 1991); the phenomenon is better understood by considering knowledge to be distributed across the different social organizations in which these children take part. Likewise, scientific literacy in everyday community life then means to be competent in finding whatever one needs to know at the moment one needs to know it. Our research in one community showed that it is exactly in this way that an environmentalist group concerned about the health of the watershed in which their community lies draws on resources distributed across this community to bring about changes (while avoiding conflict) to attitudes and practices (Lee & Roth, 2003).

In contrast to the current ideology of scientific literacy as a property of individuals, we further propose to think about it as a characteristic of certain everyday *situations* in which citizen science occurs.

[…]

Cultural–historical activity theory

At the outset of this review, let us emphasize that activity theorists use the term "activity" differently than it is often used in education. Consistent with cultural–historical activity theory, we conceive of activity as something that is motivated both at the societal and individual level; activity is a collective system that has a complex mediational structure and often takes the form of an institution. What students engage in at school are tasks, motivated by tangible teacher-set goals to which students often do not subscribe, over which they have no or little control, and which require relatively short-lived actions. In most theories of human

knowing, individual action is the central unit of analysis. However, these theories have difficulties accounting for the distributed and situated nature of knowing and learning and for the
nature of human activity as mediated by artifacts and culture (Engeström, 1999). These
theories also fail to address the "continuous, self-reproducing, systemic, and longitudinal–
historical aspects of human functioning" (p. 22). In studying science in the community, we
have successfully used activity theory to frame the water- and watershed-related activities of
adults and seventh-grade science students (Lee & Roth, 2002; Roth & Lee, 2002a).

Theories are based on basic ontologies, that is, sets of fundamental entities and processes
that define the domain. In cultural–historical activity theory, there are six such basic entities: human subjects (individuals or groups), objects (artifacts and motivations), tools, rules,
community, and division of labor (Engeström, 1987). In activity theory, activities constitute
the unit of analysis; because activities involve more than one person and in fact entire communities, they are theorized as systems. Activity systems are defined and motivated by the
relationship between individuals or groups (subject) and the primary object, which exists as
concrete object and as vision of the forthcoming product, the material conditions (tools,
materials), and knowledge of extant material and social conditions (Saari & Miettinen,
2001). For example, an environmental group that attempts, while avoiding conflict, to bring
about changes in the attitude and practices of the Oceanside municipality published a call
in a local newspaper for community participation in protecting and finding out more about
the Henderson Creek watershed. The seventh-grade students taught by one of us decided to
follow the call. They chose Henderson Creek as the *object* of their inquiry and thereby to
construct facts and knowledge *(outcomes)*, which they subsequently wanted to make available to their community during an open-house event of the environmental group.

Relations between the different activity-system constitutive entities are never direct;
rather, all relations are theorized as being mediated by other entities. For example, the *tools*
used by particular student research groups (*subject*) mediated their relation to Henderson
Creek (*object*) leading to quite different knowledge facts (representations) of the creek
(*outcomes*). Doing speed measurements and correlating these to animal species frequen-
cies lead to different *outcomes* than audiotaped birdcalls and journalistic impressions
accompanied by photographs. To use another example from our research: the children's
choice to focus on Henderson Creek was motivated by the *community* in the sense that the
children responded to the call, published in a local newspaper, by an environmental activist
group to contribute to the existing knowledge about the creek. Two further entities that are
considered by activity theory are *rules* and *division of labor*. Rules, for example, include
those that mediate the relationship between individuals and members of the community or
those that govern tool-use within specific communities. Division of labor may refer to the
different roles that students take within their research groups or the roles of teachers, parents, and other community members. All entities are constitutive of a culture (or community of practice) and are understood as continuously undergoing historical change.

[…]

Rethinking scientific literacy

[…]

In cultural–historical activity theory, agency, knowing, and learning are not properties
of individuals but are understood in terms of situated and distributed "engagement in

changing processes of human activity" (Lave, 1993, p. 12). Individual agency, knowing, and learning are understood to be subsets of generalized agency, knowing, and learning available to society. That is, human activities (including conversations) are irreducibly social phenomena that are more than the sum of the contributions of individuals. That is, because division of labor and the associated uneven distribution of knowledge and skill across communities are fundamental to the emergence and development of human society (Holzkamp, 1983), we propose, firstly, to think about scientific literacy as a collective rather than individual practice.

Our second point concerns scientific knowledge, which, in a truly democratic context, we view as one resource among many that may be relevant to the issues at hand. [...]. It is only through inter- and multidisciplinary approaches that the increasingly difficult problems in an ever more complex society can be solved in a satisfactory manner (Fourez, 1997; Maxwell, 1992).

The third point in our proposal concerns lifelong participation in collective endeavors. If students learn to participate in a particular strand of collective life, such as environmental campaigning, environmental stewardship, or hatching and raising endangered fish (e.g., Roth, 2002), their participation can continue beyond the spatial and temporal markers of school life. Participation in, and therefore learning about, issues where science can make relevant contributions can become lifelong endeavors.

Over a three-year period, we studied science in one community and, at the same time, cotaught a science unit to three seventh-grade classes. In the course of our work, these science units were explicitly planned to allow participation in a community-relevant issue. In the following two sections, we provide a detailed description of this work to articulate our perspective on scientific literacy.

Community water problems as curricular topic

[...]

In Oceanside, water has always been a problem. The climate has long favored hot dry summers and wet winters, with concomitant shortages and excesses of water available to the nonaboriginal residents, who, with their recent developments, have exacerbated the issue. There are small clusters of suburban development interspersed with the farmers' fields. Storm drains and ditches channel rainwater—along with the pollutants of suburbia, lawn chemicals, and car leakage—into Henderson Creek and its tributaries and away from these newly developed areas. The municipality of Oceanside introduced an industrial park to the watershed, which is carefully contained within a four-block boundary. The drains of its machine shops and biotechnology labs empty into a ditch (affectionately called "stinky ditch"), which in turn, empties into Henderson Creek. To increase its potential to carry away water in a rapid manner, the creek itself has been deepened and straightened, and much of the covering vegetation has been removed, thereby increasing erosion and pollution from the surrounding farmers' fields. These physical changes have led to increased erosion and silt load in the wet winter months, and are responsible for low water levels and high water temperatures during the dry summer months when (legal and illegal) pumping for irrigation purposes taxes the creek.

As a consequence of these developments, water is shed much more quickly and the water quality declines and water levels become extreme, high in the winter (more than 8000 l/s) and low in the summer (less than 10 l/s). During many summers, insufficient water supply requires the community to limit the amount available to residents. Other residents, with individual wells that draw on the local aquifers, have found their water biologically and chemically contaminated and sometimes have to get their water from gas stations about 5 km away.

The Henderson Creek Project (HCP) arose from the concerns about water quality of three watershed residents: a farmer, a professor of environmental law and policy at the local university, and a research scientist working at a nearby lab, who obtained funding from a federal agency concerned with stream restoration. The HCP is an environmental group that attempts to bring about change of attitudes and practices regarding water and the watershed, but without engaging in confrontation as can often be observed with other local but especially national and international groups (e.g., Greenpeace). The HCP is headed by a coordinator and a five- to seven-member steering committee, and enlists the support of many other people (e.g., hired high school and university students doing summer jobs) and institutions within the region.

[...]

Science education: as/for participation in the community

Science educators have been encouraged to involve their students in ways that allow them to develop a keen appreciation of the places where science and technology articulate smoothly with one's experience of life (Hodson, 1999). Given the water-related problems in Oceanside, it was not difficult to enroll teachers in a project where students would learn science by contributing to the activities initiated by the HCP—investigating the Henderson Creek watershed and contributing the results to the community at large. Over a two-year period, we cotaught with regular teachers science to three seventh-grade classes each lasting 2–4 months. In these classes, students designed and conducted their own projects in and along Henderson Creek with the intent to report their findings at an open-house event organized each year by the HCP. Fundamentally, we wanted to provide students with the opportunity to participate as active citizens in community-relevant affairs by contributing to the knowledge and representations available in and to the community. Other students at the middle and high school also conducted research in the watershed as part of their involvement in a regionally funded "Streamkeepers" program or in science fair competitions. In this way, students already participated in creating knowledge available to the community and the HCP. Members of HCP, the authors, parents, and First Nations elders have contributed in various ways to the teaching of the children by providing workshops, talks, and assistance in framing research and collecting data.

The science units began with articles from the community newspaper that described aspects of the environmental and water-related problems in and around Oceanside. For example, the following excerpt from one of these articles highlights that a revitalization of the ocean surrounding the peninsula where Oceanside is located needs to begin with improving the health of Henderson Creek and its tributary.

Group is a Bridge over Troubled Waters

If the waters of the Pat Bay and Georgia Straight are to be revitalized, the streams and creeks that feed them must be safe. A group at [Oceanside] wants to begin the process by breathing life back into [NAME] Creeks.

The damage […] was caused by channeling the creeks and removing gravel from the area. Straightening the creeks (ditching) not only makes the water move through the remaining culvert too quickly to support rearing beds, but removes the surrounding vegetation. That, in turn, erodes the environment on which birds and other species depend for survival.

Chief […] spoke about the abundance of fish, shellfish, and other wildlife in the area during his youth …

But for the long-term work, project coordinators said *the wider community must be involved* … (Reimche, 1998, p. 9, our emphasis)

The teachers read the article with the students and asked questions about the need for revitalizing the ocean; children had no difficulties in answering given that some parents fished as a hobby or for a livelihood. First Nations students were able to contribute to the understanding of the need for action by comparing their oral history about the abundance of fish in the creek and ocean inlet with their current virtual absence. At the end, teachers and students discussed how to respond to the call by the environmental group and become involved. The students began generating ideas, often related to cleaning up the creek and to finding out more about Henderson Creek and its problems. After a field trip to different sites along the creek (because of parent involvement, we had six to eight cars and vans available each field day and in each class), the students began framing initial investigations and even entire programs of research.

When we began our project in school science classrooms, we still believed that all students should engage in their activities in ways that would foster scientific practices conceived in a traditional way—designing experiments, graphing results, and so forth. That is, our model for school science was influenced by laboratory rather than community science. However, we soon realized that a considerable number of students were attracted by the project but had little interest in measuring series of variables and representing results in the form of correlations. While these students still participated in the data collection, the subsequent data analyses and activities that focused on mathematical representations generally turned them off. Particularly girls and indigenous students felt disenfranchised by such an approach and preferred to generate different forms of knowledge such as film, narratives, photographs, and interviews. Taking our lead from other activities in the community, where different representational forms were legitimately used, we began to encourage students to investigate on their own terms, choosing their data collection and representational tools that best fit their interests and needs. (We find this approach more democratic than forcing every student to engage in the same activity in the same way and at the same time.) A large variety of very different representations of the creek and the adjoining areas began to proliferate: there were audio-recorded descriptions, videotaped records of the watershed and student activities, photographs, drawings, and other representations. That is, because we made it possible for students to create representations of their interest and that met their needs, the total representations actually increased and provided a richer image of Henderson Creek and its problems. Furthermore, this change provided forms of knowing and learning that led to an increasing participation of students who traditionally have felt alienated and excluded because science lessons emphasized ways of knowing foreign to them. […]

Parents, activists, aboriginal elders, scientists, graduate students, and other Oceanside residents were an integral part of the science units—they constituted the relevant *community* in the context of which our seventh-graders learned. This community was constituted by an interpenetration of school and village life more generally. For example, every other week the classes spent one entire afternoon (12.00–2.30 p.m.) in and around the creek. Parents assisted both in driving children to the different sites along the creek and participated in teaching by asking productive questions, scaffolding, and supervising children. Members of the HCP also contributed by giving presentations, and by assisting in teaching students how to use particular tools and how to do research in the creek and in analyzing data and organisms brought back to the classroom. Students from classes that had already completed or were near completion of their unit talked about their work in another class that was just beginning, and assisted their peers during field work and data analysis.

This involvement of residents therefore integrated the children's activities with activities in Oceanside in two ways. First, the community came to the school, assisting students and teachers in their activities. Second, the student activities were concerned with a pressing issue of the community; the science lessons took children out of the school and into the community. That is, the children's activities were motivated by the same concerns that drove the activities of other community members. In terms of our model, there is therefore legitimate (peripheral) participation because the motives that drive the activity system share many elements. It is this overlap with the everyday activity in Oceanside [motivation, subjects (community), and tools] that makes the children's work "authentic." Rather than preparing for a life after school or for future science courses, children already participated in and contributed to social life in the community. It is in the process that learning was occurring.

Because the very organization of traditional science and science education has diminished the resilience of girls, First Nations, and other underrepresented groups (Aikenhead, 2001; Hammrich, 2002), we explicitly avoided the reproduction of internal relations and discourses of laboratory (professional) science. Instead, we emphasized "coming to knowing" (Aikenhead, 2001) that validates cultural knowledge and designed the units to emphasize personal relevance, cooperation, and interdependence and observation, verbal expression, and writing skills. Consistent with Aikenhead's recommendations, our students had opportunities for talking within their own personally relevant framework without sanctions for being unscientific and for immersing themselves in their everyday (gendered, aboriginal) culture as they engaged in their investigations. Thus, students chose their investigations, partners, and ways in which they wanted to represent the results of their activities. They did not have to debate or critique others' representations and interpretations but we assisted them to reflect why others might come to different conclusions. Although we asked students to interpret the data of their peers, we emphasized the value of multiple interpretations rather than argumentation, formation of alliances to defeat alternative interpretations, and disagreement. Thus, in the classrooms involved in our studies, students characteristically helped one another in gathering data, understanding details of their collections, interpreting the data, and in formulating future plans of actions.

[…]

Data sources

The data sources we collect include extensive field notes, publications produced and appropriated by the activists, videotapes of public events, audiotaped interviews, newspaper clippings, informal interviews, and texts and inscriptions from the region that relate to the issues of watershed management and ecological restoration. On several occasions, we videotaped groups of HCP members and other interested local residents who walked sections of Henderson Creek with different consultants. The HCP drew on these consultants for advice on how to improve the creek, find the best trout habitat, and how to expand the healthier sections of the creek. We used two cameras to videotape all classroom instruction—having obtained the equivalent of one entire school year of science instruction, spread over three classes. We interviewed a range of participants in the HCP, students, and local residents—all interviews were audio- or videotaped.

School science in the community

[…]

Diversity of projects and representational forms

In designing the unit, we took our cues from the activities of others in the community concerned with the health of the local watershed and its main water-carrying body, Henderson Creek, and allowed students to pursue investigations of their own interests. Because people in the community created and used various representations of the watershed, creek, and the pressing issues, we changed from an initial focus on "scientific representations" (e.g., graphs) and encouraged students to create representations that best met their needs of expressive forms. That is, students had considerable control over their objects of inquiry and the means used for producing the outcomes of their engagement (e.g., the representations).

Although the activity-system-defining object was the same in most instances for all student groups, Henderson Creek and the watershed it drains, different tools and rules mediated the relations in different ways leading to very different outcomes (Table 12.1). Nevertheless, the various outcomes ultimately contributed in their own ways to the totality of the findings generated by one or more classes. We understand that the students' activities were authentic in the sense that their goals were motivated in the same way and by the same concerns that other goals in the community were motivated. Table 12.1 also shows how different members of the community in general and the activist group in particular participated in the activity system that describes the students' activities. Other similarities with the activity systems in the community are some of the tools (colorimeter, rules). Not surprisingly, some of the *outcomes* of the student-centered activity system were therefore similar to those created elsewhere in Oceanside by adults or university students. For example, the use of colorimeter, pH meter, or dissolved-oxygen meter all led to numeric representations of stream health (Lee & Roth, 2001). In the same way, middle school students and college students working for the HCP as a summer job produced very similar graphical representations. Furthermore, forms designed by scientists (water quality assessment, physical assessment) assisted students in their summer job and middle school students in producing representations (*outcomes*) that could be used by HCP members to pursue other goals (e.g., getting grants, proposing restoration work).

It has been suggested that if the science curriculum allows students to pursue questions of their interest and to use representational tools (instruments, camera, discourse) of their own choice, disinterest and exclusion characteristic of traditional science courses (e.g., Eisenhart et al., 1996) seldom become an issue (Holzkamp, 1993). Framing their research agendas, having control over their research questions and the form of the representations, our students articulated what they have learned in a great variety of ways.

> We are studying Henderson Creek to find out about what water and creatures are like at the different sites. One of the things we are trying to find out is the quality of the water. The water quality determines what creatures live there. The quality depends on the depth, the width, the bottom (whether it is sandy, rocky, or gravely), the temperature and the speed of current. We will take samples of the creatures and then the next day count them and look at them under a microscope. We will make graphs displaying all the different information we got. There will be professors there with us to help us and tell us how to do it. (Magda, May 5, 1998)

Kathy and her teammates conducted a series of interviews to find out "what the community thinks." They interviewed the mayor of Oceanside, the coordinator of HCP, Meagan McDonald, a WSÁNEC elder, and other community members. They transcribed and analyzed the interviews. The transcriptions of the interviews were subsequently made public as part of one of the posters during the open-house event.

Kathy: Has it been just the last ten years that the fish have been dying off?
Meagan: Actually, it has been the last fifty years that the cutthroat trout have declined in size, in range, and in numbers. So there is still a dwindling population of fish, but they are not as healthy as they were or should be.
Kathy: Did people ever fish in Henderson Creek?
Meagan: Yes, they did. We know that because of the anecdotal information and first-nation history. The last time people really fished there was around thirty to forty years ago. It was the settlers and First-Nations people who fished there.
Kathy: What polluted Henderson Creek?
Meagan: There used to be a large wetland area in the middle of the Henderson Creek watershed that was drained in the late 1800s, then converted to ditches. So in that loss of the habitat from the draining, the gradual decline in water quality from things like losing the tree cover, the water temperatures would increase because there was not enough shade for the water.

We propose to look at such conversation not in terms of one person (Meagan) teaching something to another (Kathy). Rather, we suggest that scientific literacy arises from the order of interaction, the relation between questions and answers. The interview provided an occasion to interact with a central member of the HCP, a person experienced in environmental campaigning and familiar with many technical aspects that affect the health

Table 12.1 Outcomes in an activity system (Grade 7 Science Class) as Mediated by the Tools

Subject	Object	Tools	Community	Rules	Division of Labor	Outcome(s)
John, Tim	Henderson Creek	Stop watch, tape measure, ruler	Oceanside, parents [Mr. Goulet], activists, scientists	Repeated timing and averaging	Roles in research team (timer, releaser, measurer)	Correlation between speed and profile
Grade 7 students [John et al., Lisa et al.]	Henderson Creek	Tape, stopwatch, Serber sampler	Teachers, students from other classes [Davie]	For use of stopwatch, tape, sampler	Roles in research team, role in knowledge production of community	Classification and frequency of organisms; stream speed
Michelle et al., Kathy et al., Chris	Henderson Creek, shore	Cassette recorder, camera	Teacher, Michael, Stuart, Oceanside	Aesthetics	Roles in research team, role in knowledge production community	Radio-like reportage, slides, web site
Gabe	Student researchers	Videotape	Class	Quality of informational content	Role as "historian" of knowledge construction	Processes of investigating environmental health
Jodie et al.	Henderson Creek	Dissolved oxygen meter, Serber sampler	Teacher, Michael, Meagan, Oceanside	For use of D-O meter	Roles in research team, role in knowledge production of community	Dissolved-oxygen levels, organism-type/oxygen-level correlations

of a watershed. In fact, Kathy had sought out Meagan to conduct the interview; Kathy and her peers owned the project of which the interview was a part. Meagan's answers, which allowed a historical perspective on the problems of Henderson Creek to emerge, were occasioned by Kathy's informed questions. It is the interview situation in the context of the children's Henderson-Creek-related projects that allowed a scientifically literate conversation to appear. [...]

Gabe, an aboriginal student from the local WSÁNEC' reservation, who hardly engaged in any school-related task, did not want to work within a peer group. He was not interested in conducting investigations as others did but wanted to work with a video camera to document the activities of others and to interview them about their investigations while they were actually collecting or analyzing data.

Gabe: Can you talk about your observations?
Nicole: Right now, we are taking the moisture and pH of the soil in different locations.
Liza: And we are trying to find out whether it is any different when we are going through the plants.
Nicole: Yeah, and we are looking at the bugs and stuff as well. We are having a good time.

As Kathy in the previous example, Gabe had chosen the object of his work in this classroom. He was not forced to do some routine laboratory task for the sake of doing the task but rather had chosen something that fit his interest and cognitive needs. That is, he chose not to research the creek itself but to document the research conducted by others. It is evident that he was not just doing something else but also participating in the collective activity of the group, thereby encountering science as a strand in the activities of others. In fact, his journalism contributed to self-reflexivity in this classroom, for science is not just a strand of the events but those participating are giving accounts of what they have done and were presently doing. Science talk and (reflexive) talk *about* science arose here from the interaction of students pursuing different, personally relevant and meaningful goals of their interests. As critical science educators, we are interested in facilitating the emergence of such personally experienced, publicly visible, collective praxis rather than making individuals "acquire information necessary for scientific literacy" (Korpan et al., 1997, p. 516) so that they "possess a basic vocabulary of scientific concepts" (Flower, 2000, p. 38).
    [...]
Failure and marginalization occur in contexts where individuals and groups have no control; expansive learning occurs where people control the object of activity and the means of production (Holzkamp, 1993). This is the case for Kathy and Gabe, who not only chose what they wanted to do but also how they wanted to do it, the tools and instruments to use, and the assessment of the extent to which they had achieved what they had set out to achieve. In this sense, neither the aboriginal Gabe nor the woman Kathy had been marginalized but rather have become central, active participants in a collective engaged in finding out more about the physical characteristics and health of Henderson Creek.
    Mr. Goulet, the parent of a female student, enjoyed the project activities and requested to come along on every field trip. He did not consider his task as one of supervising and watching out for children but one of scaffolding student investigations. We talked to him about the importance of letting students frame goals and asking productive questions that lead to further inquiry rather than to definite answers. He took every possible occasion as a

starting point for allowing students to learn. For example, one day we recorded him as he worked with a group of boys who had decided that they would find out the relationship between the cross section and speed of the water. He questioned the boys attempting to assist them in coming up with creative means for measuring the width of the creek although it was too deep to step into it let alone cross it. He actively participated in measuring the depth of the stream, swollen by the recent winter storms. Ultimately, the group decided to measure the width of the creek by tying a piece of wood at the end of a string and launching it to the other side of the creek. By pullying, they brought the piece of wood to lie on the bank, which allowed them to mark the string at their own side. They measured the length of string between the mark and the end of the string after the wood had been pulled across. The fact that the wood had floated gave rise to a "teachable moment."

Mr. Goulet:	Why did it float instead of sinking?
John:	Like this one is too big but if it was smaller.
Mr. Goulet:	It would have sunk?
John:	Yeah, but if it was heavier, then it would have sunk.
Mr. Goulet:	Right, so how would you figure out whether that would sink or not?
Tim:	We'll say, this will generally sink.
Mr. Goulet:	What would be a way to find out? Why would this [hammer] sink?
Tim:	Because this is more compact in weight.
Mr. Goulet:	So, if compare this to the same amount of water, I would be heavier. So?
John:	It would sink.

Here, in the context of Mr. Goulet's questions to John and Tim, a conversation about sinking and floating emerged. The transcript shows that a qualitative theory involving the notions of "compactness in weight" and "relative weight to water" came to explain sinking and floating. Here again, scientific literacy characterizes the situation and might have not been observable if aspects of the situation had been changed (e.g., written test about "density"). Importantly, learning was made possible by a resident of Oceanside present to participate with and guide students in producing representations of Henderson Creek.
[...]

Reporting to the community

Given the different tools that the children had used to conduct investigations and construct their representations, the variety of the displays came as no surprise. There were maps, photographs, drawings of invertebrate organisms, instruments and tools, live invertebrates and microscopes to view them, larger organisms in a glass tank, interview transcripts, and a variety of scientific representations (graphs, histograms). The type of representations used was little different from those used in the various exhibits by the environmental activists. That is, the children's representations were a reflection of those that are characteristically used in a community-based science. We provide several brief descriptions and transcripts to articulate scientific literacy in the community involving children.

Michelle and her three (female) teammates had been more interested in qualitative than in quantitative representations of the creek. For example, one of their projects involved a tape recorder, used to record bird songs and verbal descriptions of several sites along the creek, and a camera for saliently depicting some issue identified by the girls. Accordingly, their exhibit contained photographs, exemplifying, for example, the differences between the creek where it had been turned into a ditch and where it was in a natural state. The work Michelle and her classmates had conducted in the field was represented in textual rather than graphical, mathematical, or other form. A table on the right panel of their exhibit lists the qualitative differences between different parts of the creek. The following explanation is characteristic of the information provided as results from her research.

There were no fish in the ditches, just some little bugs, but no fish. But in the creek, in Centennial Park, there were cut throat trout and stickleback. And the creek is much cleaner, because the ditch is next to the road. And people who are driving by are dumping garbage into the ditch, out of their cars and as they are walking by. So we found much more garbage, like we found pop cans, drinking things from McDonalds, French-fry cases, and things like that. (Michelie, May 29, 1999)

Important aspects of the open-house event were students' contacts and interactions with visitors of all ages. The seventh-grade students and children younger than themselves interacted in ways that were as involved as interactions involving adult visitors. In every situation, aspects of scientific literacy emerged in often unexpected and surprising ways. Thus, in his regular classes, Chris interacted very little with his peers. They saw in him a "computer nerd." Teachers often found it difficult to work with him, "get and keep Chris on task," or to get him to achieve to his potential. On the other hand, Chris thrived in the science unit, where he built a web site using his own and others' photos and texts. During the open-house event, there were many interactions involving Chris that allowed scientific literacy to become visible as a collective practice. It is in and through the interaction that the adult comes to use the stereomicroscope properly and to see an entity as "arthropod" rather than as a "mosquito larvae."

Adult: Have you got any insects?
Chris: Yeah, yeah. But don't move it [glass container under microscope] around so much because I got it focused.
Adult: (*Approaches microscope.*) You got it focused?
Chris: Yeah. (*Adult only views through one lens of the two-lens stereomicroscope.*) You can look through both. Then you can see them better.
Adult: What's these little ones in here? Are these mosquito larvae?
Chris: No, there are no mosquito larvae in there.
Adult: You see the little ones (*points towards glass*)?
Chris: Yeah, the little ones that are swimming around, those are arthropods. They like to swim on the side first. They are neat critters.
Adult: Yeah, and that is what the trout feed on, aye?
Chris: Well, I guess.
Adult: (*Looks at drawings on display, points to one.*) Oh, this is what fly larvae look like. Thanks.

This excerpt exhibits the choreography of an interaction in which Chris contributed in a significant way to produce the appearance of scientific literacy rather than its opposite, the "scientific ignorance" other authors (e.g., Shamos, 1995) seem to detect in the general population. We do not want to claim that Chris is more knowledgeable than the adult and that Chris' knowledge is somehow transferred or reconstructed by the adult. Rather, we want to claim that it is in the interaction, in the questions and answers that scientific literacy emerges. The adult's questions are as much a part of collective scientific literacy as the answers they solicited from the student. Questions and answers mutually solicit one another, leading to a collective phenomenon that cannot be predicted from individual characteristics. As any other conversation, the topics covered cannot be predicted in advance but emerge from the dialectical relation of individuals that constitute the conversation unit.

In another situation, Jodie came to interact with Miles Magee, one of the cofounders of the HCP. Unbeknownst to Jodie, Miles Magee is a political scientist living in the community interested in assisting local people in empowering themselves concerning the environmental health of their community. Miles was very interested in the outcomes of the students' investigations and interacted with a number of them. In one instance, he asked Jodie about an instrument on exhibition (colorimeter), the same type of instrument that the university summer work-study students have been using in order to conduct and produce water quality assessments. In the course of their interaction, knowledgeability relating to a particular instrument and its operation was being produced.

Miles: What is this?

Jodie: A calori … meter. It measures the clarity of the water.

Miles: Ah! A calori … a colorimeter?

Jodie: You take the clear water and you put it in this glass and then here [puts it into instrument] (*pushes a few buttons*) and you take the standard, which is like the best there is. And then you switch this (*takes different bottle*) and put the one with the water from the creek. (*Covers sample.*) And then you scan the sample. And then you see what the thing floating in the water is.

Miles: Over-range, what does that mean?

Jodie: (*Pushes a number of buttons.*)

Miles: Oh, it is when it is over the range, I see.

Jodie: First I have to do the standard again. (*Does standard.*) Then I take the creek water. (*Enters bottle into instrument. Pushes buttons.*)

Miles: Oh, I see. This is really neat.

This interaction did not lead to a contrast between an all-knowing adult (expert) and a child; there was no belittling. Rather, the conversation involving Miles and Jodie allowed the articulation of an honest request for understanding and an illustration of the operation of the device. Scientific and technological literacy emerged from the dialectic tension between a request for information and the production of an answer in the form of a demonstration. In this way, Jodie helped many adult visitors to the open-house event to learn about colorimetry and how to measure the clarity or opacity of water.

"Measures" of "success"

Enacting science in the community presents severe problems for assessment (Jenkins, 2002), especially when task orientation is replaced by an orientation to social and community values (Fusco & Barton, 2001). For example, one group of Austrian students regarded the formal school evaluation as a "devaluation" of the environmental work that they had done (Posch, 1993). Their own assessment criteria were based on real-life evaluation, as they had encountered it while dealing with the people in the community. The interactions at the open-house event involving students, activists, and community members not only led to the emergence of scientific literacy but also to the emergence of the legitimacy of the children's activities. From the perspective of the environmental activists, the children had contributed in a significant way to the success of the open house by contributing to its content and by being a drawing factor—the children's presence encouraged the participation of many parents and relatives alike. That is, the activists recognized the contributions of the seventh-grade students as the outcome of a legitimate activity of the type that they had called for in the (earlier featured) newspaper article. The results of the students' investigations were mentioned in a newspaper article and in a web publication.

[...]

These publications, which emphasized the contribution of the children's work to the overall project of environmental health in the Henderson Creek watershed, added further to underscore the legitimacy of the activity. When considered in terms of the notion of "legitimate peripheral participation" (Lave & Wenger, 1991), these children participated in the affairs of their local village community and contributed in more than marginal ways to knowing and learning available in their community about environmental health.

In the lived experiences of the children, the interactions in and with the community played an important role. When asked to reflect about what they had done and learned, many children spontaneously talked and wrote about the relation between community and their own activities.

> I worked very hard on the map and proceedings. During this course I learned about fieldwork: I learned how to collect samples of the creek and take temperatures and speed. I also did some work with the community. It taught me about working with others and working in the community. I noticed that ever since our Henderson Creek article was published in the *Peninsula News Review* that the public has begun to notice the creek. (Sally)
>
> In the Henderson Creek group the work that I have done and help with includes: Worked on the model of the creek, typed out the descriptions of the sites with help from Davie, Brandon, and Steve cut them out. I was at the cultural center. What I've learned from all this is about the problem of the creek, how to work with the public (community). The thing I learned was how much other people knew about Henderson Creek. Like Mr. Herbert as the Mayor of Oceanside he knew lots about it. How to work productively and still have fun with your friends. How to use special equipment like "D" nets, microscopes, colorimeter and all sorts of things. (Jodie)

Sally had noticed that the (above-mentioned) newspaper article had led community members ("public") to notice the creek that some (including teachers) did not even know to exist. Sally's comment may also imply how important the newspaper article was to the gratification she (and her peers) received from being acknowledged in a public forum and therefore as a legitimate contributor to the social life of the community. Jodie's comment addresses his emergent awareness of existing knowledge and expresses a certain amount of pride in being able to participate in the use of scientific equipment.

Scientific education as everyday praxis

In this chapter, we argue for a different way of looking at scientific literacy and use a case study of lessons that provide a context where it makes sense to take such a perspective. We formulate our perspective in terms of three propositions. First, scientific literacy more broadly and scientific knowledge more narrowly are aspects that characterize social activities rather than individuals. Because the division of labor is a fundamental process that links individual life and societal processes, individuals do not need to be knowledgeable in every domain. Rather, they need to be able to participate in collective activity and to locate knowledge when and where they need it. Not everybody needs to be able to bake bread or repair lawnmowers; people simply need to know where to get the bread and where to get the lawnmower fixed. In a similar way, we suggest that not everybody needs to know about chemical concentrations or molecules in fertilizers, but they should know, for example, where to go to get advice on concentrations of nitrogen and phosphorus for the particular problem at hand (e.g., garden center). The focus on participation makes us start theorizing and planning curriculum with collective processes; these can then be interrogated in terms of the opportunities they provide for individual participation.

Second, in a democratic society, all forms of knowledge that contribute to a controversial or urgent issue are to be valued; science is but one of these different forms of knowledge. The photo reportage and interviews of community members contribute to community knowledge in just as important ways as the correlations between stream speed and the frequency of particular organisms. Third, the students participated in activities that are not only like but also fundamentally oriented to the same goals and in the same context as those of other people in the community. [...]

Our study showed that children generally participated in activities with similar motives as those of adults, and they participated in a variety of forms of conversations with adults other than the regular teachers. If the motives underlying school science and environmental stewardship or volunteerism are similar, based on the nature of tools, rules, divisions of labor, and community, we can expect individuals (subjects) to move along trajectories that do not exhibit discontinuities characteristic of other transitions. That is, children who participate in activities that contribute to the knowledge available in their community will develop into adolescents and adults, but they can continue to participate in the activities relating to environmental health without experiencing a discontinuity. [...]

Current efforts in rethinking scientific literacy have many shortcomings, which impede with the development of achieving their goals of broad participation [e.g., Science for All Americans (AAAS, 1989)]. In some situations, these reform efforts are more damaging then helpful: "colonization under the guise of 'science for all' undermines students' self-identities as Aboriginal people, identities which are fundamentally essential to the economic development, environmental responsibility, and cultural survival of Aboriginal peoples" (Aikenhead, 2002, p. 288). Aikenhead further suggests that this is also the case for other often-disenfranchised individuals and groups, including many white middle-class students. These reform agendas fail to sufficiently address the wide gap between school and everyday knowledge. They pay insufficient heed to the fact that students constitute a heterogenous clientele; furthermore, it makes little sense to treat citizens as though they were a homogenous group (Jenkins, 1999). In the case study we presented, students pursued investigations of their interest, drawing on those tools that best responded to their (intellectual, motivational, and emotional) needs, and produced a large variety of representations of stream and watershed health. In this context, different strands can emerge, including those that are characterized by representations and forms of discourse typical for scientific laboratories and scientific communities. The important implication of such an approach is that the standards of argument and rules of interaction cannot privilege a single strand (e.g., science) but need to be appropriate to mediate the contributions of multiple strands. [...]

In our proposal, knowing and learning are taken as aspects of culturally and historically situated activity. Learning is discernable by noticing self and others' changing participation in changing social practices. It is discernable from the particular relationships that they have achieved with others in their community at large. Because interaction and participation cannot be understood as the sum total of an individual acting toward a stable environment, learning cannot be understood in terms of what happens to individuals. Rather, if learning is situated and distributed, educators must focus on enabling changing participation, that is, enabling new forms of societal activity that is collectively generated. We are therefore particularly interested in forms of participation that are continuous with out-of-school experiences and therefore have the potential to lead to lifelong learning rather than to discontinuities between formal and informal learning settings.

Science and scientific literacy for the students in our case study constituted the outcome of a lived curriculum. Rather than studying to be admitted to higher levels of learning (science as propaedeutic), students actively participated in the social life of their community by contributing to the available database on the health of one local stream. For these students, science was a lived curriculum, in which students "have a feeling that they are involved in their own development and recognize that they can use what they learn" (Hurd, 1998, p. 411). Our venture in science curriculum development recognizes the socialization of students into the community, and relegates to science a place next to other forms of knowledge relevant to culture, our lives, and the course of our democracy. A lived science (technology) curriculum requires a collective endeavor involving not only science but also disciplinary knowledge in the social sciences, humanities, ethics, law, and political science. However, an interdisciplinary approach, which gives science an epistemologically equal place among other forms of knowledge rather than an epistemologically exceptional status, does not necessarily lead to a different science education. [...]

Based on our research of science in and for the community, we propose a different way of approaching science and science education, a way that acknowledges the limitations of science—which does not mean that scientific efforts become undervalued. Acknowledging the nature of science as it is and can be practiced in the community opens the door to richer understandings of science as a "profoundly creative and imaginative activity tempered by a scrupulous honesty in the face of experimental evidence" (Jenkins, 1999, p. 708). Such an approach permits groups and communities to enact different relations between scientific and other forms of knowledge, including various forms of situated knowing (e.g., traditional, relational). Rather than privileging disciplinary science, we ought to foster situations that allow the negotiation of different forms of knowledge geared to particular (controversial) problems as these arise in the daily life of a community.

Teachers are often held to connect or to assist students in "connecting" school science to their everyday lives; but teachers experience difficulties in assisting students to make such connections (Cajas, 1999). Even if such connections exist (e.g., in simulated problem contexts), the problem-solving activity may still be unrelated (e.g., Lave, 1988). The solution to build bridges ("connect") between formal academic discourse and everyday life remains fraught by the presence of the gap between in- and after-school experiences. Rather than pursuing the making of connections, we argue that educators should involve students in the real thing. There is no gap if the students' activities already constitute an aspect of everyday out-of-school activity. That is, science education transcends traditional propaedeutic approaches that attempted to *prepare* students *for* subsequent levels of schooling and life after school, and provides students with opportunities to *engage in* everyday (relevant) activities that shape community and their own identities alike. The issue is one of going about engaging in and contributing to the solutions of everyday-life contentious issues rather than making connections to bridge an artificial divide.

[…]

References

Aikenhead, G. (2001). Integrating Western and Aboriginal sciences: Cross-cultural science teaching. Research in Science Education, 31, 337–355.

Aikenhead, G. (2002). Cross-cultural science teaching: Rekindling traditions for aboriginal students. Canadian Journal of Science, Mathematics, and Technology Education, 3, 287–304.

American Association for the Advancement of Science (AAAS). (1989). Science for all Americans: Project 2061. Washington, DC: AAAS.

American Association of University Women (AAUW). (1992). Agenda for action. Washington, DC: Author.

Cajas, F. (1999). Public understanding of science: Using technology to enhance school science in everyday life. International Journal of Science Education, 21, 765–773.

Eisenhart, M., Finkel, E., & Marion, S. F. (1996). Creating the conditions for scientific literacy: A re-examination. American Educational Research Journal, 33, 261–295.

Engeström, Y. (1987). Learning by expanding: An activity-theoretical approach to developmental research. Helsinki: Orienta-Konsultit.

Engeström, Y. (1999). Activity theory and individual and social transformation. In Y. Engeström, R. Miettinen, & R.-L. Punamäki (Eds.), Perspectives on activity theory (pp. 19–38). Cambridge, England: Cambridge University Press.

Flower, M. J. (2000). Unsettling scientific literacy. Liberal Education, 86(3), 36–45.

Fourez, G. (1997). Scientific and technological literacy as a social practice. Social Studies of Science, 27, 903–936.

Fusco, D., & Barton, A. C. (2001). Representing student achievements in science. Journal of Research in Science Teaching, 38, 337–354.

Hammrich, P. L. (2002). Gender equity in science and mathematics education: Barriers of the mind. In J. Koch & B. Irby (Eds.), Defining and redefining gender equity in education (pp. 81–98). Greenwich: Information Age Publishing.

Hazen, R. M., & Trefil, J. (1991). Science matters: Achieving scientific literacy. New York: Doubleday.

Hodson, D. (1999). Going beyond cultural pluralism: Science education for sociopolitical action. Science Education, 83, 775–796.

Holzkamp, K. (1983). Grundlegung der Psychologie [Foundations of Psychology]. Frankfurt/M: Campus Verlag.

Holzkamp, K. (1993). Lemen: Subjektwissenschaftliche Grundlegung [Learning: Subject-centered scientific foundations]. Frankfurt/M: Campus Verlag.

Hurd, P. D. (1998). Scientific literacy: New minds for a changing world. Science Education, 82, 407–416.

Hutchins, E. (1995). Cognition in the wild. Cambridge, MA: MIT Press.

Irwin, A., & Wynne, B. (Eds.). (1996). Misunderstanding science? The public reconstruction of science and technology. Cambridge, England: Cambridge University Press.

Jenkins, E. (1999). School science, citizenship and the public understanding of science. International Journal of Science Education, 21, 703–710.

Jenkins, E. (2002). Linking school science education with action. In W.-M. Roth & J. Dèsautels (Eds.), Science education as/for sociopolitical action (pp. 17–33). New York: Peter Lang.

Keller, E. F. (1983). A feeling for the organism. New York: W. H. Freeman.

Korpan, C. A., Bisanz, G. L., Bisanz, J., & Henderson, J. M. (1997). Assessing literacy in science: Evaluation of scientific news briefs. Science Education, 81, 515–532.

Latour, B. (1988). The pasteurization of France. Cambridge, MA: Harvard University Press.

Lave, J. (1988). Cognition in practice: Mind, mathematics and culture in everyday life. Cambridge, England: Cambridge University Press.

Lave, J. (1993). The practice of learning. In S. Chaiklin & J. Lave (Eds.), Understanding practice: Perspectives on activity and context (pp. 3–32). Cambridge, England: Cambridge University Press.

Lave, J., & Wenger, E. (1991). Situated learning: Legitimate peripheral participation. Cambridge, England: Cambridge University Press.

Lee, O. (1999). Science knowledge, world views, and information sources in social and cultural contexts: Making sense after a natural disaster. American Educational Research Journal, 36, 187–219.

Lee, O., & Fradd, S. H. (1996). Literacy skills in science learning among linguistically diverse students. Science Education, 80, 651–671.

Lee, S., & Roth, W.-M. (2001). How ditch and drain become a healthy creek: Representations, translations and agency during the re/design of a watershed. Social Studies of Science, 31, 315–356.

Lee, S., & Roth, W.-M. (2002). Learning science in the community. In W.-M. Roth & J. Désautels (Eds.), Science education as/for sociopolitical action (pp. 37–64). New York: Peter Lang.

Lee, S., & Roth, W.-M. (2003). Of traversals and hybrid spaces: Science in the community. Mind, Culture, & Activity, 10, 120–142.

Levitt, N. (1999). Prometheus bedevilled: Science and the contradictions of contemporary culture. New Brunswick, NJ: Rutgers University Press.

Maxwell, N. (1992). What kind of inquiry can best help us create a good world? Science, Technology, & Human Values, 17, 205–227.

Posch, P. (1993). Research issues in environmental education. Studies in Science Education, 21, 21–48.

Reimche, J. (1998, December 16). Group is a bridge over troubled waters. Peninsula News Review, 9.

Rodriguez, A. J. (1998). Busting open the meritocracy myth: Rethinking equity and student achievement in science. Journal of Women and Minorities in Science and Engineering, 4, 195–216.

Roth, W.-M. (2002). Taking science education beyond schooling. Canadian Journal of Science, Mathematics, and Technology Education, 2, 37–48.

Roth, W.-M., & Lee, S. (2002a). Breaking the spell: Science education for a free society. In W.-M. Roth & J. Désautels (Eds.), Science education as/for sociopolitical action (pp. 65–91). New York: Peter Lang.

Roth, W.-M., & Lee, S. (2002b). Scientific literacy as collective praxis. Public Understanding of Science, 11, 33–56.

Roth, W.-M., & McGinn, M. K. (1998). Inscriptions: A social practice approach to "representations." Review of Educational Research, 68, 35–59.

Saari, E., & Miettinen, R. (2001). Dynamics of change in research work: Constructing a new research area in a research group. Science, Technology, & Human Values, 26, 300–321.

Saxe, G. (1991). Culture and cognitive development. Hillsdale, NJ: Erlbaum.

Scribner, S. (1986). Literacy in three metaphors. In N. Stein (Ed.), Literacy in American schools: Learning to read and write (pp. 7–22). Chicago: University of Chicago Press.

Shamos, A. (1995). The myth of scientific literacy. New Brunswick, NJ: Rutgers University Press.

Tobin, K., Seiler, G., & Walls, E. (1999). Reproduction of social class in the teaching and learning of science in urban high schools. Research in Science Education, 29, 171–187.

13

Growing up Digital: How the Web Changes Work, Education and the Ways People Learn

John Seely Brown

In 1831 Michael Faraday built a small generator that produced electricity, but a generation passed before an industrial version was built, then another 25 years before all the necessary accoutrements for electrification came into place—power companies, neighborhood wiring, appliances (like light bulbs) that required electricity, and so on. But when that infrastructure finally took hold, everything changed—homes, work places, transportation, entertainment, architecture, what we ate, even when we went to bed. Worldwide, electricity became a transformative medium for social practices.

In quite the same way, the World Wide Web will be a transformative medium, as important as electricity. Here again we have a story of gradual development followed by an exploding impact. The Web's antecedents trace back to a U.S. Department of Defense project begun in the late 1960s, then to the innovations of Tim Berners-Lee and others at the Center for European Nuclear Research in the late 1980s, followed by rapid adoption in the mid- and late-1990s. Suddenly we had e-mail available, then a new way to look up information, then a remarkable way to do our shopping—but that's barely the start. The tremendous range of transformations wrought by electricity, so barely sensed by our grandparents a century ago, lie ahead of us through the Web.

No one fully knows what those transformations will be, but what we do know is that initial uses of new media have tended to mimic what came before: early photography imitated painting, the first movies the stage, etc. It took 10 to 20 years for filmmakers to discover the inherent capabilities of their new medium. They were to develop techniques now commonplace in movies, such as "fades," "dissolves," "flashbacks," "time and space folds," and "special effects," all radically different from what had been possible in the theater. So it will be for the Web. What we initially saw as an intriguing network of computers is now evolving its own genres from a mix of technological possibilities and social and market needs.

Challenging as it is, this chapter will try to look ahead to understand the Web's fundamental properties; see how they might create a new kind of information fabric in which learning, working, and playing co-mingle; examine the notion of distributed intelligence; ask how one might better capture and leverage naturally occurring knowledge assets; and finally get to our core topic—how all of this might fold together into a new concept of "learning ecology." Along the way, too, we'll look frequently at learning itself and ask not only how it occurs now, but how it can become ubiquitous in the future.

From: *Change*, March/April 2000, pp.11–20. Reprinted with permission of the Helen Dwight Reid Educational Foundation. Published by Heldref Publications, 1319 Eighteenth St., NW, Washington, DC 20036-1802. Copyright © 2000.

A new medium

The first thing to notice is that the media we're all familiar with—from books to television—are one-way propositions: they push their content *at* us. The Web is two-way, push *and* pull. In finer point, it combines the one-way reach of broadcast with the two-way reciprocity of a mid-cast. Indeed, its user can at once be a receiver and sender of "broadcast"—a confusing property, but mind-stretching!

A second aspect of the Web is that it is the first medium that honors the notion of multiple intelligences. This past century's concept of "literacy" grew out of our intense belief in text, a focus enhanced by the power of one particular technology—the typewriter. It became a great tool for writers but a terrible one for other creative activities such as sketching, painting, notating music, or even mathematics. The typewriter prized one particular kind of intelligence, but with the Web, we suddenly have a medium that honors multiple forms of intelligence—abstract, textual, visual, musical, social, and kinesthetic. As educators, we now have a chance to construct a medium that enables all young people to become engaged in their ideal way of learning. The Web affords the match we need between a medium and how a particular person learns.

A third and unusual aspect of the Web is that it leverages the small efforts of the many with the large efforts of the few. For example, researchers in the Maricopa County Community College system in Phoenix have found a way to link a set of senior citizens with pupils in the Longview Elementary School, as helper-mentors. It's wonderful to see—kids listen to these "grandparents" better than they do to their own parents, the mentoring really helps their teachers, and the seniors create a sense of meaning for themselves. Thus, the small efforts of the many—the seniors—complement the large efforts of the few—the teachers.

The same thing can be found in operation at Hewlett-Packard, where engineers use the Web to help kids with science or math problems. Both of these examples barely scratch the surface as we think about what's possible when we start interlacing resources with needs across a whole region.

The Web has just begun to have an impact on our lives. As fascinated as we are with it today, we're still seeing it in its early forms. We've yet to see the full-motion video and audio possibilities that await the bandwidth we'll soon have through cable modems and DSL; also [...] the new Web appliances, such as the portable Web in a phone, and a host of wireless technologies. As important as any of these is the imagination, competitive drive, and capital behind a thousand companies—chased by a swelling list of dot-coms—rushing to bring new content, services, and "solutions" to offices and homes.

My belief is that not only will the Web be as fundamental to society as electrification, but that it will be subject to many of the same diffusion and absorption dynamics as that earlier medium. We're just at the bottom of the S-curve of this innovation, a curve that will have about the same shape as with electrification, but a much steeper slope than before. As this S-curve takes off, it creates huge opportunities for entrepreneurs. It will be entrepreneurs, corporate or academic, who will drive this chaotic, transformative phenomenon, who will see things differently, challenge background assumptions, and bring new possibilities into being. Our challenge and opportunity, then, is to foster an entrepreneurial spirit toward creating new *learning* environments—a spirit that will use the unique capabilities of the Web to leverage the natural ways that humans learn.

Digital learners

Let's turn to today's youth, growing up digital. How are they different? This subject matters, because our young boys and girls are today's customers for schools and colleges and tomorrow's for lifelong learning. Around 1996 we at Xerox's Palo Alto Research Center started hiring 15 year olds to join us as researchers. We gave them two jobs. First, they were to design the "workscape" of the future—one they'd want to work in; second, they were to design the school or "learningscape" of the future—again, with the same condition. We had an excellent opportunity to watch these adolescents, and what we saw—the ways they think, the designs they came up with—really shook us up.

For example, today's kids are always "multiprocessing"—they do several things simultaneously—listen to music, talk on the cell phone, and use the computer, all at the same time. Recently I was with a young twenty-something who had actually wired a Web browser into his eyeglasses. As he talked with me, he had his left hand in his pocket to cord in keystrokes to bring up my Web page and read about me, all the while carrying on with his part of the conversation! I was astonished that he could do all this in parallel and so unobtrusively.

People my age tend to think that kids who are multiprocessing can't be concentrating. That may not be true. Indeed, one of the things we noticed is that the attention span of the teens at PARC—often between 30 seconds and five minutes—parallels that of top managers, who operate in a world of fast context-switching. So the short attention spans of today's kids may turn out to be far from dysfunctional for future work worlds.

Let me bring together our findings by presenting a set of dimensions, and shifts along them, that describe kids in the digital age. We present these dimensions in turn, but they actually fold in on each other, creating a complex of intertwined cognitive skills.

The first dimensional shift has to do with literacy and how it is evolving. Literacy today involves not only text, but also image and screen literacy. The ability to "read" multimedia texts and to feel comfortable with new, multiple-media genres is decidedly nontrivial. We've long downplayed this ability; we tend to think that watching a movie, for example, requires no particular skill. If, however, you'd been left out of society for 10 years and then came back and saw a movie, you'd find it a very confusing, even jarring, experience. The network news shows—even the front page of your daily newspaper—are all very different from 10 years ago. Yet Web genres change in *a period of months*.

The new literacy, beyond text and image, is one of information navigation. The real literacy of tomorrow entails the ability to be your own personal reference librarian—to know how to navigate through confusing, complex information spaces and feel comfortable doing so. "Navigation" may well be the main form of literacy for the 21st century.

The next dimension, and shift, concerns learning. Most of us experienced formal learning in an authority-based, lecture-oriented school. Now, with incredible amounts of information available through the Web, we find a "new" kind of learning assuming pre-eminence—learning that's discovery based. We are constantly discovering new things as we browse through the emergent digital "libraries." Indeed, Web surfing fuses learning and entertainment, creating "infotainment."

But discovery-based learning, even when combined with our notion of navigation, is not so great a change, until we add a third, more subtle shift, one that pertains to forms of reasoning. Classically, reasoning has been concerned with the deductive and abstract. But our observation of kids working with digital media suggests bricolage to us more than abstract logic. Bricolage, a concept studied by Claude Lévi-Strauss more than a generation ago, relates to the concrete. It has to do with abilities to find something—an object, tool, document, a piece of code—and to use it to build something you deem important. Judgment is inherently critical to becoming an effective digital bricoleur.

How do we make good judgments? Socially, in terms of recommendations from people we trust? Cognitively, based on rational argumentation? On the reputation of a sponsoring institution? What's the mixture of ways and warrants that you end up using to decide and act? With the Web, the sheer scope and variety of resources befuddles the non-digital adult. But Web-smart kids learn to become *bricoleurs*.

The final dimension has to do with a bias toward action. It's interesting to watch how new systems get absorbed by society; with the Web, this absorption, or learning process, by young people has been quite different from the process in times past. My generation tends not to want to try things unless or until we already know how to use them. If we don't know how to use some appliance or software, our instinct is to reach for a manual or take a course or call up an expert. Believe me, hand a manual or suggest a course to 15 year olds and they think you are a dinosaur. They want to turn the thing on, get in there, muck around, and see what works. Today's kids get on the Web and link, lurk, and watch how other people are doing things, then try it themselves.

This tendency toward "action" brings us back into the same loop in which navigation, discovery, and judgment all come into play *in situ*. When, for example, have we lurked enough to try something ourselves? Once we fold action into the other dimensions, we necessarily shift our focus toward learning *in situ* with and from each other. Learning becomes situated in action; it becomes as much social as cognitive, it is concrete rather than abstract, and it becomes intertwined with judgement and exploration. As such, the Web becomes not only an informational and social resource but a *learning medium* where understandings are socially constructed and shared. In that medium, learning becomes a part of action and knowledge creation.

Creating knowledge

To see how all these dimensions work, it's necessary to look at knowledge—its creation and sharing—from both the standard Cartesian position and that of the *bricoleur*. Knowledge has two dimensions, the explicit and tacit. The explicit dimension deals with concepts—the "know-*whats*"—whereas the tacit deals with "know-*how*," which is best manifested in work practices and skills. Since the tacit lives in action, it comes alive in and through doing things, in participation with each other in the world. As a consequence, tacit knowledge can be distributed among people as a shared understanding that emerges from working together, a point we will return to.

The developmental psychologist Jerome Bruner made a brilliant observation years ago when he said we can teach people *about* a subject matter like physics—its concepts, conceptual frameworks, its facts—and provide them with explicit knowledge of the field, but *being* a physicist involves a lot more than getting all the answers right at the end of each chapter. To be a physicist, we must also learn the practices of the field, the tacit knowledge in the community of physicists that has to do with things like what constitutes an "interesting" question, what proof may be "good enough" or even "elegant," the rich interplay between facts and theory-formation, and so on. Learning to be a physicist (as opposed to learning about physics) requires [...] looking at the deep interplay between the tacit and explicit. That's where deep expertise lies. Acquiring this expertise requires learning the explicit knowledge of a field, the practices of its community, and the interplay between the two. And learning all this requires immersion in a community of practice, enculturation in its ways of seeing, interpreting, and acting.

The epistemic landscape is more complicated yet because both the tacit and explicit dimensions of knowledge apply not only to the individual but also to the social mind—to what we've called communities of practice. It's common for us to think that all knowledge resides in individual heads, but when we factor in the tacit dimension—especially as it relates to practices—we quickly realize how much more we can know than is bounded by our own knowledge. Much of knowing is brought forth in action, through participation—in the world, with other people, around real problems. A lot of our know-how or knowing comes into being through participating in our community(ies) of practice.

Understanding how intelligence is distributed across a broader matrix becomes increasingly critical if we want to leverage "learning to learn," because learning to learn happens most naturally when you and a participant are situated in a community of practice. Returning to Bruner's notion of learning to be, recall that it always involves processes of enculturation. Enculturation lies at the heart of learning. It also lies at the heart of knowing. Knowing has as much to do with picking up the genres of a particular profession as it does with learning its facts and concepts.

Curiously, academics' values tend to put theory at the top in importance, with the grubbiness of practice at the bottom. But think about what you do when you get a PhD. The last two years of most doctoral programs are actually spent in close work with professors, *doing* the discipline with them; these years in effect become a cognitive apprenticeship. Note that this comes after formal course work, which imparted relevant facts and conceptual frameworks. Those frameworks act as scaffolding to help structure the practice developed through the apprenticeship. So learning *in situ* and cognitive apprenticeship fold together in this notion of distributed intelligence.

I dwell on this point because each of us has various techniques, mostly invisible, that we use day in and day out to learn with and from each other *in situ*. This is seen all the time on a campus, where students develop techniques for learning that span in-class and out-of-class experiences—all of campus life is about learning how to learn. Colleges should appreciate and support such learning; the key to doing so lies in understanding the dynamic flow in our two-by-two matrix.

If we could use the Web to support the dynamics across these quadrants, we could create a new fabric for learning, for learning to learn *in situ*, for that is the essence of lifelong learning.

Repairing photocopiers

Talk about a "two-by-two conceptual framework of distributed intelligence" can be terribly abstract; let me bring this to life, and move our argument ahead, with a story from the company where I work. When I arrived at Xerox, back in the 1980s, the company was spending millions and millions of dollars a year training its 23,000 "tech reps" around the world—the people who repair its copiers and printers. Lots of that training—it was like classroom instruction—seemed to have little effect. Xerox wanted me to come up with some intelligent-tutoring or artificial-intelligence system for teaching these people troubleshooting. Fortunately, before we did so, we hired several anthropologists to go live in their "tribe" and see how they actually worked.

What the anthropologists learned surprised us. When a tech rep got stuck by a machine, he or she didn't look at the manual or review the training; he or she called another tech rep. As the two of them stood over the problematic machine, they'd recall earlier machines and fixes, then connect those stories to a new one that explained some of the symptoms. Some fragment of the initial story would remind them of another incident, which suggested a new measurement or tweak, which reminded them of another story fragment and fix to try, and so on. Troubleshooting for these people, then, really meant construction of a narrative, one that finally explained the symptoms and test data and got the machine up and running again. Abstract, logical reasoning wasn't the way they went about it; stories were.

This example demonstrates the crucial role of tacit knowledge (in the form of stories) within a community of practice (the tech reps). But the anthropologists had more to tell us. What happened to these stories? When the reps got back to the home office, awaiting the next call, they'd sit around and play cribbage, drink coffee, and swap war stories. Amazing amounts of learning were happening in the telling and hearing of these stories. In the telling, a story got refined, added to, argued about, and stored away for use.

Today, brain scientists have helped us understand more about the architecture of the mind and how it is particularly well suited to remembering stories. That's the happy part. The sad part is that some Xerox executives thought storytelling had to be a waste of time; big posters told the reps, "Don't tell war stories!" Instead, people were sent back for more training. When people returned from it, what did they do? Tell stories about the training, of course, in attempts to transform what they'd been told into something more useful.

Let me add here that these studies convinced us that for powerful learning to occur, you had to look to both the cognitive and the social dimensions. They also led us to ask, How can we leverage this naturally occurring learning?

Our answer to that question was simple: two-way radios. We gave everybody in our tech rep "community of practice" test site a radio that was always on, with their own private network. Because the radios were always on, the reps were constantly in each other's periphery. When somebody needed help, other tech reps would hear him struggling; when one of them had an idea, he or she could move from the periphery to the (auditory) center, usually to suggest some test or part to replace, adding his or her fragment to an evolving story. Basically, we created a multiperson storytelling process running across the test site. It worked incredibly well.

In fact, it also turned out to be a powerful way to bring new technicians into this community. A novice could lurk on the periphery and hear what was going on, learn from it, maybe ask a question, and eventually make a suggestion when he or she had something to contribute. In effect, the newcomer was a cognitive apprentice, moving from lurker to contributor, very much like today's digital kids on the Web.

The trouble with this scenario is that all these story fragments were being told through the ether, and hence were lost to those reps not participating at the moment. Some of these fragments were real gems! So we needed to find a way to collect, vet, refine, and post them on a community knowledge server. Furthermore, we realized that no one person was the expert; the real expertise resided in the community mind. If we could find a way to support and tap the collective minds of the reps, we'd have a whole new way to accelerate their learning and structure the community's knowledge assets in the making. We wanted to accomplish this, too, with virtually no overhead.

The answer for us was a new, Web-based system called Eureka, which we've had in use for two years now. The interesting thing is that the tech reps, in co-designing this system to make their ideas and stories more actionable, unwittingly reinvented the sociology of science. In reality, they knew many of the ideas and story fragments that floated around were not trustworthy; they were just opinions, sometimes crazy. To transform their opinions and experiences into "warranted" beliefs, hence actionable, contributors had to submit their ideas for peer review, a process facilitated by the Web. The peers would quickly vet and refine the story, and connect it to others. In addition, the author attaches his or her name to the resulting story or tip, thus creating both intellectual capital and social capital, the latter because tech reps who create really great stories become local heroes and hence more central members of their community of practice.

This system has changed the learning curve of our tech reps by 300 percent and will save Xerox about $100 million a year. It is also, for our purposes here, a beautiful example of how the Web enables us to capture and support the social mind and naturally occurring knowledge assets.

Building knowledge assets

What are some other emergent ideas—in the workplace or on campus—that might help us capture, refine, and share knowledge assets in the making? Are there ways to capture assets that are left just lying on the table, as it were, and use them to make learning more productive in classrooms, firms, even a region? The answer, now, is yes. Here is one examples, among many I've seen around the country, especially as entrepreneurs start to see this as ripe territory.

The example I encountered was at Standford University. It comes from Professor Jim Gibbons, the former dean of engineering. He discovered the basis of building knowledge assets accidentally some years ago and has been refining it since. Jim had been teaching an engineering course that enrolled several Hewlett-Packard people. Partway through the course, the H-P students were transferred and were no longer physically able to come to class. What Jim did was simply videotape the classes and send them the tapes.

The twist, though, is that once the engineers received the video they'd replay it in their own small study group, but in a special way. Every three minutes or so they'd stop the tape and talk about what they'd just seen, ask each other if there were any questions or ambiguities, and resolve them on the spot. Forward they would go, a few minutes at a time, with lots of talk and double-checking, until they were through the tape and everybody understood the whole lesson. What they were doing, in terms we used earlier, was socially constructing their own meaning of the material.

The results were that students taking the course this way outperformed the ones actually taking the classes live. Today, the approach has been tried with other H-P engineers, with college students, even with California prison inmates; most of the students who've tried it got half a grade point better grades than the regular students. This account is not meant as a commentary on regular Stanford classes! Rather, it is used to describe an elegantly simple idea, low-tech and low-cost, about how forming study groups and letting them socially construct their own understanding around a naturally occurring knowledge asset—the lecture—turns out to be an amazingly powerful tool for learning. Think about what this suggests for distance learning—or for on-campus students.

[...]

Toward a learning ecology

An ecology is basically an open, complex, adaptive system comprising elements that are dynamic and interdependent. One of the things that makes an ecology so powerful and adaptive to new environments is its diversity. Recall that with the prior examples of knowledge performances, it was the diversity of comments that gave texture to the knowledge asset and enabled it to be used in ways that might never have been originally imagined.

Let's consider a learning ecology, particularly one that might form around or on the Web. As a start down this path, consider the Web as comprising a vast number of "authors" who are members of various interest groups, many of which embody a lot of expertise in both written and tacit form. Given the vastness of the Web, it's easy these days to find a niche community with the expertise you need or a special interest group whose interests coincide exactly with your own.

Recall the famous *New Yorker* cartoon of a dog in front of a computer, saying, "On the 'Net nobody knows you are a dog." Online, a kid need not necessarily reveal himself as a kid. Indeed, I've watched a seven year old from New York have a conversation about penguins with an expert at a university in another state. The professor may have sensed that the person he was talking with wasn't a real expert on penguins, but he probably didn't know he was communicating with a second-grader, either. Furthermore, at this child's school there was no one, including his teachers, who shared his interest in penguins. He found the right interest group through navigation. He linked, he lurked, he finally asked a question, and had this brief conversation with an expert. And I can tell you, the professor's momentary effort truly inspired him.

With the Web, these virtual communities of niche interests spread around the world as they interweave with local, face-to-face groups, in school or outside. A new, powerful fabric for learning starts to emerge, drawing strength from the local and the global. A cross-pollination of ideas happens as local students, participating in different virtual communities, carry ideas back and forth between those communities and their local ones.

Now recall our emphasis that informal learning often involves the joint construction of understanding around a focal point of interest, and one begins to sense how these cross-linked interest groups, both real and virtual, form a rich ecology for learning. Of course, not all these conversations, even if focused and well intended, lead to productive learning. As we said earlier in discussing digital kids, judgment, navigation, discernment, and synthesis become more critical than ever.

Regional learning

I've been struck, living in Silicon Valley and spending time in other high-tech regions, by how each region can be analyzed with respect to the quality and diversity of its knowledge producers and knowledge consumers.

The classic way to view knowledge production in a region is to list all the educational institutions one can think of—universities and colleges, schools, libraries, museums, civic centers—and to see these as the region's *producers* of knowledge, with the region's citizens, students, firms, government, and voluntary organizations as their *consumers*.

The region is geographically compressed enough, you start to get all kinds of informal, face-to-face connections between knowledge producers and consumers-students work part-time in surrounding firms, new firms spin out of universities, employees are retrained on campus, different people frequent common hang-outs, and so on and on.

In the 1970s and 1980s we were preoccupied with science parks; in the 1990s, all these connections produce what I think of as learning parks. Such learning parks bring increasingly rich intellectual and educational opportunities to their region. If top-quality schools and universities once primed the pump for science parks, we now see learning parks pushing resources the other way. In the relation between leading-edge firms and universities, for example, the firms increasingly provide adjunct professors, guest lectures, thesis supervision, internships for students, sabbaticals for faculty, and workplace experience for scholars of all ages. So the traditional producers of knowledge (the faculty) are also becoming consumers of the knowledge that their traditional consumers (graduate students, firms in the region) produce. This is very healthy indeed.

Now lets overlay on top of this physical social region on the Web, and look back to the example of students participating in local face-to-face groups but tying also into virtual ones. A key understanding is that on the Web there seldom is such a thing as just a producer or just a consumer; on the Web, each of us is part consumer and part producer. We read and we write, we absorb and we critique, we listen and we tell stories, we help and we seek help. This is life on the Web. The boundaries between consuming and producing are fluid, which is the secret to many of the business models of Web-based commerce.

From a region's standpoint, the great opportunity here is that the Web helps establish culture that honours the fluid boundaries between the production and consumption of knowledge. It recognizes that knowledge can be produced wherever serious problems are being attacked and followed to their root. Furthermore, with the web it is easier for various experts to act casually – in the academy or in the firm – and to mentor or advise students of any age. On top of this, the Web's great reach provides infinite access to resources beyond the region. The power of this reach comes fully into play when Web resources act to cross-pollinate and provide new points of view for a region's communities of practice.

[...]

Let me end with a brief reflection on an interesting shift that I believe is happening: a shift between using technology to support the individual to using technology to support relationships between individuals. With that shift, we will discover new tools and social protocols for helping us help each other, which is the very essence of social learning. It is also the essence of lifelong learning—a form of learning that learning ecologies could dramatically facilitate. And developing learning ecologies in a region is a first, important step toward a more general culture of learning.

Index

Page numbers followed by (Figure) or (Table) refer to Figures or Tables, e.g.: cerebral cortex, 21(Figure 2.1)
Page numbers shown as roman numerals refer to the Introduction at the front of the book.

abacus, and mathematical skill, 59
accountability, and cultural hybridity, 147
achievement
    gender differences in, 90–1, 161
    mathematical achievement, 61
    measures of success in science education, 187–9
    see also assessment; gender, testing and assessment
acquisitionism, 120–4, 125, 131
activity
    action, learning and the Web, 196
    and communication, 126–7
    cultural-historical theory of, 175–6
    diversity of, in school science project, 181–5,
        183(Table 12.1), 188
    family relationships and literacy, 136–8, 145
    and knowledge, 7
    and practice, 124, 168–70
    ritualized, and learning, 128–9, 130, 131
    social, and positional identities, 156–8
    see also interaction
'activity system', 73, 74
adaptive expertise, and thinking, 55–7
African communities, values of intelligence and
        maturity in, 52
African-American women, and positional
        identities, 152–3
agency
    and identities in learning, 162–3
    knowing and learning, 178–9
Aikenhead, G., 180, 189
Alperstein, J. F., 91
Alternative Assessment Project see portfolios
American Indian culture, and cognitive
        development, 52, 56
Anderson, J. R., 14, 15
Argyris, C., and Schön, D., 72–3, 76
assessment
    and curriculum, 10–11, 16
    measures of success in science education, 187–9
    and nature of tasks, 11–12
    in portfolio systems, 108, 110, 111–14, 117–18
    self-assessment, 12, 104, 113–14, 116, 118
    techniques of, 94–5
    and testing

assessment cont.
    as cultural activities, 95–8, 96(Figure 6.4)
    as isolated activities, 89–92, 89(Figure 6.2)
    as social activities, 92–5, 92(Figure 6.3)
    validity of, 12–13
    see also gender, testing and assessment; portfolios
        and assessment in teacher education
attention spans, 195
authenticity
    knowledge and curriculum, 9–10
    of portfolio assignments, 116

Bacon, F., 163
Baird , J., 88
Bakhtin, M., 77, 79, 107, 140, 158
Baron-Cohen, S., 28
behaviour, and positional identities, 156–7
behaviourism, learning and assessment, 90
Ben-Ari, E., 56
Benavot, A., 3
Bennett, R., 88
Berlin, B., 62
Bernstein, B., 3
Bjørlykke, B., and Økland, N., 111, 115
Black, I., 103
Black, P., 90, 93, 95
    and Wiliam, D., 10, 87
blindness, and language development, 24
blood oxygenation level dependent (BOLD), 22
Bloor, D., 96
Blount, B. G., 51
blue-collar children see class, literacy and gender
Boaler, J., 11
BOLD (blood oxygenation level dependent), 22
Boreham, N., 71, 73; author of Chapter 5
Bourdieu, P., 158
boys
    subject cultures and gender, 166, 168,
        169, 171
    working-class reading and textual practices,
        135–6, 138, 141–3, 145
    see also children; fathers; gender; husbands;
        masculinity
Braille readers, neuroimaging studies of, 26

brain development, 20–2, 21(Figure 2.1)
    see also mind; neuroscience
Bredo, E., ix, 5, 6, 7
bricolage, 196
Broadfoot, P., 88
Brown, A. L., 6
    and Ferrara, R. A., 10
Brown, J. S., 103, 107; author of Chapter 13
    and Duguid, P., 65, 71
Bruer, J. T., 28
Bruffee, K., 64, 106
Bruner, J., 4–5, 8, 14, 88, 162, 196
    and Haste, H., 95–6

Cain, C., author of Chapter 10
Cajas, F., 190
Cameron, D., 151
Capital High School, Washington, D.C., 152–3
caste, and positional identities, 149, 150–1, 151–2,
    154, 155, 158
Castro-Caldas, A., 24
Cazden, C. B., and John, V. P., 51
cerebral cortex, 21(Figure 2.1)
CERI, 87
Chaiklin, S., and Lave, J., 71
Chao, R. K., 56
Chatwin, B., 62
children
    as digital learners, 195–6
    intelligence, and maturity, 52–4, 56–7,
        60–1, 62–3
    and learning on the Web, 200
    neuroimaging studies of, 22–3, 24, 25, 26
    number learning in young children, 120–3,
        128–30, 131
    and positional identities, 149–50,
        156, 157, 158
    subject cultures and gender, 163–71
    underrepresented groups and science education,
        179, 180, 189
    see also class, literacy and gender; schooling;
        science education; subject cultures
China, cultural values and cognitive development,
    53–4, 60–1
"citizen science", 175
claims see medical claims
Clancey, W. J., 15
class, literacy and gender, 135–7
    fictional worlds and school
        textualities, 138–42
    home and family relationships, 136–8
    home and school reading practices, 141–3
    hybrid discourses of instruction, 140, 146–7
    and kindergarten literary practices, 135–6
    reading and writing masculinities, 143–6
    see also caste; positional identities

classification, of knowledge, 43–4
Cobb, P., ix, 93, 96
cognition
    and communication, 126–7
    neuroscientific studies of, 26–7
    see also cognitive neuroscience; metacognition;
        situated cognition
cognitive development see thinking
cognitive neuroscience
    educational implications of studies in, 23–7
    neuroimaging tools for, 22–3
    see also neuroscience
cognitive testing, 50–2
    see also thinking
Cole, M., 60
    and Griffin, P., 65
collaboration, 6
    and cultural tools for thinking, 63–7
    and group work, 15–16
    in portfolio systems, 106–7, 112–13
collective activity, 83–4, 108–10, 112–13, 124
    communication as, 126
    workforce training and tacit knowledge, 198–9
    see also organisational learning
commognition, 126–7
communication
    and mathematics learning, 130–1
    Net-based, 108–10, 114–15
    and thinking, 125–7
community water problems, 177–81
    see also science education
community(ies)
    of practice, 5–6, 41, 107, 197
    virtual, 200
computers
    cultural values and cognitive development, 64–5
    digital portfolios, 106, 108–9, 111, 112–13, 114–15
    see also World Wide Web
Connell, P., 161
Connell, R. W., 153
control
    of operating procedures by workforce, 75–6, 77,
        78–9, 80–3
    students', of science education, 182, 184, 189–90
    students', of teacher education, 113, 114
Cooper, B., 11
Crook, C., 64
cultural activities see sociocultural practices
cultural authenticity, 9
cultural tools
    for organisational learning, 82–3
    portfolios as, 106
    for thinking, 57–67
cultural values, and thinking, 50–4
    see also sociocultural practices; thinking
cultural-historical activity theory, 175–6

curriculum, 3–16
    and assessment, 10–11, 16
    concepts and levels of, 3–4
    and group work, 15–16
    and knowledge and learning, 8–11
    science, 190–1
    and transfer, 14–16

dairy workers, 7
Dasen, P. R., 52
Davidson, M., 14
Davies, B., 163
Davis, N. Z., 144
Dehaene, S., 25
Descartes, R., 163
dialogue
    and organisational learning, 77–8, 84
    in portfolio systems, 109–10, 111, 114–15
dichotomies, 43–4
    see also participation/reification duality
digital learners, 195–6
    see also World Wide Web
digital portfolios, 106, 108–9, 111, 112–13, 114–15
discourse(s)
    hybrid and primary, and early literacy,
        140–1, 146–7
    mathematics as, 127–30
distributed cognition, 63–7
domains, 9–10
dualities, 43
    see also participation/reification duality
Duell, O. K., 7
Dunphy, D., 71
dyscalculia, 25
dyslexia, 24, 25
Dyson, A. H., 140, 162
Dysthe, O., 106, 107

Eckert, P., and McConnell-Ginet, S., 152
ecology of learning, 200
education see engineering education; organisational
        learning; pedagogy; schooling; teacher education
Eisenhart, M., 174
Elbert, T., 26
Ellis, S., 51, 54, 60
Elwood, J., 91, 93, 97; author of Chapter 6
    and Comber, C., 94
    and Murphy, P., 93, 94
embodiment
    of fictions, and school textualities, 138–42
    and mediated positional identities, 155–8
emotion, neuroscientific studies of, 27
enacted curriculum, 3
enacted texts, 138–40
endorsed narratives, mathematical, 127–8
Engelsen, K. S., 111, 115; author of Chapter 7
Engeström, Y., 71, 72, 73, 76, 176

engineering education, and knowledge assets, 199–200
English language, testing and study of, 90, 97–8
entanglement, 97
entitlement, and positional identities, 153–4
environment, and brain development, 21–2
Epstein, D., 91
Eraut, M., 71
ERP (event related potential) studies,
        22–3, 24, 25, 27
Eureka (Web-based training system), 199
Evens, H., and McCormick, R., 14
event related potential (ERP) studies, 22–3, 24, 25, 27
examination systems, 94, 110, 112, 114
    see also assessment; gender, testing and assessment
'expansive learning', 73
experienced curriculum, 3–4
experience(s)
    cognitive neuroscience studies of, 25–6
    of meaning, 32, 39
    subject-cultures and gender, 166–70
expertise
    adaptive, and thinking, 55–7
    and community knowledge, 199
explicit knowledge, 196–7

Fagiolini, M., and Hensch, R. K., 20
families
    and children's intelligence and maturity, 53–4, 56–7
    girls, subject cultures and gender, 169, 170, 171
    relationships in, gender and literacy, 136–8, 140,
        141–6
    see also children; fathers; mothers; parents
fathers
    class, literacy and gender, 136, 137, 138,
        141, 145, 146
    girls, subject cultures and gender, 169, 170
    see also children; families; gender; husbands;
        mothers; parents
femininity, subject cultures and identity, 163–4, 170
    see also gender; girls; mothers; women
Fenwick, T., 71
fictions, embodied, and school textualities, 138–42
figurative identities, 151, 157
Fitch, W. T., 23
Flower, M. J., 184
fMRI (functional magneticresonance imaging), 22
food, and positional identities, 151, 154
Fordham, S., 152–3
Fordor, J., 88
formative assessment, 112–14
'forms of life', 96–7, 98, 124
"fossilization", 157
Fourez, G., 177
Francis, B., 93, 98
Fuller, A., and Unwin, L., 72
functional magneticresonance imaging (fMRI), 22
Fusco, D., and Barton, A. C., 174, 187

Gardner, H., 10, 11
Gauvain, M., 65
GCSE examinations, 94
Gearing, F., 150, 154
Gee, J. P., 140, 147
gender
    and academic achievement *see* subject cultures
    equated with sex group, 90
    and 'forms of life', 96–7, 98
    and group work, 16
    literacy and identity, 137–8, 139–40, 143–5
    neuromyths of, 28
    and positional identities, 149–50, 151,
        152–3, 153–4
    and scientific literacy, 163–4, 174
    and tiering, 94
    see also class, literacy and gender;
        subject cultures
gender, testing and assessment, 87–99
    assessment and models of learning, 88–92
    testing and assessment
        as cultural activities, 95–8, 96(Figure 6.4)
        as isolated activities, 89–92, 89(Figure 6.2)
        as social activities, 92–5, 92(Figure 6.3)
generalization, and specificity, 54–5
genes, and language development, 23–4
Gergen, K. J., 79
Gibbons, J., 199
Gilbert, R., and Gilbert, P., 139–40
Gipps, C. V., 10, 93, 95, 106
    and Murphy, P., 11, 95
girls
    academic achievement, 161
    and positional identities, 149–50, 156, 157, 158
    science education and the community, 179, 180
    subject cultures and gender, 164–5, 166–7, 168,
        169–70, 171
    see also children; femininity; gender; mothers;
        women
Gladwin, T., 62
Glaser, R., 9–10
Goddard, H. H., 50
Goldstein, H., 89, 90
Goodnow, J. J., 52, 54
Goodson, I. F., 3
Gorard, S., 161
Gossen, G. H., 53
Goswami, U., *author of Chapter 2*
Grayling, A. C., 96–7
Greenfield, P. M., ix, 51
Greeno, J. G., 10, 13, 16, 106
group work
    and curriculum, 15–16
    and knowledge assets, 199–200
    and portfolio processes, 106–7, 112–13
    see also collaboration; collective activity;
        organisational learning; teamwork

Hammrich, P. L., 180
Hamp-Lyons, L., and Condon, W., 103
Hargreaves, A., 87, 95
Hatano, G., 54, 55, 59
    and Inagaki, K., 61
Hawkins, J., 64
Hazen, R. M., and Trefil, J., 173
HCP (Henderson Creek Project), 178–88
Heath, S. H., 56
Heim, S., 24
hemispheres (of brain), 23–4, 27
Henderson Creek, 176, 177
Henderson Creek Project (HCP), 178–88
Herbert, N., 96
Hicks, D., x, 170, 171; *author of Chapter 9*
'higher functions', 72
Hodson, D., 178
Holland, D., 166, 170–1; *author of Chapter 10*
Hollins, M., 24
Holmberg, R., 78
Holzkamp, K., 177, 182, 184
home relationships *see* children; families; fathers;
        mothers; parents
Hurd, P. D., 190
husbands, and positional identities, 153–4
Hutchins, E., 63, 175
hybrid discourses, in early literacy, 140, 146–7

ICT, digital portfolios, 106, 108–9, 111, 112–13, 114–15
identity
    gendered, and early literacy, 137–8,
        139–40, 146
    and nature of knowledge, 8
    of participation, 34
    and primary schooling, 140
    and self-assessment, 116
    subject cultures and learning, 162–3
    see also positional identities
immigration, and cognitive testing in US, 50
implicit learning, neuromyths of, 28
individual, as learner, 89–90, 89(Figure 6.2), 93
individualized learning, 123, 124
    mathematics learning as individualized discourse,
        128–30
    scientific literacy as, 174
    thinking and communication, 125–6
individually-contained self, 79–80
informal learning, 200–1
information navigation, 195
intelligence, and maturity, 50–4
interaction
    and communication, 126–7
    and learning as social activity, 106–7, 123,
        125, 130
    in school science project, 182–8
    see also activity; negotiation of meaning;
        relationships

international tests, and gender difference, 90–1
Irvine, J., 51
Ivinson, G., and Murphy, P., 97, 170

Jackson, S., 22
James, P., 165
Japan
    cultural values and cognitive development, 55–6,
        59, 61, 62, 64
    positional identities in, 156
JCGQ, 90, 91
Jenkins, E., 175, 187, 189, 190

Kenya, values of intelligence and maturity in, 53
kindergarten, textual practices in, 135–6
Kingsolver, B., 50
Klenowski, V., 103
knowledge
    classification of, 43–4
    and concepts of learning, 5, 7–14, 93, 106–7, 117–18
    creation of, and the Web, 196–7, 201
    and curriculum, 9–10
    metacognitive, 6–7
    and organisational learning, 75–6, 78–9, 80–1
    and positional identities, 154–5
    scientific, 177
    and scientific literacy, 173–4, 175, 189, 190
    sociocultural theories of, 105–8
    symbol-processing and situated cognition,
        8(Table 1.1.)
knowledge assets, 199–200
Kobayashi, Y., 64
Kondo, D. K., 155–6, 158
Korpan, C. A., 184
Kotthoff, H., and Baron, B., 162

Lachicotte, W., author of Chapter 10
Lakoff, R., 151
language
    cultural values and cognitive development,
        53, 62, 107
    neuroscientific studies of, 23–4
    portfolio model of Norwegian, 108, 109
        (Figure 7.3), 111, 111(Figure 7.5), 115
    and positional identities, 150, 151, 152, 153–4
    testing and achievement, 90, 97–8
Latour, B., 175
Lave, J., ix, 6, 9, 12, 14, 59, 60, 123, 162, 176–7
    and Wenger, E., 5, 6, 8, 14, 71, 73, 88, 107, 162,
        168, 173, 188
league tables, 161
learning
    acquisitionist discourse on, 120–3
    concepts of, and knowledge, 5, 7–14, 93, 106–7,
        117–18
    concepts of, and the mind, 4–7

learning cont.
    gendered concepts of, 137–8, 164–70
    knowledge, and positional identities, 154–5, 190
    models of, the mind and assessment, 88–9, 88
        (Figure 6.1)
    optimal periods for, 28
    portfolio potential for, 115–16
    as process, and identity, 162–3
    sociocultural theories of, 105–8
    Web as new environment for, 194,
        195–6, 198–201
    see also organisational learning; participationism
learning ecology, 200
learning phases, and portfolio system, 104–5,
    105(Figure 7.1), 112–14
Leathwood, C., 95
Lebra, T., 55–6
LeDoux, J., 27
Lee, L. C., 53–4
Lee, O., 173
    and Fradd, S. H., 173
    and Roth, W. M., 175, 176, 181
Lee, S., author of Chapter 12
left brain/right brain learning, 24, 27
Lemann, N., 89
Leont'ev, A. N., 72, 73, 83, 125
levels of analysis, and participation, 6
Lévi-Strauss, C., 196
Levinson, S. C., 62
Levitt, N., 174
Lewis, C. C., 61
lifelong participation, 177, 189–90
Lillard, A. S., 62
Lillis, T. M., 98
literacy
    concepts of and the Web, 194, 195
    neuroimaging studies of, 24–5
    scientific, 173–5, 176–7
    sociocultural values and thinking, 58–9, 141–3
    see also class, literacy and gender; reading
literature, portfolio model of Norwegian, 108,
    109(Figure 7.3), 111, 111(Figure 7.5), 115
Lloyd, G., 163
Lucy, J. A., and Gaskins, S., 62
Lundvall, B-A., 71
Lunt, I., 10
Lutz, C., 150
    and LeVine, R. A., 52
Lykes, M. B., 155

Maguire, E. A., 26
Mahoney, P., 161
Maquet, P., 26
Marcus, G. F., and Fisher, S. E., 23
Martin, M. O., 91
Martini, M., and Kirkpatrick, J., 56

masculinity
    literacies and identity, 137–8, 139–40, 143–5
    subject cultures and identity, 163–4, 165
    see also fathers; gender; husbands; masculinity
Massey, G. C., 51
mathematics
    neuroscientific studies of, 25
    and participationism *see* participationism
    portfolio model of, 110–11, 110(Figure 7.4)
    sociocultural values and thinking, 59–61, 65–6
    testing and achievement, 91, 94
maturity, and intelligence, 50–4
Maurer, D., 20
Maxwell, N., 177
Mayan Indians, values of intelligence and
        maturity in, 53
McConnell-Ginet, S., 152
McCormick, R., 14; *author of Chapter 1*
McDermott, R. P., 88, 150, 162
McGinn, M., 95, 96
McLaughlin, M., and Vogt, M. E., 102
meaning, 31–45
    negotiation of, 32–4, 39
    and participation, 34–5
    participation/reification duality, 34, 38–45,
        39(Figure 3.1)
    and practice, 31
    and reification, 35–8
    shared, and organisational learning, 78–80
media *see* computers; digital portfolios;
        World Wide Web
mediated positional identities, 155–8
mediating tools *see* cultural tools
medical claims processing, as negotiation
        of meaning, 32, 33–4, 35, 39–40
Mehan, H., 50
men *see* fathers; gender; husbands
Mercer, N., 16
Merchant, C., 163
Messick, S., 12–13
metacognition, 6–7, 12
Mexico, cultural values and cognitive development,
        53, 56–7
Miller, K. F., 61
Minami, M., and McCabe, A., 62
mind
    and concepts of learning, 4–7
    learning, assessment and gender, 88–9, 88
        (Figure 6.1), 96–7
    see also neuroscience
Miura, I. T., 60
Moore, F., 96
Moreno, R. P., 51
Morgan, C., *author of Chapter 5*
Morrison, H., 96
Moss, G., 12

mother-tongue (Norwegian), portfolio model of,
        108, 109(Figure 7.3), 111, 111(Figure 7.5), 115
mothers
    and child's intelligence and maturity,
        53, 56, 62–3
    class, literacy and gender, 137, 138, 142, 146
    and young children's number learning, 120–3, 128
    see also children; families; femininity; gender;
        girls; parents; women
motivation
    for learning, 130
    and students' control of science education,
        182, 184, 189–90
multiprocessing, 195
Murphy, P., 3–4, 10, 12, 15, 16, 88, 89, 95; *author
        of Chapters 1 and 11*
    and Elwood, J., 94
    and Ivinson, G., 95, 97
    and McCormick, R., 11
    and Whitelegg, E., 161
musical experience, neuroimaging studies of, 26
Myers, M., 59
myths, about neuroscience, 27–8

NAEP, 90, 91
narrative structure
    cultural values and cognitive development, 62–3
    endorsed mathematical narratives, 127–8
    workforce training and tacit knowledge, 198–9
national assessments, 91
Naudada (Nepal), positional identities in, 149–50,
        151, 152, 153–4, 156–7, 158
navigation, of information, 195
negotiation, of meaning, 32–4, 39
neuromyths, 27–8
neuroscience, 19–29
    brain development, 20–2, 21(Figure 2.1)
    educational implications of studies in, 23–7
    neuroimaging tools, 22–3
    neuromyths, 27–8
    and teaching, 19–20
    see also mind
Neville, H. J., 22, 24
Newman, D., 10, 11
Nicolopoulou, A., 60, 65
Noon, M., and Blyton, P., 82
Norway *see* portfolios and assessment in teacher
        education
Norwegian language, portfolio model of, 108,
        109(Figure 7.3), 111, 111(Figure 7.5), 115
numbers
    sociocultural values and thinking, 60–1, 65–6
    young children's number learning, 120–3,
        128–30, 131
Nunes, T., 55, 60
    and Bryant, P., 122

Oakeshott, M. J., 63
O'Barr, W., and Atkins, B., 151
objectification, and positional, identities, 158
Oceanside, Henderson Creek Project (HCP), 178–88
Ochs, E., 64
OECD, 27, 90, 91
oil refinery, organisational learning project, 73–4
operating procedures, workforce control of, 75–6,
    77, 78–9, 80–3
operative knowledge, 7, 12
organisational learning, 71–84
    background to project in, 73–4
    cultural tools used, 82–3
    dialogue and relational practices, 76–8, 84
    and power relationships, 80–2
    procedures and competence development
        initiative, 74–6
    and shared meaning, 78–80
    sociocultural perspective of, 72–3
"Other", and identity, 153
Otnes, H., 103, 110, 115

Pantev, C., 26
Papert, S., 65
parents
    class, literacy and gender, 136, 137, 138
        141, 145, 146
    girls, subject cultures and gender, 169, 170
    and science education project, 184–5
    see also children; families; fathers; mothers
Parker, L. H., and Rennie, L. J., 161
participation
    in community see science education
    learning as, 107–8, 137
    lifelong, 177, 189–90
    and meaning, 34–5
    peripheral, and subject cultures, 167–70
    and planes of analysis, 6
    in summative assessment, 116–17
participation/reification duality, 34, 38–45, 39
    (Figure 3.1), 117
participationism, 120–31
    and acquisitionism, 120–3, 125, 131
        solutions to acquisitionist dilemmas, 123–4
    and mathematics learning
    as individualized mathematics
        discourse, 128–30
    mathematics as discourse, 127–8
    teaching and learning, 130–1
    thinking and communication, 124–7
Paulson, F. L., 103
Pea, R. D., 65
    and Gomez, L. M., 64
pedagogy
    concepts of, 13–14

pedagogy cont.
    gender and academic achievement, 161
    neuroscience and teaching, 19–20
    of organisational learning, 84
    and participation/reification duality, 42
    staff training and tacit knowledge, 198–9
    Web as new environment for, 198–200
    workshops and literacy teaching, 143–4
Pentland, B. T., and Reuter, N., 82–3
Penuel, W. R., and Wertsch, J. V., 162
performance see achievement; assessment; gender,
        testing and assessment
personal authenticity, 9
PET (positron emission tomography), 22, 26
petrochemicals company, organisational learning
        project, 73–4
Philips, S. U., 51
Piaget, J., 5, 15
Pinkerton, M., 96
Pirie, M., 91
planes of analysis, and participation, 6
Plank, G. A., 56
play, and figured identities, 157
plowing, as gendered work, 149–50
Polynesia, cognitive development and adaptive
        expertise, 56
portfolios and assessment in teacher
        education, 102–18
    critical aspects of, 115–17
    model of analysis for, 103–5, 105(Figure 7.1)
    research findings, 112–15
    and sociocultural theories of learning, 105–8
    at Stord/Haugesund University College, 110–12
    at Vestfold University College, 108–10
Posch, P., 188
positional identities, 149–58
    cross-cutting markers and categories of, 151–3
    embodiment versus mediated identities, 155–8
    relative social positions, 153–5
    social position becomes disposition, 155
    of students, and subject cultures, 163–7
positron emission tomography (PET), 22, 26
power relationships
    and organisational learning, 80–2
    and portfolio systems, 113
practice(s)
    and activity, 124, 168–70
    and meaning, 31
    see also relational practices; sociocultural practices
Presentation Portfolio (PP), 104
privilege, and identity, 151–2, 153–4
problem solving, 6
Procedures and Competence Development
        Methodology, 74–6
    see also organisational learning

process, and product, 107–8
psychology, and 'higher functions', 72
quantum theory, 97

Read, B., 93, 98
reading
  neuroscientific studies of, 24–5
  working-class boy's textual practices, 135–6, 138,
    141–3, 145
  see also class, literacy and gender; literacy
Reading Workshop, 143
reasoning, learning and the Web, 196
reflection, 113–14, 116
regional learning, 201
reification, 35–8, 107–8, 115–16, 117
reification/participation duality, 34, 38–45, 39
    (Figure 3.1), 117
Reimche, J., 179
relational identities, 150–1, 155, 158
relational practices, and organisational
    learning, 77–80, 84
relational self, 79–80
relationships, interpersonal
  and adaptive expertise, 55–7
  and cognitive tests, 50–1
  and distributed cognition, 64
  and ecologies of learning, 201
  family, gender and literacy, 136–8, 145
  and relational identities, 150–1, 155, 158
  teacher-student, and gender, 165
Religion, portfolio model of, 109(Figure 7.2), 115
REM sleep, 26
Resistant Materials workshops, subject cultures and
    gender, 165–70
Resnick, D. P., and Resnick, L. B., 59
Reynolds, D., and Farrell, S., 13–14
right brain/left brain learning, 24, 27
ritualized action, and learning, 128–9, 130, 131
"roaming", 136, 137–8
Röder, G., 24, 26
Rodriquez, A. J., 174
Rogoff, B., x, 5–6, 55, 65, 95; *author of Chapter 4*
  and Waddell, K. J., 54
romance, studies of, and identity, 157, 158
Roschelle, J., and Berend, S., 106
Roth, W. M., 11; *author of Chapter 12*
  and Lee, S., 175, 176
routines, mathematical, 128
Rust, C., 93

Saari, E., and Miettinen, R., 176
Sadler, R., 93
Säljö, R., 106
Salomon, G., 106
Saxe, G. B., 60

Schaffer, D. W., and Resnick, M., 116
Schatzki, T. R., 78
Schein, E., 72
Schliemann, A. D., 55, 60
Schoenfeld, A., 12
schooling
  cultural values and cognitive development, 50–1,
    55–7, 60–1, 62–3
  first/second grade literacy practices, 140–6
  kindergarten literacy practices, 135–6
  seventh grade science education, 177, 178–89
  single-sex science and technology classes, 164–71
  see also class, literacy and gender; learning;
    subject cultures; engineering education;
    organisational learning; pedagogy; teacher
    education
Schrage, M., 63, 64
Schwartz Cowan, R., 163
science
  subject cultures and gender, 163–5
  testing and achievement, 91
  see also neuroscience; science education
science education, 173–91
  community water problems as curricular topic, 177–81
  and participation in community, 178–80
  and cultural-historical activity theory, 175–6
  as everyday praxis, 189–91
  Henderson Creek Project
    measures of success, 187–9
    projects and representational forms, 181–5
    reporting to community, 185–7
    and scientific literacy, 173–5, 176–7
scientific knowledge, 177
scientific literacy, 173–5, 176–7
Scribner, S., 7, 60, 174
  and Cole, M., 58–9
Seegers, M., 113
self, and organisational learning, 79–80
self-assessment, 12, 104, 113–14, 116, 118
self-communication, thinking as, 125–6
self-education, 138
self-esteem, and nature of knowledge, 8
Senge, P., 77
Serpell, R., 52
sex groups, testing and achievement, 91–2
  see also gender; single-sex classes
Sfard, A., ix, 162; *author of Chapter 8*
shared meaning, and organisational
    learning, 78–80
Shepard, L., 87
Sherwin, S., 79
single-sex classes, subject cultures and gender, 164–71
situated approach, 5–6
situated cognition, 8(Table 1.1.), 107
Skilbeck, M., 4

Skinner, D., 149, 155; *author of Chapter 10*
   and Holland, D., 158
sleep, neuroscientific studies of, 26–7
Snyder, W. M., and Cummings, T. G., 71
social activities *see* sociocultural practices
social class *see* caste; class
social constructivism, 5, 93–4
social relationships *see* caste; class; interaction;
      positional identities; relationships
sociocultural practices
   cognitive development and academic
         achievement, 61
   learning and gender, 162, 163–4
   and organisational learning, 72–3, 78, 83, 84
   and participation, 35
   reading at school and home as, 141–3
   and scientific literacy, 175
   testing and assessment
      as cultural activities, 95–8, 96(Figure 6.4)
      as social activities, 92–5, 92(Figure 6.3)
      and theories of knowledge and learning, 105–8
   and thinking *see* thinking
   see also class, literacy and gender; participationism
sociolinguistics, and positional identities, 150, 151, 152
specificity, and generalization, 54–5
specified curriculum, 3
speech, and positional identities, 151, 152,
      153–4, 158
   see also language
Standford University, engineering education,
      199–200
status *see* class; positional identities
stereotype, and positional identities, 151–2, 165–6
Sternberg, R., 53
Stevenson, H. W., 60, 61
Stigler, J. W., 59
Stobart, G., 94
Stord/Haugesund University College, 110–12
Strauss, S., 19–20
stress, neuroscientific studies of, 27
students *see* children; class, literacy and gender;
      schooling; science education; subject cultures
subject cultures, 161–71
   and agency and identities in learning, 162–3
   challenges to and peripheral participation, 167–70
   and positioning of students, 163–4
      in resistant materials lessons, 165–7
      in science lessons, 164–5
success, measures of in science
      education, 187–9
summative assessment, 105, 111–12, 114, 116–17
Super, C. M., and Harkness, S., 51, 52
Sutherland, G., 95
Swisher, K., and Dehyle, D., 51
symbol-processing, 5, 6, 8(Table 1.1.), 11
synaptogenesis, 28

tacit knowledge, 196–7
Tannen, D., 152
tasks, nature of, 11–12
taxi drivers, neuroimaging studies of, 26
Taylorist principles, 75, 82
teachers
   gender and testing, 97–8
   literacy practices and gender, 136, 143, 144–5
   subject cultures and views of gender, 161–2,
         164–7, 168, 169, 170–1
   see also portfolios and assessment in teacher
         education
teaching methods *see* pedagogy
teamwork, in organisational learning, 75–6, 77
   see also collaboration; collective activity;
         group work
technology, subject cultures and
         identity, 163–4
Temple, E., and Posner, M. I., 25
testing *see* assessment; cognitive testing; gender,
         testing and assessment
thinking, 49–67
   an adaptive expertise, 55–7
   and cognitive development, 49–50
   cultural tools for, 57–63
      collaborative use of, 63–7
   and cultural values of intelligence and
         maturity, 50–4
   generalization and specificity of, 54–5
   participationist views on, 124–7
tiering, 94
Tobin, K., 174
tools *see* cultural tools
Topping, K., 104
training *see* organisational learning; pedagogy;
         schooling; teacher education
transfer, and curriculum, 14–16
Trosset, C. S., 154
Turner, T., 150

Ueno, N., and Saito, S., 60
understanding, and learning, 131
United Kingdom
   league tables and gendered achievement, 161
   organisational learning project in, 73–4
   testing and achievement in, 90–1, 94
   see also subject cultures
United States
   cultural values and cognitive development in, 50,
         53, 56–7, 59, 60–1
   early literacy learning in see class, literacy and
         gender
   engineering education in, and knowledge assets,
         199–200
   positional identities in, 151, 152, 157
   science education and the community, 177–89

Vai people, cognitive skills and literacy, 58
validity, of assessment, 12–13
verbal duelling, 53
Vestfold University College, 108–10
video game cultures, and gendered identities, 139–40
Vince, R., 80
Vines, A., 116
virtual communities, 200
visualization, and mathematical skills, 59
Von Glaserfeld, E., 7, 12, 93
Vygotsky, L. S., 49, 72, 82, 93, 107, 157, 158

Wajcman, J., 164
Ward, M. C., 51
water *see* community water problems; science
    education
Web *see* World Wide Web
Weber-Fox, C. M., and Neville, H. J., 24
Weisner, T. S., 53
Welsh language, 154
Wenger, E., ix, 107, 108, 115, 116, 117, 162–3, 165,
    170; *author of Chapter 3*
Wertsch, J., 54, 65–6, 72, 96, 106
White, M., 56, 61
Whiting, B. B., and Whiting, J. W. M., 51
Whorf, B., 62
Willingham, W. W., and Cole, N. S., 90, 95
Wittek, L., 114, 117
Wittgenstein, L., 96, 125, 126
wives *see* femininity; gender; girls; mothers;
    parents; women
Wober, M., 52

Wolf, D. P., 59
Wolof people, and cognitive testing, 51
women
    dress and identity, 155, 156
    speech and identity, 149–50, 151, 152–3, 153–4
    see also femininity; gender; girls; mothers
workforce
    and organisational learning, 74, 84
        control of operating procedures, 75–6, 77,
            78–9, 80–3
    training and tacit knowledge, 198–9
working class children *see* class, literacy
        and gender
workshops, reader's and writer's, 143–4
World Wide Web, 193–201
    and digital learners, 195–6
    and knowledge asset building, 199–200
    and knowledge creation, 196–7
    and a learning ecology, 200
    as new medium, 194
    and regional learning, 201
    workforce training and tacit knowledge, 198–9
writing, working-class boy's Writer's Notebook,
        138–9, 143–4

Xerox company, 195, 198–9

Yancey, K. B., and Weiser, I., 103

Zago, L., 25
Zambia, values of intelligence and maturity in, 52
Zeichner, K., and Wray, S., 103